Contents

HOW TO USE THIS BOOK

Finding Your Course

The 136 golf courses in this book are presented by their geographical location, on a region-by-region basis. Within each of the eight major Irish regions presented here, the courses are arranged loosely by their geographical proximity. Use the regional map to locate your course and then go to the appropriate number within the chapter for a full course description. Some major courses, such as Ballybunion or Royal County Down, have been given more in-depth descriptions, including a diagram of the course layout. The selection of the 136 courses here reflects the author's opinion of the courses that you should try to visit. However, there are now over 440 golf courses across Ireland (with more being developed) and most are worth playing.

Golf Course Yardages

There is almost a 50-50 variation in the way that Irish golf courses are measured. Some are measured in imperial yards while others are in metric. In this book, both measurements are given. Overall course yardages are for the maximum length of the course, either from the championship tees or from the medal tees. Each course uses different colour tee markers although, in the vast majority of cases, blue markers signify championship tees and white markers indicate medal tees. Yellow or green markers tend to denote visitors' or societies' tees and red markers indicate ladies' tees. Tiger tees (black) are found on some of the newer courses and are seldom, if ever, used. Visitors are rarely allowed to use the white competition tees – although, in the case of low-handicap players, requests can be made in advance. In most cases, the course starter will inform you what tee you should play from.

Club Facilities

Most clubs offer a range of facilities, and it is only the more remote or smaller clubs that do not cater for the usual golfing requirements. Changing rooms are commonly provided, usually with a separate area for visitors. Showers are available at the majority of clubs and most provide a towel service. However, it is advisable to pack your own towel, just in case.

Most Irish golfers use trolleys, although some still prefer to carry their bags, and there is a growing trend of electric trolleys. Most clubs offer trolleys and electric trolleys for hire. If you require an electric buggy, it is recommended that you check availability in advance.

Visitors' Restrictions

Visitors are welcome in most Irish clubs, but there are restrictions at certain times, especially at weekends, when club member competitions take place. There may also be restrictions mid-week when many clubs have a ladies' day or competitions open to five-day members. There are also a growing number of pay-and-play facilities with no weekend restrictions.

You will find, in practice, that handicap certificates are rarely requested on the majority of Irish courses, although it makes sense to keep your certificate and/or letter of introduction from your club with you.

Key to Green Fees

For each course we have provided a rough guide to green fees to play a round of 18 holes.

In the Republic of Ireland, the currency is the euro and this is indicated by the symbol €.

€	= **up to €19 (up to $22)**
€€	= **€20 to €29 ($23–33)**
€€€	= **€30 to €39 ($34–45)**
€€€€	= **€40 to €49 ($46–56)**
€€€€€	= **€50 to €59 ($57–68)**
€€€€€€	= **€60 to €69 ($69–79)**
€€€€€€+	= **€70 and over ($80 or over)**

In Northern Ireland, the currency is the pound Sterling, and this is indicated by the symbol £.

£	= **up to £19 (up to $31)**
££	= **£20 to £29 ($32–48)**
£££	= **£30 to £39 ($49–65)**
££££	= **£40 to £49 ($66–81)**
£££££	= **£50 to £59 ($82–99)**
£££££+	= **£60 and over ($100 or over)**

These green fees are based on the most expensive (weekend) rates that you are likely to pay. Most clubs offer lower rates mid-week. Golfing societies can command rates that are slightly cheaper than the normal green-fee rates. Club members are also often entitled to sign in a number of guests at discounted green-fee rates.

Introduction

Golf in Ireland

It's true that Ireland didn't invent the game of golf, although at times it may seem that way to the outside world. We'll leave the Scottish (the most likely) and the Dutch to fight it out for the right to win that particular argument and simply assert that the Irish have adopted the game, taken it to their hearts, added a touch of mystique and nurtured it into something special.

There are now over 440 courses in Ireland as a whole, and the number is growing year by year. Already Ireland has more golf courses per head of population than any other country in the world. Not only that; there are just over 150 genuine links courses in the world – and Ireland has over 35 per cent of them, dotted like diamonds in an emerald necklace all along its coastline.

Left: Kilkenny Castle, on the banks of the River Nore, is one of the finest examples of Norman architecture in Ireland. Above: The James Joyce statue in Dublin.

Many of the linksland courses' names readily trip off foreign tongues – Ballybunion, Royal Portrush, Royal County Down, Lahinch and Portmarnock. All of these are famous far beyond the Irish shore. They are magnificent courses, but there are many more. Newer links courses such as Bally-liffin (Glashedy), The European and Doonbeg have come to join their ranks. While most visiting golfers come to Ireland to savour the delights of the links, the addition of quality parkland courses has certainly added to the many attractions of Ireland as a golfing destination. Add in the renowned hospitality of the people, and the mix is truly intoxicating.

Oldest National Union

In Ireland, it is accepted that the Scottish introduced the game to the country. The first recorded mention of 'goff' in Ireland can be traced back to a Scot, the Honourable Laird of Braidstone, Hugh

Montgomery, who found his way to the Ards Peninsula, County Down, and made some land available to a school at Newtown for the purpose of playing. That was in 1606. However, the first verifiable playing of golf in Ireland was *c.* 1762 in the seaside town of Bray, County Wicklow, when a notice appeared in *The Dublin Journal* newspaper advising members of the 'goff club' to dine in a member's house.

It is known that small bands of golfing pioneers started to form their own clubs from the early 1880s – the first organized golf in Dublin took place on a 12-hole course laid out in Phoenix Park – and, by 1891, a band of dedicated golfers took the initiative to form a national union. On 12 October 1891, a meeting in the Railway Hotel, in Portrush, County Antrim, was held for the purpose of establishing the Golfing Union of Ireland. As such, the GUI, which to this day administers the sport in Ireland, is the oldest established national governing golfing body in the world.

Irish Golf Today

Golf in Ireland is, today, at the peak of its popularity. There are more Irish people playing golf now than at any other time in history. There are also more dedicated golf tourists travelling to Ireland than ever before – in 1988, the figure was 52,000; by 2000, the number had increased to 250,000. The number of golf courses has also significantly increased. In the 1990s alone, 110 new courses were developed, bringing the number in the country to over 440. Although the majority of courses cater for strong club memberships, they also cater for visitors, and players – no matter what their handicap – will find a venue that suits

them. On some of the major courses, you won't get a round unless you book, often well in advance; elsewhere, there are times when you can simply drive up and tee off within minutes. We have selected 136 courses across the price spectrum and of varying landscapes and degrees of difficulty – but all of which you will be able to book and play.

The Island of Ireland

The total area of the island is 32,595 square miles/84,421sq. km. There are two administrative areas in Ireland: the Republic of Ireland (Eire), which is an independent state with its seat of Government in Dublin, and Northern Ireland, which is part of the United Kingdom and is governed from London. There are four provinces – Leinster (the East), Munster (the South), Connacht (the West) and Ulster (the North). In all, there are 32 counties – 26 of them are in the Republic and six of them in Northern Ireland. The only province that has counties in both the Republic and Northern Ireland is Ulster (three of them, Donegal, Cavan and Monaghan, are in the Republic's jurisdiction; six of them, Antrim, Down, Armagh, Tyrone, Fermanagh and Derry, are in Northern Ireland). The Golfing Union of Ireland administers amateur golf in Ireland, and the sport is an all-island one; there are no boundaries when it comes to golf.

Ireland is an island that, for its size, offers great diversity. Landscape and people are what bring most visitors to Ireland – both the Republic and the North. Once there, few are disappointed by what they find. An Irishman, it is often said, can talk the hind legs off a donkey. What is perhaps more of a surprise is the variety that this small island packs into

IRELAND

Enlarged area maps showing the location of golf courses
appear on the following pages

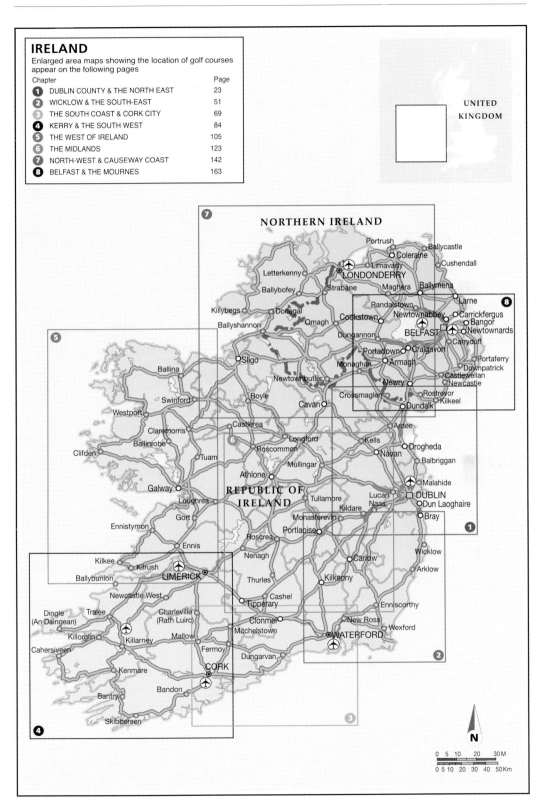

UNITED KINGDOM

NORTHERN IRELAND

REPUBLIC OF IRELAND

N

0 5 10 20 30 M

0 5 10 20 30 40 50 Km

the countryside – mountains, lakes, fertile flatlands, rugged coastlines. Then, of course, there are also the golf courses. There is a wide diversity here, too – from famous links courses amidst towering dunes to heathland courses on cliff tops and inland courses that suck in the beauty of trees, rivers and mountains.

TRAVELLING TO IRELAND

By Air

The main cities of Dublin, Belfast, Cork and Limerick (Shannon) all have international airports and are well provided with road and rail links. Dublin is the main gateway, with land or airline connections available to regional airports (Knock, Cork, Galway, Derry, Waterford and Kerry). There are also flights from various UK cities to all of the regional airports. Flight times from London to the Republic of Ireland are between an hour (to Dublin) and an hour and a half (to Cork, Knock, Shannon, Waterford and Kerry).

Flights from London to Belfast are about one hour and 15 minutes. Flights into Ireland from the United States land at Dublin and Shannon airports. Aer Lingus, Ireland's national airline, flies direct out of Boston, New York, Chicago and Los Angeles. Of the US airlines that operate direct services to the Republic, Delta flies from Atlanta to both Shannon and Dublin.

Airports

Dublin – Tel: +353 (0)1-8141111
Cork – Tel: +353 (0)21-313131
Shannon – Tel: +353 (0)61-471444
Waterford – Tel: +353 (0)51-875589
Kerry – Tel: +353 (0)66-64644
Donegal – Tel: +353 (0)75-48232
Belfast – Tel: +44 (0)28-9448 4848

By Ferry

In an attempt to compete with airlines, ferry services have been greatly upgraded in recent years. There are also catamaran or high-speed services on each of the main routes, Holyhead–Dún Laoghaire, Fishguard–Rosslare, Liverpool–Dublin, Cairnryan–Larne and Stranraer–Belfast, which cut sailing times almost in half. Ferry prices vary enormously depending on the time of year you travel. Most ferry companies have peak seasons of July, August and Christmas, and some also operate higher fares on bank holidays. Generally, mid-week crossings are cheaper throughout the year, and many companies also offer special off-peak deals. From Europe, the routes operating into Ireland are Cherbourg–Rosslare, Roscoff–Cork and Cherbourg–Dublin.

TRAVELLING WITHIN IRELAND

By Plane

There is no major internal flight structure in place. Most internal flights operate from Dublin, servicing all of the regional airports, including Cork, Shannon, Kerry, Galway and Derry.

By Train

Trains are an option, but for golfers they lack the required flexibility, especially if they are trying to reach the golf course from the terminal. Iarnród Éireann (Irish Rail) operates Intercity trains from Dublin to various cities, and the Enterprise service, run jointly with Northern Ireland Railways, is in service on the Dublin–Belfast route. In the Greater Dublin area, a number of suburban services operate. The most frequent service is DART (Dublin Area Rapid Transit), an electrified system operating along the east coast. LUAS, a light rail tram system, was due to come into operation in Dublin in 2003. In Northern Ireland, you will find only three short train routes: Belfast–Derry, Belfast–Larne, Belfast–Bangor.

By Bus

Bus Éireann operates throughout the Republic of Ireland and its services are reliable, if infrequent. You can travel by bus between all major towns, but this can be time consuming and can involve several connections. Bus fares are generally lower than train fares, especially mid-week. Private buses also operate on many of the major bus routes. Northern Ireland has an excellent network of regular bus services and there are good express links between those towns not served by a rail link.

Bus Éireann also operates a range of coach tours throughout Ireland, and there is a wide variety of coach tours from the Europa Bus Centre in Belfast to places of interest, such as the Glens of Antrim, the Causeway Coast, Fermanagh Lakelands and Sperrin Mountains. If you intend to do a lot of travelling by bus in Ireland, then ask at any major bus terminal about the 'Emerald Card', which can be used in both the north and south. For tourists who want to see a bit more of the major cities, open-top bus tours are now a familiar sight in Dublin, Cork and Belfast.

One of the best ways to see the many sights of Dublin is to take an open-top bus tour.

By Car

The most popular and versatile way of visiting Ireland on a golf holiday is by car. The advantages of having a vehicle at your disposal are obvious, including transporting your clubs and luggage directly to the hotel door or clubhouse car-park. Fly-drive tickets purchased in your home country are possibly the most economical way of hiring a car, as prices in Ireland can be expensive. International car-hire companies are found at all the major airports and ferry terminals. You can find local and international car rental companies in the Yellow Pages in Northern Ireland and in the Golden Pages in the Republic.

IRELAND'S CLIMATE

Ireland's climate, determined by the pressure systems of the North Atlantic, is notoriously variable and cannot be relied upon at any time of the year. Each year produces weeks of beautiful weather – the problem lies in predicting when they are likely to arrive. In recent years, late spring and early autumn have seen some of the best of the weather, with May and September the most pleasant months. Geographically, the south-east is the driest and sunniest part of the country and the north-west is the wettest, but regional variations are not particularly pronounced. The overall climate throughout Ireland is mild, due to the warming effects of the Gulf Stream. Even in the wetter zones, mornings of rain are often followed by afternoons of blue sky and sunshine. Anyway, a downpour on a windswept headland can be exhilarating, and provides as good a pretext as any for retiring to the local pub, the hub of Irish society.

GOLFING INFORMATION

Generally, the Irish golfing season opens on St Patrick's Day, 17 March. Irish links courses have found in recent years that the season is getting longer and longer, with foreign visitors travelling in groups as late as the end of October, especially as links courses, being generally well-drained, are playable all year round. Through the winter months, many inland courses will close temporarily if there has been a frost, in order to avoid damage to the grass.

Golf Club Opening/Closing Times

Irish golf clubs generally open for business between 7am and 7.30am in the late spring, summer and early autumn months and close whenever the sun sets (although the bar stays open!). Normally, some part of the morning and/or afternoon is reserved purely for the use of members. It is usually advisable to check in advance about tee-time availability for visitors, but there tends to be a fair degree of flexibility – unless you are playing at one of the major clubs, where green times are at a premium (and often limited).

Although most Irish clubs are termed members' clubs, they are generally open to the public for green-fee traffic, certainly mid-week. In many clubs there may be a small area or bar reserved for the use of members – but, generally, members

The Rock of Cashel in County Tipperary – once home to the Kings of Munster – is now a major tourist attraction.

DRIVING IN IRELAND

• To drive in Ireland you must have a current driving licence; foreign nationals will also need an international driving permit.

• Ireland (along with Britain) is one of the few countries in the world where you drive on the left-hand side of the road.

• The national speed limit in the Republic is 60mph/98kph, except where posted otherwise; in Northern Ireland, speed limits are 30–40mph/ 50–60kph in built-up areas, 70mph/110kph on motorways.

• Passengers must wear seat belts.

• In remote areas, watch out for wandering cattle, unmarked junctions and potholed minor roads.

• A cause of some confusion are 'slow lanes' or 'passing lanes', indicated by a broken yellow line, where you can pull over to the left for the car behind to overtake. However, use these lanes with care, as they have poor surfaces and can end with no warning.

• Be careful if you take a car into Dublin city centre – theft and vandalism are prevalent. It is advisable to leave your car in a supervised car-park.

• Ireland has been very slow to convert to metric measures, although on the main roads the new (green) signs are in kilometres. In many rural areas, however, you will mostly find the old black-and-white fingerpost signs in miles. Most people tend to think and talk in miles, too.

• Fuel is predominantly unleaded and is available almost everywhere.

• In large towns, a disc parking system is in operation: discs can be bought in newsagents and have to be displayed on the car when parked in certain designated areas.

• In the Republic, the Irish Automobile Association (IAA) operates a 24-hour emergency breakdown service. In Northern Ireland, the Automobile Association (AA) and the Royal Automobile Club (RAC) also offer 24-hour emergency breakdown services.

and visitors tend to converge in the same location for a bit of *craic* (good fun). The Irish are great humorists and the 19th hole can often be the most entertaining place in a club.

At weekends, tee times tend to be harder to come by, especially in the major cities. Most clubs hold their competitions on Saturday or Sunday, but golf has become so popular in Ireland in recent years that many clubs are having to extend their weekend club competitions to take in two days so that members can be facilitated.

The golden rule is always to phone ahead to make a reservation; that way, no one is likely to be disappointed.

There has been an increase in the municipal and pay-to-play courses in Ireland in recent years, especially in Dublin, where it is possible to book a tee time on-line at www.dublingolf.com (courses include the links at Corballis and the parkland courses in Stepaside, Elmgreen and Grange Castle). There are also municipal courses in Waterford, Limerick and Belfast.

What to Wear at the Golf Club

The weather in Ireland is so variable that it is always best to be prepared for anything. Pack your rain gear, even though you may not need it, and always have a woollen sweater handy, just in case the weather changes suddenly – it has been known to happen.

Most golf clubs adhere to dress codes. Usually, this means that no denims are allowed – either on the course or in the clubhouse – and tracksuits and shell suits are also on the banned list. Collarless shirts are also frowned upon in most clubs. There are one or two more traditional clubs that insist on gentlemen wearing a

The Customs House in Dublin (lit up here by a spectacular firework display) was designed by James Gandon in 1790.

jacket, collar and tie in the main lounge, although this may not be enforced until late evening. Usually, such notices are clearly displayed.

ACCOMMODATION

There is a wide range of accommodation, and most of it is of a very high standard. Bed-and-breakfast establishments (B&Bs) tend to have a very good rating. Guest houses, hotels, country houses and town houses are all graded by the Tourist Boards – Bord Fáilte in the Republic, the Northern Ireland Tourist Board (NITB) in the North – and, if approved, they will display a sign to indicate this.

Accommodation can be difficult to find in Dublin, Cork and Galway during the peak tourist season and during festivals, so it is imperative to book your accommodation in advance.

Bed-and-breakfast accommodation in the Republic varies enormously, but most B&Bs are clean, warm and welcoming. Many historic houses are run as B&Bs, and they can be surprisingly cheap. However, if you are travelling alone, don't be surprised if you are asked to pay for a double room.

You will find each region in Ireland is highly accustomed to dealing with golfers and their requirements. Many golf-orientated hotels will even book your tee times for the days that you are staying with them and suggest or even provide excursions for non-golfing guests.

If you are travelling independently and looking for accommodation, call in at the local Tourist Information Office (listed at the end of each regional chapter). The Tourist Information Office will often be able to find suitable accommodation for you at short notice.

If you would prefer to look after your own accommodation, then you can buy *The Accommodation Guide* from Bord Fáilte, which has comprehensive, graded lists of B&Bs and hotels. You can also check Family Homes of Ireland's website (www.family-homes.ie), which co-ordinates quality B&Bs. In Northern Ireland, the NITB has a booklet, *Where to Stay in Northern Ireland*, which is on sale at its tourist offices.

Another excellent guide to Ireland's fine country houses and restaurants is Ireland's *Blue Book*, which is on sale in all tourist offices and most books stores nationwide. In the North, *A Taste of Ulster Guide* is available in tourist offices.

Travel lodges and inns are a recent innovation in the Irish market and, although lacking character, they are ideal for families and small groups and can work out to be less expensive than B&Bs. Hotels tend to be more expensive, and the quality in this sector of the tourism market has grown significantly over the past decade. Virtually all hotels have bars and restaurants, and it is also worth scouring the national newspapers for special offers, especially in the off-peak tourist season.

Accommodation in the Republic and Northern Ireland can be booked in advance through the Tourist Board-approved agency Gulliver Info Res. There is a nominal charge for the service and a non-refundable deposit taken on your credit card as soon as you make the reservation. Call the following numbers to make a reservation – all calls are free:

From within the Republic of Ireland – Tel: 1800/668668
From the UK or Northern Ireland – Tel: 0800/668 66866
From the USA – Tel: 001/1800 668 66866

FOOD AND DRINK

Ireland has only recently discovered the joys of eating out, and restaurants have responded well to the new challenge. The quality and variety of restaurants throughout Ireland has improved no end in recent years, and you are now likely to find restaurants with locally produced fine produce alongside Chinese, Thai, Italian and Tex-Mex restaurants. Irish food is generally meat orientated and is of a very good standard – steaks, in particular, are excellent. You will also find that the catering in golf clubs is usually of a good standard.

Drink plays a large part in Irish culture, and to travel throughout Ireland without visiting a pub would be to miss out on an experience. The pub is far more than just a place to drink, especially in rural areas – it is the hub of the community and often the cultural centre, too. In the west, don't be surprised to find an impromptu traditional music session start at the drop of a hat.

There has been a liberalization of the opening hours of pubs throughout Ireland in recent years. The classic Irish drink is stout: Guinness (it tastes better in Ireland than anywhere else, especially around Dublin, where it is brewed), Murphy's and Beamish are the three most popular stouts. Irish whiskeys – the word is taken from the Irish *uisce beatha*, meaning 'water of life' – may seem expensive, but the measures are larger than those in Britain. Popular whiskeys include Paddy's, Powers, Jamesons, and Bushmills. If you come into a clubhouse bar after a cold day, ask for a 'hot whiskey' – served with lemons and cloves – to cheer you.

BOOKING YOUR GOLF VACATION

Most first-time visitors are advised to purchase a package from a recognized golf tour operator specializing in or including Ireland in its brochure. There are a large number of reputable Irish golf tour specialists dealing with travel packages to Ireland. The advantage of booking a trip through a golf tour operator is that most elements of your visit are prearranged. The disadvantage is that the vacation might be slightly more expensive than if you book a holiday yourself. Tour operators can negotiate lower rates on accommodation, car rental and golf, however, so their comprehensive service can be good value.

SWING – South West Ireland Golf Ltd – is a company that represents a number of courses (links and parkland) in the south-west of the country, including Waterville, Ballybunion, Tralee, Killarney, Dooks, The Old Head, Ceann Sibeal (Dingle), Dromoland Castle, Shannon and Adare. SWING can be contacted by phone on +353 (0)66-7125733 or via their website: www.swinggolfireland.com.

West Coast Links is the marketing brand representing seven links courses in the north-west of the country. These are Connemara, Carne, Enniscrone, Rosses Point, Murvagh, Ballyliffin and Rosapenna – the so-called 'Magnificent Seven'. You can contact them on +353 (0)91-526737 or via their website: www.westcoastlinks.com.

In the Republic, an organization called the Irish Golf Tour Operators Association (IGTOA) is the umbrella body for all golf tour operators, and it can organize golf holidays that cover the entire island.

DAY TO DAY ESSENTIALS

Currency

The basic unit of currency in the Republic of Ireland is the euro (you can use euro banknotes and coins anywhere in the euro zone: Austria, Belgium, Finland, France, Germany, Greece, Ireland, Italy, Luxembourg, the Netherlands, Portugal and Spain), which is based upon 100 cents to the euro. Coins are in denominations of 1, 2, 5, 10, 20 and 50 cents, €1 and €2 and can be easily distinguished as they vary in design, size and colour. The common sides of the euro coins show three outlines of the European Union set amid its 12 stars. While all eight coins have identical common sides, the other sides feature country-specific designs.

GOLF TOUR OPERATORS

J D Golf Tours, Shannon, County Clare Tel: +353 (0)61-364000 www.jdgolf.ie

Eire Golf Tours, Killarney, County Kerry Tel: +353 (0)64-31638 www.irishgolftravel.com

Carr Golf and Corporate Travel, PO Box 6385, Dublin 15 Tel: +353 (0)1-8226662 www.carrgolf.com

Ireland Golf, Tralee, County Kerry Tel: +353 (0)66-7123733 www.irelandgolf.com

Easi-Golf, Ballinteer, County Dublin Tel: +353 (0)1-4941447

Golf and Travel Services Ltd, Killarney, County Kerry Tel: +353 (0)64-44000

Irish Golf Tours Ltd, Tramore, County Waterford Tel: +353 (0)51-381728 www.irishgolftours.com

Delaney Marketing, Dún Laoghaire, County Dublin Tel: +353 (0)1-2802641 www.dmc.ie

Golf Events Ltd, Eagle House, Wentworth, Dublin 2 Tel: +353 (0)1-6768633

Travelling The Fairways, Temple Bar, Dublin 2 Tel:+353 (0)1-6770454

Speciality Ireland, Murrintown, County Wexford Tel: +353 (0)53-39962

Golf & Incentive Travel, Ballybrit, County Galway Tel: +353 (0)91-773339

Guidelines Tourism, Bangor, County Down Tel: +44 (0)28-9146 5697

Lynchpin Ireland, 4 Dhu Varren Gardens, Portrush, County Antrim Tel: +44 (0)28-7082 3232

N I Golf Tours Ltd, Portballintrae, BT57 8SB Tel: +44 (0)28-2073 2612 www.northernirelandgolftours.co.uk

Travelbreak, 128-130 Cavehill Road, Belfast Tel: +44 (0)28-9071 4614

Wrightlines, Lurgan Road, Banbridge, County Down Tel: +44 (0)28-4066 2126 www.wrightlines.com

Irish pubs have tremendous character – this is the Julianstown Inn in Julianstown, County Meath.

Euro coins can be used anywhere in the euro zone, regardless of their national sides. There are seven euro banknotes – €5, €10, €20, €50, €100, €200 and €500 – all of which have several features to help blind and partially sighted people to identify them.

The basic unit of currency in Northern Ireland is the pound Sterling, as in Britain, which is based upon 100 pennies to the pound. Coins are in denominations of 1p, 2p, 5p, 10p, 20p, 50p, £1 and £2; notes are in denominations of £5, £10, £20 and £50. Prices quoted in this book are in euros for the Republic and pounds Sterling for Northern Ireland. Note that if you are travelling from the Republic to Northern Ireland or vice versa, you will need to change currency.

Carrying money

If you have a PIN, the easiest way to draw cash is with a cashpoint card or credit card.

Most sizeable towns throughout Ireland have at least one bank with a cash dispenser that will accept Visa and/or Mastercard/Access, and most also accept Cirrus. Most large department stores, petrol stations, hotels and restaurants in Ireland accept the major credit cards. However, credit cards are less useful in rural areas, especially in smaller establishments, so it is advisable to carry some cash.

Travellers' cheques

Travellers' cheques are widely accepted in Ireland and are preferable to carrying large amounts of cash. They are available for a small commission from any bank.

Banks

The main high-street banks in the Republic are Bank of Ireland and Allied Irish Bank. Smaller banks include Ulster Bank, TSB, National Irish Bank and First Active. All are open Monday to Friday 10am to 4pm, and there is also a late opening during the week, normally on Thursday. Please note that there may sometimes be regional variations. In the North, the main high-street banks are Bank of Ireland (linked with Barclays), First Trust (AIB) and Ulster Bank (linked with NatWest). There are also bureau de change offices and, sometimes, banking facilities at all the major airports and ferry terminals in the Republic and the North.

Electricity

The electrical current throughout the Republic is 230V AC. In the North, it is 240V AC. Plugs everywhere are British-style large three-pin; in other words, British plugs will work everywhere. An adapter and transformer are needed for North American appliances. Most hotels and guesthouses provide hairdryers and irons.

Passports and Visas

If you are an EU national, you can enter the Republic with either a national ID card or a passport, and you are entitled to stay for as long as you like. Travellers from the USA, Canada, Australia and New Zealand are required to show a passport and can stay for up to three months. All other visitors to the Republic should contact the Irish Embassy as regulations vary. In the North, British regulations apply. Citizens of all countries of Europe (except Albania, Bulgaria, Romania and the republics of the former Soviet Union, with the exception of the Baltic states) can enter Northern Ireland with just a passport or national ID card for up to six months. UK and Irish citizens need no ID or passport. US, Canadian, Australian and New Zealand citizens can enter for up to six months with just a passport.

Health

There are no inoculations required for travellers to Ireland.

Embassies

Britain

17 Grosvenor Place, London SW1X 7HR
Tel: +44 (0)20 7235 2171

USA

2234 Massachusetts Avenue NW, Washington DC 20008 Tel: +001 (202) 462-3939
345 Park Avenue, 17th Floor, New York, NY 10154 Tel: +001 (212) 319-2552
535 Boylston Street, Boston, MA 02116 Tel: +001 (617) 267-9330
400 N Michigan Avenue, Chicago, IL 60611 Tel: +001 (312) 337-1868
44 Montgomery Street, Suite 3830, San Francisco, CA 94104 Tel: +001 (415) 392-4214

Foreign embassies in Ireland include:
British Embassy, 31 Merrion Road, Dublin Tel: +353 (0)1-2053700
United States Embassy, 42 Elgin Road, Dublin Tel: +353 (0)1-6688777
French Embassy, 36 Ailesbury Road, Dublin Tel: + 353 (0)1-2601666
German Embassy, 31 Trimleston Road, Dublin Tel: +353 (0)1-2693011
Swedish Embassy, Dawson Street, Dublin Tel: +353 (0)1-6715822

PUBLIC HOLIDAYS

Public holidays in the Republic and in the North include New Year's Day, St Patrick's Day (17 March), Easter Monday, Christmas Day and 26 December (St Stephen's Day in the Republic, Boxing Day in the North). On the main public holidays, virtually everything outside the cities is closed, except garages, pubs and restaurants.

Newpapers

The most widely read broadsheet papers in the Republic are *The Irish Times*, *The Irish Independent* and *The Irish Examiner*. *The Star* is the principal tabloid.

In the North, the *Belfast Telegraph*, an evening paper, is the biggest selling paper, but *The Irish News* and *The Newsletter* are both popular. *The Irish Times* and *The Irish Independent* are also widely available.

British newspapers are generally available on the same day, both in the North and in the Republic.

Maps and Brochures

There is no shortage of information supplied on Ireland, and much of it is free. It is well worth contacting the local office of either the Irish Tourist Board (Bord Fáilte) or the Northern Ireland Tourist Board (NITB); there are numerous regional offices around the country. Every tourist office carries a plethora of free guides and brochures, as well as some very good books and guides that are for sale.

All the main bookshops around Ireland are also well stocked with good guides. A variety of large-scale maps of Ireland are available, but for general touring the four Ordnance Survey Ireland Holiday Maps (covering the north, west, east and south at a scale of 1:250,000), give more contour details and are probably the best all-purpose maps.

Phones

There are fully automatic pay-phones in kiosks throughout Ireland, with instructions for use clearly on display. Pay-phones take coins (usually 10c, 20c, 50c or €1 in the Republic, or 10p, 20p, 50p or £1 in the North) or phonecards, which are widely available from shops and hotel reception desks. It is worth carrying a phonecard with you, as cash phones are rare nowadays in rural locations. International dialling codes in the Republic and Northern Ireland follow the European standard – to call the Republic of Ireland the code is 353, and for Northern Ireland, as part of the UK, it is 44. The cheapest times to make international calls are between 8pm and 8am mid-week and through the weekend.

Useful Operator Numbers

In the Republic: Operator dial 10; Directory Enquiries within Ireland (including Northern Ireland) dial 1190; International Directory enquiries dial 1198; International Operator services dial 114. In Northern Ireland: Operator dial 100; Directory enquiries dial 192; International Directory Enquiries dial 153; International Operator services dial 155.

Emergency Numbers

The number to summon the police (Gardai in the Republic), ambulance or fire brigade is the same in the Republic and in Northern Ireland – telephone 999 on any phone; there is no charge.

Internet Cafés

All the major Irish cities have cafés with internet access.

Postal Services

Post to and from the Republic is reasonably fast and efficient. An Post, the postal service, has offices in most towns and villages: opening hours in main offices are Monday–Friday 8.30am to 5.30pm, Saturday 9am to noon. In the North, post-office hours are Monday, Tuesday, Thursday and Friday 9am to 5.30pm, and Wednesday and Saturday 9am to 12.30pm.

Chapter 1

Dublin County & the North-East

It is often said that the Vikings who first guided their longships up the River Liffey in the 9th century to establish the town of Dublin (taken from the Gaelic *Dubh Linn*, meaning 'black pool') could not have chosen a better place in which to set up house.

Their arrival was unwelcome to the native Celts, with many battles ensuing over the years, but the history of Dublin – and, indeed, the whole of Ireland – is one of such invasion.

Today, Dublin continues to attract visitors, albeit of a less hostile nature. Approximately one-third of Dublin's inhabitants were actually born in another part of Ireland, and the city has also seen a surge in recent years in the numbers of immigrants from outside Ireland. All of this has helped make modern Dublin – the capital of the Republic of Ireland – a

cosmopolitan, bustling city of over one million inhabitants (including its suburbs), comprising one-fifth of the entire island's population.

Tourists to Dublin will find a vibrant city that successfully manages to reflect on its history and culture while, at the same time, also providing a taste for the good life. The liberalization of the country's licensing laws has resulted in longer opening hours for the numerous pubs, and there has also been an increase in the number and quality of restaurants and night-clubs, with much of the most recent development occurring in the Temple Bar area on the River Liffey's south bank.

In pure golfing terms, Dublin's inhabitants are spoilt for choice. Just 10 miles/16km north of the General Post Office in O'Connell Street, which is considered the centre of the city, lies Portmarnock Golf Club, undoubtedly one of the world's top courses. It is one of more than 60 golf facilities catering for every pocket – from municipal pay-to-.

Left: Skerries windmill in the north of Dublin county. The history of the mill can be traced back to the early 16th century. Above: The 12th-century Malahide Castle.

play facilities to more up-market developments – that lie within Dublin's county borders.

Dublin is made up of four administrative boroughs, with the area known as Fingal, in the north of the county, housing more than its fair share of top courses. Fittingly enough, as far as those arriving into the country by plane are concerned, Dublin Airport is effectively on the doorstep to the Fingal area; to the north-east, the coastal areas of Meath and Louth are within easy driving distance.

The Irish love their links courses, and it may come as some surprise to the tourist to discover that some of the best of these courses are so accessible to the capital.

The Grand Canal provides some peace and tranquillity amid the bustle of Dublin's south inner city.

Royal Dublin, Portmarnock, Portmarnock Links and The Island are among the top courses, and are situated like a necklace of jewels along the north Dublin coastline, stretching from Clontarf to Donabate.

For those on a short visit, but seeking to play as much golf as possible, the Donabate area is without question the most accommodating. There are six courses – including two links courses: The Island and the municipally owned Corballis course – in the area; Balcarrick, Beaverstown, Turvey and Donabate are the four parkland layouts.

North of Dublin, a number of treats await. Just 40 minutes' drive from Dublin Airport, along the N1 through Drogheda, is County Louth Golf Club (or Baltray, as it is more commonly known). Once a hidden gem of Irish golf, it is now very much on the tourist trail and offers one of the most demanding – yet pleasurable – experiences on a golf course. Literally next door lies Seapoint, a newer development, but one that also espouses the Irish affinity with linksland.

Golf-course development to the south of Dublin city does not compare with that in the north, primarily because the southern area is considered prime property development land. Still, the likes of Woodbrook, which has been upgraded in recent years, and long-established clubs such as the Castle and Grange will provide visitors with excellent golf.

Planning an Itinerary
Although there is a rail system, called the DART (Dublin Area Rapid Transit), that runs along the eastern metropolitan coast, serving Greystones and Bray in the south and Howth and Malahide in the north, the simple fact of the matter is that those wishing to play golf in Dublin are most

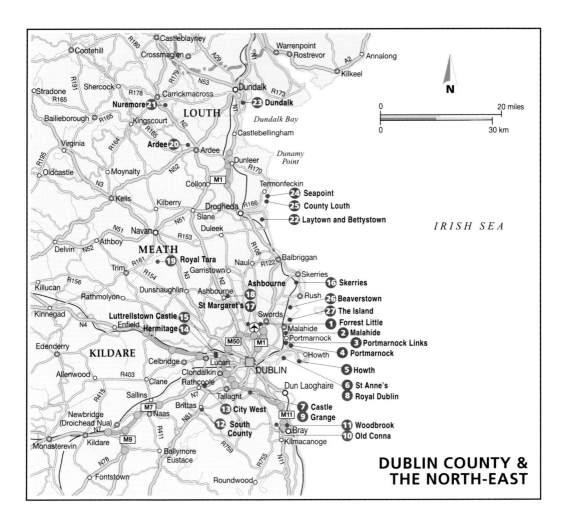

DUBLIN COUNTY & THE NORTH-EAST

likely to require road transport. Cross-city travel in Dublin's traffic can be frustrating and, as such, it is probably better to be based either on the north side or, alternatively, on the south side, where golfers have the option of adding courses in north Wicklow to the schedule. Both areas are suitable bases, with no shortage of quality accommodation and good places to eat. If you intend to undertake cross-city journeys, be prepared to endure traffic jams. Alternatively, early-morning trips may enable you to beat a rush hour that lasts considerably longer than the usual 60 minutes.

Pay-to-Play Facilities
Although the clubs around Dublin are most welcoming to visitors, there is an excellent standard of municipal and pay-to-play courses, particularly on the city's north side. Although Portmarnock Links is technically a pay-to-play course, it comes in at the premium end of the market. You will also find excellent value and quality at other facilities such as Hollystown near Mulhuddart, Deer Park in Howth, Sillogue in Ballymun, Elmgreen in Castleknock, Corballis in Donabate, Grange Castle in Clondalkin and Stepaside near Kilternan.

Forrest Little

Forrest Little Golf Club, Cloghran, County Dublin
TEL: *+353 (0)1-8401763*
FAX: *+353 (0)1-8401000*
LOCATION: *⅔ mile/1km past Dublin Airport,*
off the N1
COURSE: *18 holes, 6492yd/5902m, par 71, SSS 70*
GREEN FEES: €€€
FACILITIES: *Changing rooms and showers, full*
catering, bar, pro shop, teaching pro, club hire, buggy
hire, trolley hire
VISITORS: *Welcome – tee-time reservation advisable*

You'd imagine, given its proximity to Dublin Airport, that ear plugs would be regarded as essential accessories for a round of golf at Forrest Little. Fortunately, this is not the case as the flight paths rarely go over this fine and testing parkland course.

Forrest Little has recently strengthened its defences with some attractive water features and the remodelling of all 18 greens. All of the old greens have been raised, with the result that they contain far more subtle undulations than previously. The water features have added hugely to the aesthetics

As the golf club's name suggests, mature trees provide an omnipresent natural hazard at Forrest Little.

of what has always been a very pretty course, with its tree-lined fairways requiring accuracy off the tees. The short 7th, a par 3 across a lake, is an intimidating tee shot; apart from water, there are no fewer than six bunkers around the green.

The 12th hole, a sharp dogleg to the left, measures just 356yd/324m and is now one of the nicest holes on the course. The green has a lake – with fountain – in front of it.

The 18th, which is probably the toughest hole on the course, relies on the old-fashioned defence of mature trees. It is a par 4 of 456yd/418m and a tough driving hole: the ball must find the middle of the fairway or trees will block out the approach to the green, which is hidden by bunkers.

All in all, Forrest Little presents a good test for all standards of golfer.

Malahide

Malahide Golf Club, Beechwood, The Grange,
Malahide, County Dublin
TEL: *+353 (0)1-8461611* **FAX:** *+353 (0)1-*
8461270 **EMAIL:** *malgc@clubi.ie*
WEBSITE: *www.malahidegolfclub.ie*
LOCATION: *8 miles/13km north of Dublin,*
1 mile/1.6km south of Malahide
COURSE: *27 holes, 6672yd/6066m, par 71, SSS 72*
GREEN FEES: €€€€
FACILITIES: *Changing rooms and showers, full*
catering, bar, pro shop, teaching pro, practice area, club
hire, buggy hire, trolley hire
VISITORS: *Welcome (am) Monday, Thursday, Friday*
and Saturday, although booking is advisable

Founded in 1892 by the landscape artist Nathan Hone, Malahide's original hillside course ran alongside Malahide estuary before coastal erosion forced a move to land overlooking the waterway. Increasingly hemmed in by housing, the club made the move to a new greenfield site almost a century later, officially opening the new course and clubhouse in 1990.

Clever use of water features – with streams, ditches and lakes in play at various points – has added character, most ingeniously on the 140-yd/128-m par 3 3rd hole. Strategic bunkering and the careful use of trees add to the challenge and, no matter the time of year, the course is excellently maintained.

There are a number of blind shots, but none is too severe. Indeed, the course has matured very well and, year in and year out, seems to improve in every aspect, making it a tough enough test off the back tees for the serious player, but also a very enjoyable course for social outings. Some new holes, designed by the club's favourite son – the late Tom Craddock – tastefully complement those of the course's original designer Eddie Hackett and provide the option of playing any two of three very enjoyable nines.

3 *Portmarnock Links*

Portmarnock Hotel and Golf Links, Portmarnock, County Dublin
TEL: *+353 (0)1-8460611* **FAX:** *+353 (0)1-8462442* **WEBSITE:** *www.portmarnock.com*
LOCATION: *10 miles/16km north of Dublin; 1¼ miles/2km south of Malahide*
COURSE: *18 holes, 6846yd/6223m, par 71, SSS 73*
GREEN FEES: *€€€€€€ +*
FACILITIES: *Changing rooms and showers, full catering, bar, shop, practice area, buggy hire, trolley hire, on-site accommodation*
VISITORS: *Any time – but it is essential to book*

Although a relatively new addition to Ireland's golfing stock, Portmarnock Hotel and Golf Links, which was designed by Bernhard Langer, is steeped in history. Moreover, it has wasted little time in establishing itself as one of the country's premier pay-to-play facilities.

The course is built on land once owned by the Jameson family, of Irish whiskey fame, and, indeed, the five-star hotel that overlooks the links is their former family home.

The course itself, although not overly long, is demanding. There are many penal bunkers on the course and, after some relatively ordinary opening holes, the demands on the player become ever more difficult, with accuracy off the tees and precise iron-play a requisite.

One of the toughest holes on the outward stretch is the 5th hole, a par 4 measuring 474yd/431m off the championship tees, which has the added difficulty – apart from length and bunkers – of a series of ponds on the right-hand side for errant shots.

However, it is from the dogleg 8th hole onwards that the real character of the course is found. With the prevailing wind coming off the Irish Sea, this stretch belongs to true links golf. Once the 10th, the only par 5 on the back nine, is negotiated, there is a mix of devilishly difficult par 4s – as in the 11th – and a couple of superb par 3s – the 17th in particular demanding an accurate long-iron or wood to a raised green. The pièce de résistance is the 18th, a par 4 with towering dunes down the right and an approach to a green surrounded by yet more imposing dunes.

The 15th hole at Portmarnock Links – a dogleg par 4 – demands an accurate approach shot to a green set in dunes.

Portmarnock

Portmarnock Golf Club, Portmarnock, County Dublin
TEL: +353 (0)1-8462968 **FAX:** +353 (0)1-8462601 **EMAIL:** secretary@portmarnockgolfclub.ie
WEBSITE: www.portmarnockgolfclub.ie
LOCATION: 10 miles/16km north of Dublin; follow the coast road to Baldoyle, then on to Portmarnock
COURSE: 27 holes, 7283yd/6622m, par 72, SSS 74
GREEN FEES: €€€€€€+
FACILITIES: Changing rooms and showers, full catering, bar, pro shop, practice ground, teaching pro, club hire, trolley hire, buggy hire
VISITORS: Welcome – by prior arrangement

PORTMARNOCK

HOLE	YD	M	PAR	HOLE	YD	M	PAR
1	394	358	4	10	370	336	4
2	411	374	4	11	428	389	4
3	398	362	4	12	160	146	3
4	474	431	4	13	565	514	5
5	397	361	4	14	411	374	4
6	603	548	5	15	190	173	3
7	184	167	3	16	577	525	5
8	401	364	4	17	472	429	4
9	437	397	4	18	411	374	4
OUT	3699	3362	36	IN	3584	3260	36

7283YD • 6622M • PAR 72

The little security hut and the unimposing barrier at the entrance to Portmarnock Golf Club give barely a hint of the majestic links course that awaits down the narrow tarmac roadway. Such unpretentious obstacles to entry, though, shouldn't detract anything from the treat that awaits the first-time visitor, for this course – developed on a sandy peninsula – is among the finest to be found anywhere in the world.

In many ways, Portmarnock is the spiritual home of Irish golf. It was here that the Canada Cup – now known as the World Cup – was staged in 1960, when the legendary Americans Arnold Palmer and Sam Snead triumphed. It was also at Portmarnock that the 1991 Walker Cup match, in which Phil Mickelson and Padraig Harrington, playing on opposing teams, enhanced Portmarnock's proud tradition of playing host to major amateur tournaments. Incidentally, this match was the first of its kind to be a sell-out.

It was also on this famous north Dublin links terrain that the very first Irish Open was staged, in 1927. In more recent decades, the likes of Seve Ballesteros, Bernhard Langer, Ben Crenshaw, Ian Woosnam and Jose-Maria Olazabal have enjoyed victories here in the same championship, which was last held at Portmarnock in 1990.

So, when you find yourself standing on the first tee at Portmarnock, perhaps casting an eye across the estuary to Baldoyle, where the legendary steeplechaser Red Rum ran his first race, you will be following in some very famous footsteps indeed.

For a links, Portmarnock is rather unusual in that there are a number of small ponds

Ben Crenshaw described Portmarnock's par 3 15th hole as 'one of the greatest short holes on earth'.

hidden around the course and, as if to give the place its own unique character, small exotic trees – some of them well wind-lashed – are also evident.

For the most part, though, this is a true classic links. The small dunes provide tremendous definition, but they offer little protection against the strong winds that invariably sweep in off the Irish Sea.

Portmarnock has always been known as a fair golf course. If you strike the ball well, cope with the wind, avoid the bunkers and stay out of the rough, then you will score well. There is no real trickery either – the drive off the 5th is the only so-called blind tee shot.

Be that as it may, Portmarnock is a long, demanding course. The 1st may be a relatively gentle opening, despite the out-of-bounds right and the classical clubhouse to the left, but the beauty of Portmarnock is that it has tremendous variety while at the same time ensuring that any lapses in concentration rarely go unpunished. Indeed, the trend is set over the opening few holes, which are not intimidating in length. Miss fairway or green, though, and you will pay the price. From the 4th on, the course is a severe, if immensely enjoyable, test of golf.

Everyone who has played and savoured the delights of a round of golf on Portmarnock's championship course – there is also a third nine holes – has a favourite hole. The 6th is one of the great par 5s in championship golf (a genuine three-shot hole), while Henry Cotton once described the 14th, which plays directly towards the strand and invariably into the wind, as one of his favourite par 4s.

As if to confirm the variety of holes, and the shots required in your armoury if you are to attempt to conquer the links, the 15th is a 190-yd/173-m par 3 that plays parallel to the sea – with out-of-bounds right for shots that are steered onto the beach – and is widely considered one of the great short holes in world golf. The shot to an upturned elevated green, with a wicked hollow on the left and three bunkers for protection, is enough to put the fear of God into anyone.

As finishing holes go, the 18th – a par 4 that requires a good tee shot and then a long-iron or fairway-wood approach to a large upturned green – is a wonderful way to finish off a round of golf.

The Portmarnock course is always in tremendous condition, at whatever time of year. For any serious golfer travelling to Ireland, it must definitely be included on the 'must play' list.

5 Howth

Howth Golf Club, Carrickbrack Road, Sutton, Dublin 13
TEL: *+353 (0)1-8323055* FAX: *+353 (0)1-8321793* EMAIL: *howthgc@gofree.indigo.ie*
WEBSITE: *www.howthgolfclub.ie*
LOCATION: *8½ miles/14km north of Dublin; follow coast road to Sutton village, then up Howth Head*
COURSE: *18 holes, 6239yd/5672m, par 72, SSS 69*
GREEN FEES: €€€€
FACILITIES: *Changing rooms and showers, full catering, bar, pro shop, club hire, trolley hire*
VISITORS: *Welcome weekdays except Wednesdays – booking advisable*

Once in Dublin, it is hard to miss Howth Head. As you would expect of a course perched on top of a peninsula that juts out into the Irish Sea and overlooks Dublin Bay, Howth Golf Club offers players some spectacular views.

In fact, as if to confirm that this part of Dublin is very much golfing country, it is possible to view six other courses – Portmarnock Links, Portmarnock, Sutton, Deer Park, St Anne's and Royal Dublin – from the very first fairway, a hole known as 'Ireland's Eye', without straining your eyes.

Spectacular views apart, Howth is a hilly course with much gorse and heather. For anyone who is walking, it is quite a physically demanding course.

There are also a number of blind tee shots but, despite the proliferation of heather in relatively close proximity to the fairways, the landing areas tend to be quite generous.

On the outward journey, the dogleg par 4 5th hole allows little room for error, with the trademark heather dominating the left side.

However, it is the back nine that is most agreeable. The 13th hole, an uphill par 4 measuring 434yd/395m with a cluster of trees awaiting any pulled tee shots, is a fine hole; while the short 15th – called Farnan's – is a delightful hole that overlooks the Bay and has views across to the Wicklow Mountains.

You may be feeling rather tired by the time you finally reach the clubhouse, but a hot shower and good food should help make memories of this unique hillside course all the fonder.

The rocky outcrops at Howth Golf Club add unique character to the course. This is the 10th green.

6 St Anne's

St Anne's Golf Club, Bull Island Nature Reserve,
North Bull Island, Dollymount, Dublin 5
TEL: *+353 (0)1-8336471* **FAX:** *+353 (0)1-*
8334618 **EMAIL:** *info@stanneslinksgolf.com*
WEBSITE: *www.stanneslinksgolf.com or*
www.stannesgolfclub.ie
LOCATION: *5 miles/8km north of Dublin, along the*
coast road
COURSE: *18 holes, 6235yd/5669m, par 70, SSS 70*
GREEN FEES: €€€€
FACILITIES: *Changing rooms and showers, full catering,*
bar, pro shop, club hire, buggy hire, trolley hire
VISITORS: *Welcome – booking advisable; restrictions*
apply on Tuesdays (women's day)

Not many courses can boast of being located on UNESCO nature reserves, but Bull Island – the smallest such wildlife sanctuary in the world – can boast of two such courses. St Anne's, originally a nine-hole course founded in 1921, lies to the north of the island. It is a testing but nonetheless enjoyable course, now extended to 18 holes, and is suitable for players of all levels. Although not unduly long, the course requires precision golf; a number of holes, particularly on the front nine, have out-of-bounds lurking that leave little room for error. As on all links courses, wind is inevitably a factor here.

St Anne's, with a well-established reputation for being particularly friendly to visitors and societies, is always in very good condition and includes some holes that wouldn't be out of place on more illustrious courses. The 9th – known as 'Furze' – is one of the newer holes created by the club's long-time professional Paddy Skerritt. It has a ditch and a lake adjacent to the fairway, putting the onus on accuracy, both off the tee and on the approach to the green. The 18th, a par 4 measuring 402yd/366m, is a dogleg in true links tradition. The drive must find the valley on the right to leave an approach to a green protected on the left by a mound and on the right by a deep pot bunker.

7 Castle

Castle Golf Club, Woodside Drive, Rathfarnham,
Dublin 14
TEL: *+353 (0)1-4904207* **FAX:** *+353 (0)1-*
4920264 **EMAIL:** *leslie@castlegolfclub-dublin.com*
LOCATION: *7 miles/11km south of Dublin, through*
Terenure
COURSE: *18 holes, 6306yd/5733m, par 70, SSS 70*
GREEN FEES: €€€€
FACILITIES: *Changing rooms and showers, full*
catering, bar, pro shop, club hire, trolley hire
VISITORS: *Welcome weekdays – booking*
advisable

It's hard to believe that you are so close to a capital city when playing at the Castle Golf Club, a tight tree-lined parkland course with gentle undulations and invariably in excellent condition.

Deemed good enough to play host to the Irish PGA championship in its time, the opening hole – down what appears to be a tunnel of trees and demanding accuracy – sets the tone for the task ahead.

One of the course's feature holes is the 6th, a dogleg par 4 over a stream. Critically, the tee shot must be to the right-hand side and long enough to give you an approach shot into the green; anything left will be blocked out by trees.

The par 3 7th hole is one of the prettiest short holes on any parkland course in Dublin, again getting you to fire down a tunnel of trees, but this time over a dyke to a green set in a valley.

The back nine also has its attractions. The 10th is another par 3 that needs length as well as accuracy, as it demands a tee shot over a valley to a raised green.

The 18th is a particularly difficult hole to finish on, and it has, perhaps, an even more testing tee shot than that required on the 6th hole.

All in all, this Harry Colt-designed course – with five par 3s – is a delight that will test any golfer.

Royal Dublin

The Royal Dublin Golf Club, North Bull Island,
Dollymount, Dublin 5
TEL: *+353 (0)1-8336346* **FAX:** *+353 (0)1-*
8336504 **EMAIL:** *royaldublin@clubi.ie*
LOCATION: *3¾ miles/6km north of Dublin, along the*
coast road
COURSE: *18 holes, 6939yd/6309m, par 72, SSS 73*
GREEN FEES: *€€€€€€ +*
FACILITIES: *Changing rooms and showers, full catering,*
bar, pro shop, club hire, buggy hire, trolley hire
VISITORS: *Welcome (except Wednesdays and Sundays*
10am–12 noon); booking essential

Above: The approach shot to the finishing hole at Royal
Dublin is one of the most intimidating in Irish golf.

The sense that you're in line for something special strikes as soon as you drive over the old wooden bridge and arrive on the southern end of North Bull Island. This is no ordinary course. Indeed, its origins – on a body of land that is a designated nature reserve – provide many a tale that is best told at the 19th hole. In the early 1800s, Captain William Bligh (of *Mutiny on the Bounty* fame) was asked to find a way to provide shipping with a safe and deep approach to the River Liffey. It was on his suggestion that a breakwater – known as Bull Wall – was constructed. The resultant silt formed into Bull Island, which is where the Royal Dublin Golf Club set up home.

This is a fairly traditional links course. Laid out on flat terrain with the opening nine holes following the coastline so that the 10th tee box is the farthest point from the clubhouse, the homeward journey is entirely in the opposite direction.

Royal Dublin has played host to a number of Irish Opens – Bernhard Langer and Seve Ballesteros have both won here – but perhaps its most famous golfing-professional connection

is with Irish golfer, Christy O'Connor Snr, whose association with the club stretches back to 1959. Known simply as 'Himself', and considered one of the best players never to have won a major championship, O'Connor added to the lore of this course when winning the International Tournament here in 1966, with a finish of eagle-birdie-eagle over the closing three holes.

Given the nature of the course, the wind is a huge factor. You could quite feasibly play with the wind on your back for the outward journey, and then directly into it for the trip home – or the other way round.

The closing hole – known as 'The Garden' – is not the prettiest hole on the course, and it is easily the most daunting. It is a severe dogleg with cavernous bunkers up the left-hand side and a ditch and out-of-bounds to the right. For those who do find the fairway, the approach shot must diagonally carry the out-of-bounds area.

9 Grange

Grange Golf Club, Whitechurch Road, Rathfarnham, Dublin 14
TEL: *+353 (0)1-4932889* **FAX:** *+353 (0)1-4931404* **WEBSITE:** *www.grangegc.com*
LOCATION: *7 miles/11km south of Dublin*
COURSE: *18 holes, 6094yd/5450m, par 68, SSS 69*
GREEN FEES: *€€€€*
FACILITIES: *Changing rooms and showers, full catering, bar, pro shop, club hire, trolley hire*
VISITORS: *Welcome weekdays, except Tuesday and Wednesday pm – booking advisable*

You might say that Paul McGinley, who is a World Cup of Golf winner for Ireland and who learned so much of his craft on this tree-lined course, is slightly biased in nominating the 4th hole at Grange as one of his all-time favourites. However, such a high regard for the course – which is located in south Dublin's prime property belt – is not unique.

Grange is full of character, and even some recent remodelling to facilitate the development of a motorway has not diluted its appeal. Set in the foothills of the Dublin mountains, the hand of the famous architect James Braid is apparent.

The course is unusual in that it starts with back-to-back par 3s. The opening hole (223yd/203m off the championship tees) represents a devilishly difficult first shot, especially for newcomers. Not only does it have trees left and right and very much in play, the tee shot is to a raised green that is heavily guarded by clever bunkering. All the way round, though, the mature trees are a factor and, as such, the overall lack of length is compensated for by the need for accuracy and good course management. Nowhere is this more true than on the finishing hole. Here the approach shot must negotiate the River Kilmashogue before players can adjourn to one of the most magnificent new clubhouses in Dublin to discuss the finer points of the round.

10 Old Conna

Old Conna Golf Club, Ferndale Road, Bray, County Wicklow
TEL: *+353 (0)1-2826055* **FAX:** *+353 (0)1-2825611* **EMAIL:** *oldconna@indigo.ie*
LOCATION: *10 miles/16km south of Dublin; turn off the N11 at the Silver Tassie pub*
COURSE: *18 holes, 7205yd/6550m, par 72, SSS 72*
GREEN FEES: *€€€€*
FACILITIES: *Changing rooms and showers, full catering, bar, pro shop, club hire, trolley hire, buggy hire*
VISITORS: *Welcome – booking advisable*

The Old Conna course has matured much faster than anyone could have hoped, and is now among the best inland courses within the south Dublin–north Wicklow catchment area. Indeed, once you escape the traffic on the N11, cutting away at the Silver Tassie pub to take what is little more than a narrow country road up towards the course, there is an immediate sense that tranquillity is close at hand.

Old Conna enjoys a prime location, with panoramic views of the Irish Sea, Bray Head and the Wicklow Mountains, and the wonderful modern clubhouse takes full advantage this.

Old Conna also benefits greatly from a significant number of mature trees, which the designer Eddie Hackett has integrated into the course. There are also a few water features – but not too many – as well as enough open spaces for those who fancy themselves as big hitters to open their shoulders.

The 13th is a long par 5 of 600yd/545m. However, as always, Hackett shows great variety with his course design, and the 13th is immediately followed by a par 4 that is a mere 292yd/265m. There is a relatively tough closing stretch of two long back-to-back par 4s – the 15th and 16th – followed by a teasing short hole and, finally, a par 5 finish with danger right off the tee and then out-of-bounds to the left of the green!

11 *Woodbrook*

Woodbrook Golf Club, Dublin Road, Bray,
County Wicklow
TEL: *+353 (0)1-2824799* FAX: *+353 (0)1-*
2821950 EMAIL: *woodbrook@internet-ireland.ie*
WEBSITE: *www.woodbrook.ie*
LOCATION: *10 miles/16km south of Dublin, turn off*
the N11 at the Shankill roundabout
COURSE: *18 holes, 6998yd/6362m, par 72, SSS 73*
GREEN FEES: *€€€€€€*
FACILITIES: *Changing rooms and showers, full catering,*
bar, pro shop, club hire, trolley hire, buggy hire
VISITORS: *Welcome – booking essential at weekends*

When you think of seaside golf in Ireland, you inevitably think of links terrain. However, Woodbrook, situated on the Dublin–Wicklow county border, and with Bray Head as an imposing backdrop, is an exception. This course, which has played host to a number of international professional tournaments in its time, certainly has a distinctive charm of its own.

To give just one example, Woodbrook is one of the few courses to have a pedestrian underpass, so golfers don't need to take their lives into their hands when crossing the railway line that splits the course. The railway track is indelibly linked with Woodbrook, especially as it constitutes the out-of-bounds on the right of the 18th fairway. Certainly, more than one title, and more than one card in club competition, has been ruined by a wayward drive onto the line!

In truth, the railway line is perilously close to around half a dozen holes, but a more natural phenomenon, the hazardous edge of the cliff top, also comes into play on a number of holes – most notably on the 9th, 10th, 11th, 12th and 14th – and, with a wind present virtually all of the time, club selection is vitally important.

The club has done wonders to offset the effects of coastal erosion on its more exposed land, and has also shown an ability to move with more modern golfing concepts by redesigning the course's greens – a task undertaken by Peter McEvoy – and defining mounds and hillocks in places.

Bray Head serves as an imposing backdrop to the 18th
hole at Woodbrook.

12 South County

South County Golf Club, Brittas, County Dublin
TEL: +353 (0)1-4583035
FAX: +353 (0)1-4583036 **EMAIL:** igolf@ireland.com
WEBSITE: www.southcountygolf.com
LOCATION: Situated 5 miles/8km from the M50; take either the N81 from Tallaght or the R114 to the village of Brittas; the course is situated on the Blessington road, across from the Blue Gardenia pub
COURSE: 18 holes, 7051yd/6410m, par 72, SSS 73
GREEN FEES: €€€€€
FACILITIES: Changing rooms and showers, full catering, bar, club hire, trolley hire, buggy hire
VISITORS: Welcome – booking advisable

Set in the foothills of the Dublin mountains, this new development has established itself as a course of real substance. Although still maturing, it is blessed with a diversity of terrain that ensures a player must produce good shot-making to score well.

The front nine is unquestionably the easier of the two loops, set as it is in more open country. Still, there are some demanding holes to be negotiated on this stretch, especially when a strong wind blows down off the mountains.

Although fairly new, the course has great character. Mounding around the greens imitates the surrounding mountains, and there is much to commend about a homeward run that cleverly incorporates the Brittas River, while two lakes also come very much into play. This is certainly true on the par 3 16th, which offers a bail-out to the left, but insists on a brave carry over water for those who need to score.

This is the beginning of a finishing run that reaches a crescendo on the 18th, a long dogleg par 4 of 396yd/360m uphill to the clubhouse.

13 City West

City West Hotel and Golf Resort, Saggart, County Dublin
TEL: +353 (0)1-4588566
FAX: +353 (0)1-4588565
LOCATION: Take the N7 off the M50 intersection, then proceed west for 2 miles/3.2km, exiting the N7 at Citywest Business park; the course is signposted
COURSE: 18 holes, 7350yd/6682m, par 70, SSS 72
GREEN FEES: €€€€
FACILITIES: Changing rooms and showers, full catering, bar, golf academy, trolley hire, buggy hire, on-site accommodation
VISITORS: Welcome – booking advisable

City West boasts one of the most intimidating finishing holes in the Dublin area. Course designer Christy O'Connor Jnr likens the shot – over water – to the two-iron that he played to the 18th at The Belfry in his 1989 Ryder Cup singles win over Fred Couples.

The resemblance may be stretching things a little too far, but there is no denying that it is a fine way to finish a course that is always enjoyable and testing.

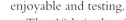
Artworks on granite rocks illustrate each hole's layout at City West.

The 18th is the signature hole, a par 4 measuring 435yd/395m, with a double lake on the left-hand side. For those who are overly concerned with safety and insist on playing their tee shot up the right, where there are mounds, then the approach into the green is narrowed considerably.

There are plenty of other fine holes that shouldn't be overlooked. The stroke index one is the 6th, which also features a lake on the left and requires an approach shot through trees to a green guarded by bunkers, while the 8th and 9th are extreme doglegs.

There is a second, executive-style course with a par of 68 that is also impressive.

14 *Hermitage*

Hermitage Golf Club, Lucan, County Dublin
TEL: *+353 (0)1-6268491*
LOCATION: *8 miles/13km west of Dublin on the N4;
the entrance gate is across the dual carriageway from
The Foxhunter pub*
COURSE: *18 holes, 6648yd/6044m, par 71, SSS 71*
GREEN FEES: *€€€€*
FACILITIES: *Changing rooms and showers, full catering,
bar, pro shop, trolley hire, buggy hire*
VISITORS: *Welcome weekdays – booking advisable*

The River Liffey, which runs through the Hermitage, has been both friend and foe in its time. Although the water is a special feature – particularly to the back of the 10th green and down the length of the par 5 11th, two of the most picturesque holes in Irish golf – it has also caused its share of grief, especially when flooding. These two holes, though, remain the centrepiece of a course that is graced by numerous mature trees.

Although relatively modest in length, the course requires creative shot-making and intelligent course management from players of all levels.

The 10th hole is especially captivating. The tee box to this pretty par 3 is in close proximity to the clubhouse (one of the most convivial you'll find anywhere) and there is a sheer drop to the green, that plays about 140yd/129m in distance.

While the course itself will beguile, and some of the par 4s on the homeward run will threaten to spoil many a card, there is also fascinating local folklore that claims things frequently go bang in the night. A hermit's cave once formed part of the topography of the course, and to this day it is claimed that the ghost of Lady Agnes moves through the trees reciting the 'Ballad of the Hermit of Lucan'. Maybe it's best not to think of such things, however, if you just happen to pull a shot into the trees.

The 10th hole at Hermitage is a classic, requiring a shot from an elevated tee to a green in a wooded valley beneath.

15 *Luttrellstown Castle*

Luttrellstown Castle Golf and Country Club, Castleknock, Dublin 15
TEL: *+353 (0)1-8089988* FAX: *+353 (0)1-8089989* EMAIL: *golf@luttrellstown.ie*
WEBSITE: *www.luttrellstown.ie*
LOCATION: *8 miles / 13km west of Dublin; head for Castleknock at M50/N3 intersection; the course is signposted*
COURSE: *18 holes, 7021yd / 6319m, par 72, SSS 74*
GREEN FEES: *€€€€€€*
FACILITIES: *Changing rooms and showers, full catering, bar, pro shop, trolley hire, buggy hire, club hire, on-site apartments*
VISITORS: *Welcome anytime – booking advisable*

The 13th-century castle at Luttrellstown has, in the past, entertained numerous members of the European aristocracy. These days, however, its patrons are more likely to include stars from the music, film and sports world – and the presence of a championship course has proven to be a major attraction.

Although the castle itself remains out-of-bounds for visiting golfers, there is a spectacular clubhouse, a solid wooden structure that would probably be more in tune with a Scandinavian landscape than an Irish one.

However, its uniqueness works. It occupies an elevated site overlooking the 18th green, with balconies for those who have already finished their rounds to relax and peer out at their fellow golfers traipsing up the finishing hole.

The course at Luttrellstown Castle is always in pristine condition. The fairways are generous enough, the rough comfortably short, and the greens large and relatively flat – all of which tends to enable those who are not regular players to get around without too much difficulty. Yet, there are some excellent holes: the 7th, a par 4 of 393yd / 357m, demands a precise tee shot to the top of a hill, and then an approach that must carry water. There is a bail-out to the left for the faint-hearted, and a further complication of a bunker at the back for any over-hit shot.

The prettiest hole on the course is probably the 11th, which doglegs left. The drive should be hit to the right of the bunker on the elbow, and the approach must skirt water on the right to find a large green. The sequence of difficult par 4s from the 13th to the 15th are the holes that will either make or break your card.

LITERARY DUBLIN

There are few cities anywhere in the world where its people share quite the same affection for literature or cultural traditions as Dublin. This is the birthplace of James Joyce, author of *Ulysses*, who suggested that if the city were ever demolished, then it could be rebuilt from the pages of his book.

The literary tradition in Dublin's 'Fair City' – as it is described in the ballad of Molly Malone – dates back to the early 18th century, when Jonathan Swift, author of *Gulliver's Travels*, was dean in St Patrick's Cathedral. Bram Stoker, who may have incorporated elements from the Great Irish Famine into his novel *Dracula*, hailed from the city's Northside. Nobel Literature Prize winners George Bernard Shaw,

Samuel Beckett, William Butler Yeats and, more recently, Seamus Heaney all sought inspiration from the city and its people, while Oscar Wilde spent his formative years here.

Ireland's literary past is not lost on modern-day authors, many of whom have enjoyed acclaim around the world. Roddy Doyle won the Booker Prize for *Paddy Clarke Ha Ha Ha* and is well-known for his Barrystown trilogy – *The Commitments*, *The Snapper* and *The Van* – that successfully capture the unique wit of the Dublin people.

The Dublin Writers' Museum in Parnell Square, close to O'Connell Street, is a comprehensive mine of information about the city's writers.

16 Skerries

Skerries Golf Club, Hacketstown, Skerries, County Dublin
TEL: *+353 (0)1-8491567* **FAX:** *+353 (0)1-8491591* **EMAIL:** *skerriesgolfclub@eircom.net*
WEBSITE: *www.skerriesgolfclub.ie*
LOCATION: *20 miles/32km north of Dublin; take the N1 and turn at Blakes Cross onto the R127 for Skerries; the club is signposted*
COURSE: *18 holes, 6717yd/6107m, par 73, SSS 72*
GREEN FEES: *€€€€*
FACILITIES: *Changing rooms and showers, catering, bar, pro shop, trolley hire*
VISITORS: *Welcome – booking advisable*

This mature parkland course is one of the most popular in north Dublin. Immaculately maintained, with undulating fairways offering panoramic views of the Mourne Mountains to the north and Howth Head to the south, there is plenty of variety.

Moreover, with five par 5s – three of them on the front nine – there is scope for big hitters to let loose. Yet, one of the course's attractions is that there are also some innocent-looking short holes that have been known to ruin many a good card. The 7th is a lovely little par 3 that has four bunkers guarding it, while the 11th is an enticing short par 4 that will often tempt players to loosen their shoulders. Indeed, the following hole, the par 3 12th, is probably the nicest on the course.

The toughest is arguably the 17th, the last of the par 5s. The tee shot is a drive through trees to a narrow fairway and you won't feel safe until you have played your third shot to a narrow green that is notoriously difficult to hold.

17 St Margaret's

St Margaret's Golf and Country Club, St Margaret's, County Dublin
TEL: *+353 (0)1-8640400* **FAX:** *+353 (0)1-8640289* **EMAIL:** *sales@stmargarets.net*
WEBSITE: *www.st-margarets.net*
LOCATION: *9 miles/15km north of Dublin and 4 miles/6.4km west of Dublin Airport; approach the course, which is signposted, either from the N1 or the N2*
COURSE: *18 holes, 6930yd/6300m, par 72, SSS 73*
GREEN FEES: *€€€€€*
FACILITIES: *Changing rooms and showers, full catering, bar, pro shop, trolley hire, buggy hire, golfing academy*
VISITORS: *Welcome – booking advisable*

On what was originally flat farmland that was transformed in the mid-1990s into an inland course of richly rolling terrain by considerable earth moving and ingenious design, St Margaret's is a superb course. Indeed, there are no perceivable weak holes on a layout that utilizes trees, hedgerows and, of course, the ubiquitous water to tremendous effect.

After a gentle opening that concentrates the mind but doesn't destroy confidence, St Margaret's winds its way with some interesting holes – including the pretty par 3 5th – until it comes to a part of the course that has similarities with no less than Augusta National. It is on the 7th and 8th that the river has been cleverly employed. The 7th runs downhill from an elevated tee and the shot to the green must be precise and committed. The 8th is a truly great par 5, measuring some 525yd/477m, where the drive must be hit over water to a fairway that has another hazard running up the right and the green on

Clever use of the River Ward at St Margaret's adds to the course's appeal.

the opposite side. The 9th hole brings you back up to the clubhouse. Then it is off again on another loop that has yet more holes to hold your interest.

The two par 3s, the 13th and the 15th, are great short holes, but the best is reserved until the very last, where the 18th, a 458-yd/416-m par 4, demands an approach from the brave, over yet another lake to a tiered green. This finishing hole typifies the essence of St Margaret's. It rewards accuracy but requires length, too, making it a true test of a golfer's body and mind.

18 *Ashbourne*

Ashbourne Golf Club, Ashbourne, County Meath
TEL: *+353 (0)1-8352005* **FAX:** *+353 (0)1-8352561* **EMAIL:** *ashgc@iol.ie or comm.mgr@iol.ie*
WEBSITE: *www.ashbournegolfclub.ie*
LOCATION: *12 miles/19km north of Dublin, on the N2*
COURSE: *18 holes, 6472yd/5884m, par 71, SSS 70*
GREEN FEES: €€€
FACILITIES: *Changing rooms and showers, full catering, bar, pro shop, trolley hire, buggy hire*
VISITORS: *Welcome – booking advisable*

A little byroad takes you from Ashbourne, once a village but now a mushrooming town, to the golf course. As you drive through the entrance gate, take a quick glance to the right – your gaze will be directed towards an area of water, mature trees and undulating terrain that local players have christened 'Amen Corner'. It may not compare to the original version at Augusta, but these few holes are, nevertheless, a little piece of heaven in this corner of County Meath. Of course, it takes some time to actually reach this part of the course – given that it constitutes the 11th, 12th, 13th and 14th holes – but you will not be disappointed by the preceding journey.

There are some nice holes on the front nine, especially the 3rd, a par 4 of 374yd/

340m, where the River Broadmeadow deviously guards the green.

However, it is the homeward run, and especially the sequence after the turn, that features the best of a course that is always well maintained and welcoming to visitors.

The 11th green at Ashbourne, the start of a local version of Augusta's 'Amen Corner'.

19 Royal Tara

Royal Tara Golf Club, Bellinteer, Navan, County Meath
TEL: *+353 (0)46-255508* **FAX:** *+353 (0)46-25508* **EMAIL:** *info@royaltaragolfclub.com*
WEBSITE: *www.royaltaragolfclub.com*
LOCATION: *30 miles/48km north of Dublin on the N3*
COURSE: *27 holes, 6494yd/5904m, par 72, SSS 71*
GREEN FEES: *€€€*
FACILITIES: *Changing rooms and showers, full catering, bar, pro shop, trolley hire, buggy hire*
VISITORS: *Welcome by arrangement*

With 27 excellent parkland holes, and a state-of-the-art clubhouse, Royal Tara boasts one of the finest golfing facilities in the country; and, for good measure, it is only half an hour's drive north-west of Dublin. The course comprises three loops of nine holes – the Cluide (blue), Tara (red) and Bellinter (yellow). The club has honoured the area's rich past by naming each hole after an aspect of the nearby hill of Tara's folklore.

Although it is possible to vary the three loops, the Cluide and Tara make up what is the official 18-hole course. With a large number of trees lining the fairways, accuracy off the tee is absolutely critical. This is brought home as early as the 2nd hole, a par 4 of 411yd/374m, which requires an uphill drive over a valley before the ball rolls downhill. Two large trees on either side will severely penalize any inaccuracy.

The 7th is another hole that reaffirms the necessity for accuracy, as there is a spinney of trees 240yd/220m down the right and more on the left. The 15th – 6th on the Tara nine – is a beautiful par 3 with the tee shot played over a valley to a green guarded by mounds.

It's worth pointing out that the 'Royal' appendage does not come via the traditional route, that is bestowed on a golf club by Britain's Royal family. Rather, it reflects the club's location, just beside the traditional seat of the ancient High Kings of Ireland.

TARA

Tara was the seat of the High Kings of Ireland in the first millennium AD. Though an important site as early as the Stone Age, it was not until the reign of the legendary King Cormac MacAirt in the 3rd century that Tara reached the pinnacle of its splendour. Na Fianna, the legendary warriors of Ireland, served King Cormac, and magnificent feasts were celebrated in the long Banqueting Hall that he built. His palace, along with Ráth Riogh (Palace of Kings), is part of the Royal Enclosure, the largest fort on the hill top. In the centre of these remains stands the Lia Fáil, the Stone of Destiny, an ancient fertility symbol that is reported to have roared its approval on the inauguration of a worthy High King. Nearby is the mound of the hostages, a passage-grave dating from 1800BC. The whole site is infused with the legends of the Meabh, the goddess of fertility and the earth.

20 Ardee

Ardee Golf Club, Ardee, County Louth
TEL: *+353 (0)41-6853227*
FAX: *+353 (0)41-6856137*
LOCATION: *2/3 mile/1km north of Ardee, off the N2 Dublin–Derry road; alternatively, approach Ardee via the link road to the N1/M1 motorway; the course is signposted*
COURSE: *18 holes, 6438yd/5852m, par 70, SSS 71*
GREEN FEES: *€€€*
FACILITIES: *Changing rooms and showers, full catering, bar, pro shop, tuition, trolley hire*
VISITORS: *Welcome weekdays – booking advisable*

Originally a rather cramped 18-hole course, Ardee has since benefited immensely from the addition of five new holes and a remodelling of the old course layout, transforming it into a parkland course that presents an excellent test for players of all standards. Add in a very convivial clubhouse atmosphere, and this club has discovered a truly winning formula. It is genuinely among the best inland courses in the north-east.

With names such as 'Cuchulainn's Crown', as in the 1st hole, and 'Ferdia', the 7th, there are obvious links with the Irish legendary figure of Cuchulainn. Indeed, the Tain Trail that purports to follow his war route goes through the town. On the course, the stretch of holes from the 12th to home may convince golfers that they, too, require bravery above and beyond the call of duty.

The 12th, a par 4 of 372yd/338m, needs a well-positioned tee shot through trees, with danger left and right. The 13th is a lovely par 3 of 190yd/172m that requires a carry over a pond (be careful not to disturb the swans!). The 14th, probably the hardest hole on the course, is a demanding par 5 to a viciously undulating green.

Ardee is a heavily wooded parkland course. At the 12th, trees come into play on both sides of the fairway.

21 Nuremore

Nuremore Hotel and Golf Course, Carrickmacross, County Monaghan
TEL: *+353 (0)42-9664016* **FAX:** *+353 (0)42-9664016* **EMAIL:** *nuremore@eircom.ie*
LOCATION: *1¼ miles/2km south of Carrickmacross, on the N2*
COURSE: *18 holes, 6706yd/6096m, par 71, SSS 69*
GREEN FEES: *€€€*
FACILITIES: *Changing room and showers, full catering, bar, pro shop, trolley hire, buggy hire, on-site accommodation*
VISITORS: *Welcome – booking advisable*

At first sight, as you drive up the approach to the Nuremore Hotel, the massively rolling hills and numerous glimpses of water can be pretty daunting. The 'Slow Please, Ducks Crossing' sign that warns oncoming motorists simply reinforces the impression that water lurks everywhere.

While it is true that the course is extremely testing, with virtually every club in the bag likely to be used, there is a great sense of fulfilment at the end of the round.

The natural drumlins of the Monaghan landscape have been used to very good effect, adding up to an excellent test of golf, as professionals have discovered in contesting the Ulster Open on this course – which also has a top-class hotel.

Water has been cleverly used on the course. A huge lake is in play between the 2nd and 5th holes on the outward journey, and the 7th fairway is literally surrounded by water. However, this hazard is even more evident on the inward run. Indeed, the tee shot off the 10th tee is very intimidating – with the edge of the lake only too willing to offer the ball a watery grave – while the par 4 13th, a dogleg left, is a fine hole that demands absolute precision off the tee.

The biggest challenge on the course, though, comes on the last hole, a 474-yd/430-m par 4 to an elevated green that has serious trouble to the right.

22 Laytown and Bettystown

Laytown and Bettystown Golf Club, Golf Links Road, Bettystown, County Meath
TEL: +353 (0)41-9827170 **FAX:** +353 (0)41-9828506 **EMAIL:** bettystowngolfclub@utvinternet.com
WEBSITE: www.bettystowngolfclub.utvinternet.com
LOCATION: Turn off the N1 at Julianstown, taking the R150 to Laytown and then the coast road to the golf club
COURSE: 18 holes, 6437yd/5852m, par 71, SSS 72
GREEN FEES: €€€€
FACILITIES: Changing rooms and showers, catering, bar, pro shop, tuition, trolley hire
VISITORS: Welcome by arrangement

Only one club in Ireland can boast that two players who subsequently went on to enjoy Ryder Cup honours each won the club's captain's prize in their amateur days – and that is Laytown and Bettystown, thanks to Des Smyth and Philip Walton.

L and B, as the club is commonly known, is a true links, with the opening nine holes taking you down the coast to the bird sanctuary at Mornington and close to the lighthouse, while much of the homeward stretch runs parallel to the coastal road.

This is a very fine course and possesses a tough par 71. The 10th is a really good par 4, measuring 420yd/382m, and requiring an accurate drive to the dogleg and then a good second shot to a well-protected green. The 18th is a par 5 back to the clubhouse, and is unusual in that it has two blind shots – dual mounds guarding the green. This is a hole that has been the downfall of many a card.

23 Dundalk

Dundalk Golf Club, Blackrock, County Louth
TEL: +353 (0)42-9321731
FAX: +353 (0)42-9322022 **EMAIL:** dkgc@iol.ie
WEBSITE: www.eiresoft.com/dundalkgc/
LOCATION: 2 miles/3.2km south of Dundalk, on the coast road
COURSE: 18 holes, 6776yd/6160m, par 72, SSS 72
GREEN FEES: €€€
FACILITIES: Changing rooms and showers, catering, bar, pro shop, trolley hire, practice ground
VISITORS: Welcome – booking advisable

The drive along the coastline to Blackrock, where Dundalk Golf Club is located on rising ground above the picturesque village, is tranquil – and the stress-free environment is maintained upon arrival at this welcoming course, which is also home to the Irish Region of the Professional Golfers Association.

Dundalk is a well-matured course with a reputation for very good greens. However, the key to conquering the course has to be accuracy off the tee, with length being the additional requirement.

This parkland course is effectively broken up into three distinct segments: an opening stretch of four tough tree-lined par 4s, then a run of holes to the 13th that include four par 5s, with a tough finishing stint to the 18th.

The feature hole on this course is the 7th. This is a slight double dogleg par 5 of 547yd/498m, with a pond in front of the green to rule

The 2nd at Dundalk – a par 4 of 403yd/366m – is part of a tough opening stretch of tree-lined holes.

out anyone's bright idea of going for the green in two. The ideal drive is a draw off the tee and then a straight or slightly faded second shot.

There are two really good holes towards the end of the round. The 16th is a sharp dogleg left of 432yd/393m to a well bunkered green; the 17th is a short hole with a tee shot to a raised green that has five bunkers as extra protection.

24 *Seapoint*

Seapoint Golf Club, Termonfeckin, County Louth
TEL: *+353 (0)41-9822333* **FAX:** *+353 (0)41-9822331* **EMAIL:** *golflinks@seapoint.ie*
WEBSITE: *www.seapoint.com*
LOCATION: *Take the R166 to Termonfeckin off the N1, north-east of Drogheda; the course is signposted in Termonfeckin*
COURSE: *18 holes, 7062yd/6420m, par 72, SSS 74*
GREEN FEES: *€€€€*
FACILITIES: *Changing rooms and showers, catering, bar, pro shop, trolley hire, buggy hire, practice area*
VISITORS: *Welcome – booking advisable*

Once you drive through the entrance gate to Seapoint Golf Club, the sight of some fine villas on the road up to the clubhouse may lull you into a mistaken sense that this is some sort of holiday course. It isn't! Indeed, this mix of heathland and links has some spectacular holes, and anyone who can play to their handicap here will have reason to be pleased.

The first part of the course is unquestionably heathland and, with water hazards very much in play, it requires a player's full concentration from the start. Invariably in good condition, as you would expect from a creation by Ryder Cup player Des Smyth, the tougher part can be found once you turn into the back nine.

These holes are carved through some fine duneland, not unlike that found on the neighbouring County Louth links. The 14th is a delightful hole, and anyone who misses the fairway will undoubtedly find trouble. Moreover, the approach shot to a small green tucked away in the corner of the course requires great accuracy.

Each hole from the 14th to the finish is superb, and the 511-yd/465-m par 5 18th means that there is no real respite until you reach the clubhouse.

The finishing holes at Seapoint are pure linksland and run along the coastline of the Irish Sea.

25 County Louth

County Louth Golf Club, Baltray, Drogheda, County Louth
TEL: *+353 (0)41-9822329* **FAX:** *+353 (0)41-9822969* **EMAIL:** *baltray@indigo.ie*
LOCATION: *5 miles/8km east of Drogheda*
COURSE: *18 holes, 6783yd/6169m, par 73, SSS 72*
GREEN FEES: *€€€€€€+*
FACILITIES: *Changing rooms and showers, catering, bar, pro shop, tuition, practice ground, trolley hire, buggy hire, on-site accommodation*
VISITORS: *Welcome – booking essential*

COUNTY LOUTH

HOLE	YD	M	PAR	HOLE	YD	M	PAR
1	433	394	4	10	398	362	4
2	482	439	5	11	481	437	5
3	544	495	5	12	410	373	4
4	344	313	4	13	421	383	4
5	158	144	3	14	332	302	4
6	531	483	5	15	152	138	3
7	163	148	3	16	388	353	4
8	407	370	4	17	179	163	3
9	419	381	4	18	541	492	5
OUT	3481	3166	37	IN	3302	3003	36

6783YD • 6169M • PAR 73

For many years, this links remained largely undiscovered, except to those in the know. Given that County Louth Golf Club lies in the quaint village of Baltray, not more than 35 miles/55km north of Dublin Airport, it is inexplicable that it took so long for word to spread. Perhaps it was a case of the Irish wanting to keep the secret all to themselves.

Nowadays, Baltray – as the course is commonly known – is the traditional Irish

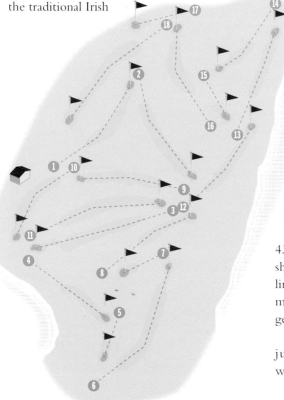

regional qualifying venue for the British Open. Many overseas players from as far afield as South Africa, Australia and the United States have used the event as an excuse to play this fine links in a competitive environment. It is also home to the East of Ireland amateur championship, which was won by Darren Clarke in the year before he turned professional.

Although the original layout was designed in the 1890s by a Scottish professional with the wonderful name of Mr Snowball, the man responsible for leaving his imprint on this imposing links course was the noted golf architect Tom Simpson. It was Simpson who, in the mid-1920s, strategically placed the bunkers and gave each green its own distinct individuality, while using the rolling hills to good effect. The dunes, it must be said, are not towering, but they don't need to be.

From the opening hole, a par 4 of 433yd/394m, you know you'll need good shot-making and a clear head to conquer a links course that is very traditional in set-up: miss the fairways, which are sufficiently generous, and there is a heavy price to pay.

If you doubted the need for shrewd judgement, then the 3rd hole, a par 5 wickedly called the 'Punch Bowl', will teach you a lesson. The drive itself is not too intimidating, but the approach shot to a green that is difficult to hold means that anyone who manages to walk away with a par can feel extremely good about themselves.

This is followed by a classic short par 4 4th hole – all of 344yd/313m – which offers immediate respite. So it goes, with the demanding 9th hole bringing you back towards the clubhouse before embarking on a back-nine loop that brings you down to some majestic holes etched out of the dunes down by the coast. Each hole from the 10th to the 16th is memorable in its own right, and the pity is that the finishing two holes don't quite live up to those that have preceded them.

In every sense, however, Baltray is a course that will reward and captivate. It is at all times challenging and, from the first tee shot, holds your interest, and is likely to make you use every club in the bag. One reason that it has not played host to a major international tournament is probably its remoteness; Baltray is situated by the mouth of the River Boyne. However, that is one of its beauties too, for the drive from Drogheda out to the course – along the river and ever-narrowing roads – increases the expectation that a true links is at hand. For those who return, and most do, this is a links that stays forever in the memory.

Perhaps the holes that will remain longest in the memory bank are those immediately after the turn, as you head back into the dunes and run up towards the neighbouring Seapoint course – but invariably the abiding memory is of a place that has all the best qualities associated with golf. A warm welcome, a great course and a fond farewell, for those who run the County Louth Golf Club are very much golfing folk.

Baltray is the traditional home of the British Open regional qualifying in Ireland. This is the 18th hole.

26 *Beaverstown*

Beaverstown Golf Club, Donabate, County Dublin
TEL: *+353 (0)1-8436439*
FAX: *+353 (0)1-8435059* **EMAIL:** *bgc@iol.ie*
WEBSITE: *www.beaverstown.com*
LOCATION: *15 miles/24km north of Dublin,
4 miles/6.4km north of Dublin Airport; take the turning
for Donabate off the M1; the course is signposted*
COURSE: *18 holes, 6637yd/6034m, par 72, SSS 73*
GREEN FEES: *€€€*
FACILITIES: *Changing rooms and showers, catering,
bar, trolley hire*
VISITORS: *Welcome – booking advisable*

A whole generation of north Dublin school children in the 1960s and 1970s spent their summers trekking to the fruit orchards and strawberry fields of Donabate to earn extra pocket money. Now, many of them are enjoying the same rich land in a different guise – as one of the finest tests of inland golf in the region.

Beaverstown, originally designed by Eddie Hackett and recently upgraded by Peter McEvoy, winds its way through the orchard. The trees are still there, giving vibrant colour and providing a magnificent hazard for the wayward, while the greens, many of them undulating, are first class. 'I'd say we've managed to take a pretty average club course and turn it into something that is right up there in the Premiership,' says McEvoy.

The 1st hole doglegs slightly to the left and has a pond lurking on its left. It is the start of a very enjoyable experience and, off the back tees, Beaverstown is quite a challenge. This is proven as early as the 4th, a par 4 of 398yd/362m, with the estuary on the right.

On the back nine, the 14th is a tough par 4, with what the locals call 'The Canal' running in front; the 16th has the most undulating green on the course.

However, the feature hole remains the 17th, even though it has been totally reversed from its original routing because of the proximity of the railway line. Fortunately it has lost nothing of its magic in doing this complete about face.

*Beaverstown is always in good condition. At the 18th,
strategic bunkering protects the green.*

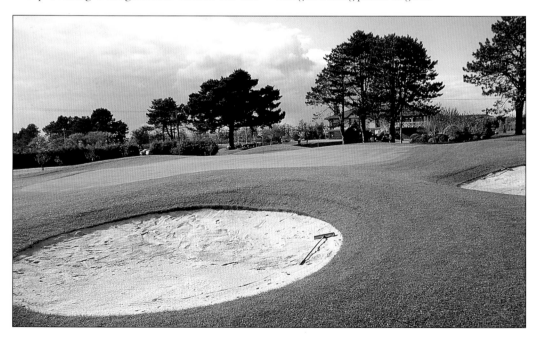

27 The Island

The Island Golf Club, Corballis, Donabate, County Dublin
TEL: *+353 (0)1-8436462*
FAX: *+353 (0)1-8436860* **EMAIL:** *islandgc@iol.ie*
WEBSITE: *www.theisland.com*
LOCATION: *15 miles/24km north of Dublin, take the turning for Donabate off the M1; the course is signposted*
COURSE: *18 holes, 6815yd/6195m, par 71, SSS 73*
GREEN FEES: *€€€€€€+*
FACILITIES: *Changing rooms and showers, catering, bar, pro shop, tuition, practice ground, trolley hire, buggy hire*
VISITORS: *Welcome – booking essential*

The Island is not, in fact, an island, but a jut of land – with magnificent sand dunes – that protrudes out from Donabate. Still, for many years, access to the course was restricted to a boat journey from Malahide, where most of the club's members lived, to a special jetty (now long gone) close to the present-day 14th hole on this marvellous, natural links.

That little boat trip added to The Island's mystique and, even though access is now entirely by road, the place still retains a special appeal. A modern clubhouse and some recent redesign work to the course by Jeff Howes, which greatly compliments the work previously carried out by Eddie Hackett and Fred Hawtree, has ensured that it is among the very top courses in the country. In addition, its proximity to Dublin Airport has made it a very popular destination for golfing tourists.

Golfing in twilight at The Island – this is the 15th, with the village of Malahide across the estuary.

The Island is a wonderful test of golf. The layout is unusual in that it opens with eight straight par 4s – indeed, the first three holes are among the toughest starts that you will find anywhere – but there is great variety to the holes and, always, the onus is on accuracy off the tee. The rough is very severe and any wayward drive will be punished.

This is a course that will make you use every club in your bag and forces great creativity. The outward nine has a mix of par 4s ranging from the 441-yd/401-m 7th hole to one immediately following that measures 305yd/278m. With an out-of-bounds on the right, the 9th doesn't actually play as the easiest hole on the course, as the score card would have you believe.

On the homeward run, however, the challenge is made even harder with the holes manoeuvring their way through spectacular dunes. The first of two par 5s arrives at the 10th, which has out-of-bounds down the right and dares you to skirt with it as the hole is a dogleg right. The 13th, a par 3 of 211yd/192m, looks delightful but has evil intent, with out-of-bounds right and a huge grass bunker in front of the green. The 14th is another classic short par 4, with probably the narrowest fairway in Irish golf. There is one great hole after another until the pièce de résistance is delivered on the 18th, a murderous par 4 of 463yd/421m, that brings you back to the clubhouse where, finally, there is some respite.

REGIONAL DIRECTORY

Where to Stay

Dublin City It is worth bearing in mind that there are many reasonably priced bed-and-breakfast guest-houses available in the Greater Dublin area, most of which can be booked through any Bord Fáilte (Irish Tourist Board) office. In terms of hotels, the choice has never been better. However, Dublin's status as one of the most desired locations in Europe makes pre-booking imperative, regardless of the time of year. **The Arlington Hotel** (+353 (0)1-8049100) is one of the most central hotels in the city, overlooking the River Liffey at O'Connell Bridge and within comfortable strolling distance of the trendy Temple Bar area, with its array of restaurants, pubs and nightlife. **The Davenport Hotel** (+353 (0)1-6073500) is located close to Merrion Square and is within easy walking distance of many museums. The food in its Lanyon's Restaurant is superb, while some of Dublin's best pubs – including O'Donoghue's – are a short walk away. One of the features of Dublin's boom times has been the arrival of a number of five-star hotels, among them the **Four Seasons Hotel** (+353 (0)1-2696446) in Ballsbridge, which has prices to match its opulence, while, across the road, **Bewley's Hotel** (+353 (0)1-6681111) provides the same convenient location at a much lower price. For those in search of a stay in the heart of Georgian Dublin, **The Schoolhouse Hotel** (+353 (0)1-6675014), with its acclaimed Satchels Restaurant and Inkwell Bar, is a viable option. Nearby, the **Merrion Hall** (+353 (0)1-6681426) is a four-star guesthouse that combines Edwardian comforts, including four-poster beds, with fine food. For economical but good accommodation in the city centre, **Bewley's Hotel** (+353 (0)1-6708122) is located in the heart of the Temple Bar area, while **Cassidy's Hotel** (+353 (0)1-8780555) is situated in Cavendish Row in the north inner city close to O'Connell Street. **Clontarf Castle Hotel** (+353 (0)1-8332321) is just north of the city centre and close to the Royal Dublin Golf Club. In west Dublin, the **City West Hotel** (+353 (0)1-4010500) is an ideal base for a golfing holiday, with its own championship course and golfing academy. **Red Cow Moran's Hotel** (+353 (0)1-4593650) is located off the M50 and its facilities include three restaurants, four bars and a night-club.

Dun Laoghaire/South Dublin **The Stillorgan Park Hotel** (+353 (0)1-2881621) is a gateway to the magnificent courses in the north Wicklow area and includes the highly regarded Purple Sage Restaurant in its complex. **The Royal Marine Hotel** (+353 (0)1-2801911) in Dun Laoghaire is particularly suitable for those using the car ferry into that port as the base for their golfing holiday. **The Radisson SAS St Helens Hotel** (+353 (0)1-2186000) is another of the newer hotel developments aimed at the top end of the tourist and business market, but it is conveniently located beside the Stillorgan dual carriageway and within short driving distance of many of south Dublin and north Wicklow's top courses.

Fingal **The Portmarnock Links and Golf Hotel** (+353 (0)1-8460611) overlooks the links course and is an ideal base for golfers wishing to savour the delights of nearby courses, including The Island and Portmarnock. It also has one of the finest restaurants in the area, Osbornes. **The White Sands Hotel** (+353 (0)1-8460003) is also a good golfing base. As its name suggests, the **Island View Hotel** (+353 (0)1-8450099) overlooks The Island Golf Club across the Malahide estuary, while the recently upgraded **Grand Hotel** (+353 (0)1-8450000) is located in the heart of this thriving north Dublin town, which has some of the best restaurants in the country.

North-East Leinster **The Nuremore Hotel** (+353 (0)42–9661438) has an attractive 18-hole championship course on its doorstep. **The Neptune Beach Hotel** (+353 (0)41-9827107) has some magnificent views of the Irish Sea but, for golfers, it is also the ideal base to discover the delights of the links courses at Laytown and Bettystown, County Louth and Seapoint. For those who prefer self-catering, contact **The Cottages** (+353 (0)41-9828104), a small development of thatched cottages virtually at the entrance to Laytown and Bettystown. **The Boyne Valley Hotel and Country Club** (+353 (0)41-9839188) in Drogheda is ideally located for those who wish to visit the Neolithic sites at Newgrange and Knowth, as well as test their golfing skills at County Louth and Seapoint. Just north of Dundalk, **The Ballymacscanlon Hotel** (+353 (0)42-9371124) has its own golf course and is a good base for courses in the region.

Where to Eat

Dublin City There has been a huge improvement in restaurant standards in Dublin and the city now boasts some international-class restaurants, unfortunately often with prices to match. However, it is still possible to get good quality food at a reasonable price, and many pubs also offer quality food with a uniquely Dublin ambience. **Captain America's** (+353 (0)1-6715266) in Grafton Street is the city's original hamburger and steak cookhouse and offers good food at affordable prices. Likewise, the **Elephant and Castle** (+353 (0)1-6793121) in Temple Bar has managed to get the mix of atmosphere, price and quality just about right. The **Bad Ass Cafe** (+353 (0)1-6712596) may not look much from the outside but the food is excellent − particularly the pizzas and pasta dishes − and also good value. **Break for the Border** (+353 (0)1-4780300), located near St Stephen's Green, is a trendy place that combines good food with loud music. More upmarket, **L'Ecrivain** (+353 (0)1-6611919) in Baggot Street is a sophisticated restaurant with mouth-watering seafood dishes, while **Patrick Guilbaud's** (+353 (0)1-6764192) is an acclaimed French restaurant in Merrion Street. **Chapter One** (+353 (0)1-8732266) is located in the Dublin Writers' Museum, Parnell Square, and is extremely popular with theatre-goers, offering a menu that ranges from duckling to venison. **QV2** (+353 (0)1-6773363) serves international cuisine with an Irish twist and has established a very good reputation. **The Eastern Balti House** (+353 (0)1-6710428) has an unrivalled reputation for Indian cuisine.

Dun Laoghaire/South Dublin Just to confirm that Ireland has international taste buds, one of the best and most popular restaurants is **Ayumi-Ya** (+353 (0)1-2831767) in Blackrock, which offers patrons traditional Japanese food in an open-seating environment. **The Vico** (+353 (0)1-2354014) in Dalkey has made a name for itself due to its ambience as much as for its food; it is essential to book to be sure of a table. **Luigi Malone's** (+353 (0)1-2786024) in Stillorgan offers tremendous variety, and anyone favouring pasta dishes is in for a special treat.

Fingal As someone who lives in this particular area, I can vouch for the gastronomic delights available for the visitor. The town of Malahide has a cosmopolitan range of really good restaurants. For Chinese food, you won't do better than **Silks** (+353 (0)1-8453331) or **The Wild Swan** (+353 (0)1-6662), while **Vinnie Vinucchi's** (+353 (0)1-8451888) will delight lovers of Italian food. **Cruzzo's** (+353 (0)1-8450599) is placed on what appear to be stilts in the Malahide Marina, looking across to The Island Golf Club. One of the finest seafood restaurants in the country is the **Red Bank** in Skerries (+353 (0)1-8491005).

North-East **The Buttergate Restaurant** (+353 (0)41-34759) in Drogheda has a reputation for fine food. **The Triple House** (+353 (0)41-22616) in Termonfeckin is close to both Seapoint and County Louth courses and is ideal for post-round meals. **The Monasterboice Inn** (+353 (0)41-9837383) near Drogheda has steaks as a speciality. **The Loft** (+353 (0)46-71755) in Navan is great for pizza and chargrilled streaks. **Banjo Sherlocks** (+353 (0)46-74688), also in Navan, has fantastic brown trout and great steaks.

What to Do

Dublin County One of the best ways to get around Dublin City and to see the sights, is to take one of the open-top bus tours. A number of companies run these tours, with O'Connell Street as a central starting point. Once you purchase a ticket, you are free to hop on and off at any of the stop-off points around this thriving city. Dublin has a rich past, as will become evident with visits to museums, **Christ Church Cathedral**, the **Royal Hospital** and **Kilmainham Gaol**. For those visitors who want to seek out information about their Irish ancestry, a visit to the **Genealogical Office** in Kildare Street should be of immeasurable assistance. For the more energetic, it is possible to take the **Viking Splash Tours** − on land and water − which trace this particular side of old Dublin's history. **Trinity College** houses the famous Book of Kells, an illustrated manuscript dating from the 8th century, which is recognized as the crowning achievement of Celtic art. Among the artefacts on view in the **National Museum** are the Tara Brooch and the Ardagh Chalice. For those who would like to know a bit more about the 'black stuff', as Guinness stout is known locally, then a visit to the **Guinness Hop Store** is worthwhile.

Fingal A visit to the 12th-century **Malahide Castle** in the north of County Dublin is a pleasant way to spend some time, and for train lovers there is the added bonus of the **Fry Model Railway**, which is also on the estate. Meanwhile, in Skerries, the conducted tour of the recently renovated **Skerries Windmill** is fascinating. For those who enjoy a brisk walk and some healthy sea air, the old harbour at **Howth** − which can be reached on the DART, the local rail network − is an option. There are also boat rides during the summer to **Ireland's Eye**, an unpopulated island that lies just off the coast.

North-East Leinster One of the most interesting and important historic sites in Europe can be found at **Newgrange**, west of Drogheda, where a mound was built in 3200BC as a burial site for local chiefs.

Tourist Information Centres

Dublin Tourism, O'Connell Street, Dublin (Lo-call, within Ireland, 1850-230330)
Dublin Tourism, Suffolk Street, Dublin 2 (+353 (0)1-6057700)
Fingal Tourism, Swords, County Dublin (+353 (0)1-8400077)
Brú na Boinne, Donore, County Meath (+353 (0) 41-9880305)
Dundalk Tourism Jocelyn Street, Dundalk, County Louth (+353 (0)42-9335484)

Chapter 2

Wicklow & the South-East

One of the most remarkable things about exiting Dublin's urban mass is that it doesn't take unduly long to find stress-free bliss. In fact, all that is required to swap houses and office blocks for a place in the countryside is 12½ miles/ 20km of dual carriage-way as the N11 heads south into County Wicklow, the so-called 'Garden of Ireland'.

County Wicklow – with its impressive mountains and valleys and innumerable golf courses – is a beautiful part of the country, which also serves as the gateway to County Wexford, part of the sunny south-east.

Although there is a railway line that travels down the Wicklow coast, connecting Dublin to Rosslare, anyone who wishes to experience the golf courses of this region in all their glory will require a car or some other means of road transport. County Wicklow's largest urban centre is Bray, which nestles the border with Dublin. The town is by-passed by a motorway, however, so for the most part, driving through the county is like revisiting nature. Moreover, there are some spectacular mountain peaks along the route.

Some stunning golf courses are to be found in the Wicklow Mountains, and it is worth an excursion up and down some of the more remote byroads in the region to savour these undulating hill-side courses. For the most part, though, the cream of Wicklow's courses lie close to the coastline. Further down the N11, in Wexford, the development of a number of new courses now gives the visiting player a mix of parkland and traditional links that will satisfy the most discerning of golfing palates.

Left: The Round Tower at Glendalough, County Wicklow, which may have served as a bell tower, a storehouse, a refuge – or simply as a landmark for approaching visitors. Above: The Croppy Boy at Druids Glen Golf Club – a symbol of the failed 1798 Rebellion.

Almost as soon as you head south from Dublin, you are hit by one golfing jewel after another. Druids Glen (No. 1) is a parkland course that has played host to three Murphy's Irish Open championships – in fact, it was here that Spaniard Sergio Garcia achieved his first ever European Tour win – while The European Club, a links course that lies alongside the spectacular strand at Brittas Bay, has three holes that have been voted among the top 500 in world golf by *Golf* magazine.

Both of these venues, which are located less than 30 minutes' drive from each other, were designed by Pat Ruddy; not only did he design the modern-day links at The European, but he owns it as well. Nowhere is the welcome to a visiting golfer more genuine than that at The European, a course that, although only designed as recently as 1992, looks as if it has been here for eternity.

Further down the coast, and slightly inland along the River Avoca, lies one of the prettiest golf courses you could ever visit. It is called Woodenbridge and, over time, it has fought an ongoing war with

Dolmens, or megalithic burial chambers, such as this one at The European Club, are remarkably commonplace.

the ravages of the flowing waters that meander through, and from time to time inundate, it. Thus far, the course has always recovered – and it is definitely worth including on any golfing itinerary.

While Wexford does not have the same spectacular scenery as its northern neighbour, this part of south-east Ireland has a lovely mix – from the newly-developed Seafield in Ballymoney, which manages to give the visitor a flavour of parkland, heathland and seaside golf all in one round, to the more traditional links courses at Rosslare and St Helen's Bay.

Along the way, it is worth stopping over at Curracloe Strand – where much of the movie *Saving Private Ryan* was shot – which is one of the many Blue Flag beaches along this coastline.

Planning an Itinerary

It is hard to imagine, when you consider the golfing treats that await in the rest of the country, but there are a large number of visitors to Ireland who choose to play in Wicklow and the south-east, and nowhere else. Certainly for those visiting from Britain, with the car ferries into Dun Laoghaire and Rosslare respectively providing the perfect starting points, it makes a great deal of sense – there are good courses, plenty of what the locals call *craic* (that's best translated as 'good fun'), good scenery and good hospitality. For the most part, it is possible to reserve tee times on courses without the need to make your booking too far in advance. Druids Glen is probably the only exception in this regard.

It is advisable to arrange your own mode of transport to make your way around Wicklow and Wexford. This way, you will be able to enjoy the mountainous terrain in Wicklow, and have

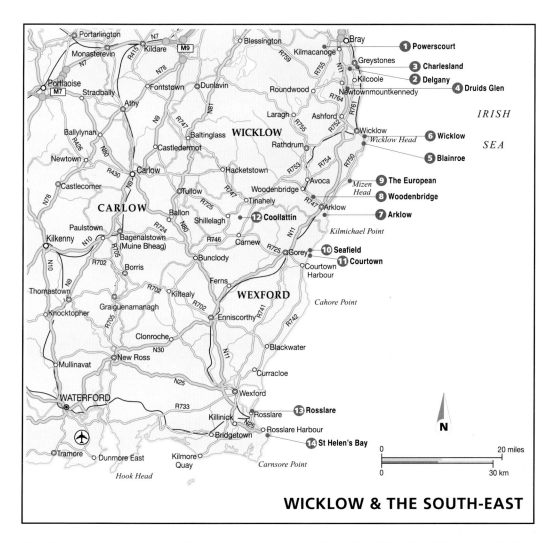

WICKLOW & THE SOUTH-EAST

the freedom to visit such diverse courses as Powerscourt, Druids Glen, The European and the lovely Woodenbridge in the east. Or better still, arrange to be driven – that way you can relax and enjoy the *craic* at the 19th as well.

The Wicklow Way

The norm when playing golf in Ireland is to walk with your clubs or spoil yourself and hire a caddie, but many non-golfing visitors to Wicklow come for some of the best hill-walking to be found anywhere in the British Isles.

In fact, the 'Wicklow Way' was the first long-distance mountain-walking route to be opened in Ireland (in 1981). It covers an 82-mile/132-km route that begins in Marlay Park in south Dublin and runs through the forests and mountains that take in Knockree, Roundwood (the highest village in Ireland), Laragh, Glenmalure, Ballygobban Hill, Tinahely, Shillelagh and Clonegal. The playwright John Millington Synge – author of *Playboy of the Western World* – spent much of his time walking in this part of the world long before such a pursuit became fashionable.

Powerscourt (No. 1)

Powerscourt Golf Club, Enniskerry, County Wicklow
TEL: +353 (0)1-2046033 **FAX:** +353 (0)1-2761303 **EMAIL:** golfclub@powerscourt.ie
WEBSITE: www.powerscourt.ie
LOCATION: 12 miles/19km south of Dublin, just off the N11 at Enniskerry
COURSE: 36 holes, No. 1 course: 7062yd/6421m, par 72, SSS 74
GREEN FEES: €€€€€€ +
FACILITIES: Changing rooms and showers, catering, bar, pro shop, trolley hire, buggy hire, on-site accommodation
VISITORS: Welcome – booking advisable

There was a time when Powerscourt was most famous for its waterfall, the highest in Ireland, and the magnificent house and gardens that sat in sylvan splendour just outside the village of Enniskerry in the foothills of the Wicklow mountains. Now, however, the fame of this most picturesque of settings is boosted by two fine championship golf courses. The No. 1 course – which has the stunning backdrop of the Sugarloaf Mountain – has played host to the Irish PGA championship and also to the Irish Seniors' Open on the European Tour.

The course is a good test, and particularly demanding if the wind blows. Yet the severely undulating greens are the feature that will linger longest in the memory – you either love them or hate them; it is as simple as that. Whatever your inclination, one thing that is beyond dispute is the quality of the putting surfaces, all of which are magnificent.

The course winds its way through mature parkland, and each hole is interesting. The opening few holes are especially pretty. The 2nd, a par 5 of 507yd/461m, requires a good drive from an elevated tee and, for the approach, you can either take the brave route or opt to lay-up to the right.

It doesn't take long for Powerscourt to bare its teeth, however. The 4th has a narrow landing area and the difficulty is compounded by out-of-bounds down the right. The 8th, a long par 4 with fairway bunkers strategically placed, is more like a three-shooter to the green for most mortals.

The beauty of the course at Powerscourt is, in my opinion, captured best on the finishing stretch. The 16th is a beautiful par 3 of 159yd/145m, with water in front of a raised green surrounded by subtle mounds and trees. This short hole contrasts superbly with the 17th, a par 5 of 544yd/490m, which has yet another water hazard guarding a green that is hard to hold.

Delgany

Delgany Golf Club, Delgany, County Wicklow
TEL: +353 (0)1-2874536 **FAX:** +353 (0)1-2873977 **EMAIL:** delganygolf@eircom.net
LOCATION: Take the N11 south from Dublin, then the turn for Delgany at Glen of the Downs
COURSE: 18 holes, 6028yd/5480m, par 69, SSS 68
GREEN FEES: €€€€
FACILITIES: Changing rooms and showers, catering, bar, pro shop, trolley hire, buggy hire
VISITORS: Welcome

With water guarding the green, it doesn't pay to be short on the par 3 16th hole at Powerscourt No. 1.

Although it is located in a beautiful part of the so-called 'Garden of Ireland' and possesses some marvellous undulating terrain, the Delgany course probably owes its good testing layout to the wisdom of the legendary Harry Vardon.

Back in 1909, Vardon played a challenge match with the Irish champion Michael 'Dyke' Moran. Afterwards, he was asked to suggest some improvements for the infant course. Vardon responded by staking out suitable locations for bunkers and extra tree-planting, and the committee took his advice on board.

The result is a fine round of golf – not overly long by modern standards – that requires a player to use his head, with course management important, and a requirement for accurate rather than long driving.

3 Charlesland

Charlesland Golf Club, Greystones, County Wicklow
TEL: +353 (0)1-2878200 **FAX:** +353 (0)1-2878200
EMAIL: info@charlesland.com
WEBSITE: www.charlesland.com
LOCATION: 5 miles/8km south of Bray; take the turning for Greystones off the N11
COURSE: 18 holes, 6785yd/6169m, par 72, SSS 72
GREEN FEES: €€€€
FACILITIES: Changing rooms and showers, catering, bar, pro shop, practice area, club hire, trolley hire, buggy hire, on-site accommodation
VISITORS: Welcome – booking advisable

With the sea as one backdrop and the imposing Wicklow Mountains as another, Charlesland – located on the outskirts of the vibrant town of Greystones, about 45 minutes south of Dublin – could be described as a 'surf and turf' kind of course. Yet designer Eddie Hackett, as ever, has managed to broaden its appeal beyond purely the aesthetics of the place and provide a course that presents a challenging but fair test of golf.

The Irish Sea accompanies the course for much of the front nine, but the homeward journey is pure parkland. Course designer Hackett remarked of the site, 'I couldn't have asked for better.'

The extension of the DART rail service to Greystones has increased its appeal for those without car transport and has made it particularly popular with day trippers. With a hotel and conference centre also on the grounds, Charlesland has proven a winner, too, for corporate outings.

The par 4s are generally tough, but the par 5s offer something back to the golfer – and the landing areas on the fairways are relatively generous. At 251yd/229m, the par 3 13th hole is by no means short. However, it is very much the feature hole, with the tee box on the highest part of the course. The ascent to the tee is gentle rather than punishing, but once you get there the shot to a green situated some 100ft/30m below can be daunting.

The 7th green at Charlesland, with the 'Little Sugarloaf' in the background.

Druids Glen (No. 1)

Druids Glen Golf Resort, Newtownmountkennedy,
County Wicklow
TEL: *+353 (0)1-2873600* **FAX:** *+353 (0)1-2873699*
EMAIL: *druids@indigo.ie* **WEBSITE:** *www.druidsglen.ie*
LOCATION: *25 miles/40km south of Dublin; take the*
N11, turning off the Newtownmountkennedy roundabout
for Druids Glen; the course is signposted
COURSE: *36 holes, No. 1 course: 7058yd/6389m,*
par 71, SSS 74
GREEN FEES: €€€€€€+
FACILITIES: *Changing rooms and showers, catering, bar,*
pro shop, tuition, golf academy, club hire, trolley hire,
buggy hire, on-site accommodation
VISITORS: *Welcome – booking essential*

DRUIDS GLEN (No.1)

HOLE	YD	M	PAR	HOLE	YD	M	PAR
1	445	405	4	10	440	400	4
2	190	173	3	11	522	475	5
3	339	308	4	12	174	158	3
4	446	405	4	13	471	428	4
5	517	470	5	14	399	363	4
6	476	433	4	15	456	415	4
7	405	368	4	16	538	489	5
8	166	151	3	17	203	185	3
9	389	354	4	18	450	409	4
OUT	3373	3067	35	IN	3653	3322	36

7058YD • 6389M • PAR 71

In many ways, it is hard to believe that Druids Glen – or, to give it its Irish name, *Gleann na Draoite* – only opened for play in 1995. To many, it seems that it has been around for much longer. As host venue to the Irish Open for four successive years, with Colin Montgomerie and Sergio Garcia numbered among its champions, this mystical place didn't waste any time establishing itself as a prime tournament venue.

The land on which Druids Glen now stands has a rich history. The resort gets its name from the discovery of an ancient druids' altar – in close proximity to the 12th green on the No. 1 course – while the two courses are built on the old Woodstock estate, a beautiful 400-year-old demesne with mature trees and undulating landscape. In addition, of course, the nearby Sugarloaf mountain provides a backdrop for a number of holes.

The sense of history is maintained in the clubhouse, built in the restored Woodstock House, which has a specially commissioned statue of a 'croppy boy' (in memory of the 1798 Rebellion). Inside, there are historical paintings and memorabilia dating back to the Great Famine that decimated the Irish population between 1845 and 1855.

Such a connection with the past helps give Druids Glen, which now boasts two fine championship courses and a five-star hotel, a rather special ambience. Pat Ruddy and Tom Craddock designed the No. 1 course, while Ruddy created the second course.

Eamonn Darcy has been the club's touring professional since it opened and, given that he regularly used the old Woodstock estate for horse riding – his other sporting passion – as a boy, the

The par 3 12th hole has an elaborately landscaped
St Brigid's Cross by the elevated tee box.

sense of continuity is preserved. 'They have created a litany of great hole thrills here,' enthused Darcy upon playing the course for the first time. Such a feeling is not just confined to Ryder Cup players, for this is a course, tough as it may be, that can be enjoyed by players of all standards.

An indication of the amount of thought that went into the course's development is the undersoil heating installed at the 8th, 12th and 13th greens to ensure that they don't fall victim to frost. Similar evidence of the care that has been taken with the course's design and construction is everywhere – from the clever use of water, to the superbly manicured greens and the pristine bunkers.

There are no weak holes on this course. Indeed, the sense of variety is immediately obvious, with the first six holes played in a loop back towards the clubhouse.

Water comes into play for the first time on the 8th hole – a pretty par 3 of 166yd/ 151m over a pond to a green set amidst mature trees. The short holes will enthrall; on the back nine, the 12th and the 17th, to an island green, are both very memorable, indeed.

Of all the holes, however, the one that is likely to remain with players the longest is the par 4 13th hole, a devilishly difficult proposition of 471yd/428m off the back stakes. When this hole was created, it was necessary to blast away much of the granite rockface on the right – and the result is a drive over an irritating stream to a low-lying fairway. Even if you find the fairway, your work is far from done because an expanse of water guards the green, which also has trees on either side. Get your par here, and you will earn the right to boast about it at the 19th.

The closing holes offer little respite. In fact, the 17th and 18th are two of the most demanding holes that you will meet anywhere. The penultimate hole is 203yd/ 185m off the championship tees, with much of the carry over water. The 18th again has water as a feature and has seen many cards suffer a watery grave.

 Blainroe

Blainroe Golf Club, Blainroe, County Wicklow
TEL: *+353 (0)404-68168* **FAX:** *+353 (0)404-69369*
LOCATION: *3 miles/4.8km south of Wicklow on the coast road or, alternatively, 4 miles/6.4km north of Brittas Bay, off the N11*
COURSE: *18 holes, 6792yd/6175m, par 72, SSS 72*
GREEN FEES: *€€€€*
FACILITIES: *Changing rooms and showers, catering, bar, pro shop, trolley hire, on-site accommodation*
VISITORS: *Welcome – booking advisable*

Blainroe enjoys a lovely setting beside the sea, just south of Wicklow Town. The tranquil nature of the site shouldn't lull anyone into thinking this is an easy day out, however, as the course itself doesn't waste any time bearing its teeth.

After an easy introduction to the course – a short par 4 that rises steadily and barely gives time to loosen the joints – the 2nd hole is a par 4 of 431yd/392m that plays even longer than its length. It is uphill all the way, with out-of-bounds on the left, and you never see the bottom of the pin when playing your second shot to a long and narrow undulating green.

The 7th tee box is the highest point on the whole course and, on a clear day, it is possible to see the mountains of Wales across the Irish Sea.

From here, the course descends onto flatter and undulating territory, and it is on the back nine that the course's two feature holes are to be found. The 14th is 331yd/303m, but it takes a brave drive with a carry of over 165yd/150m over cliffs, with the sea crashing into the rocks below, to find safety.

The 15th, a par 3 of 229yd/209m, is one of the best 'short' holes to be found anywhere in County Wicklow. With your back to the sea, and not far from the cliff edge, the challenging task is to fire a tee shot across a valley and a pond to a green that is on the same level as the tee box.

Wicklow

Wicklow Golf Club, Dunbur Road, Wicklow
TEL: *+353 (0)404-67379*
LOCATION: *32 miles/51km south of Dublin*
COURSE: *18 holes, 5969yd/5427m, par 71, SSS 70*
GREEN FEES: *€€€*
FACILITIES: *Changing rooms and showers, catering, bar, pro shop, trolley hire, buggy hire*
VISITORS: *Welcome – but booking at weekends is advisable*

Part of the charm of Wicklow is that it is situated on a cliff top, just outside the town. It has been upgraded in recent years to a fine 18-hole course, with little expense spared, and Wicklow Golf Club can proudly hold its head up in a county that is positively awash with fine courses.

The upgrading work, completed in 1994, was conducted by Pat Ruddy and Tom Craddock, who constructed nine holes and remodelled two of the old ones. As you would expect of such renowned designers, the result is a course that isn't afraid to test a player's ability.

A number of greens are quite close to the cliff, which obviously presents its own hazards for anyone playing, but – provided that you take great care – it really is a very enjoyable experience.

Perhaps the most intimidating drive comes relatively early on in the round. The 6th is a par 4 of 409yd/372m, and is known by the locals as the 'Nose Hole', as it is all carry over a craggy cliff-face.

The following hole, the 7th, is a nice uphill par 3 to a two-tiered green that seems to be surrounded by furze bushes.

The last of the four par 3s, for which Wicklow is renowned, is a bit special as well. It is the 17th hole, measuring 160yd/146m, and it demands a tee shot from an elevated tee box over a couple of lakes to a green that is surrounded by mounds and a strategically placed bunker on the right-hand side.

7 Arklow

Arklow Golf Club, Abbeylands, Arklow, County Wicklow
TEL: *+353 (0)402-32492* **FAX:** *+353 (0)402-91604*
EMAIL: *arklowgolflinks@eircom.net*
LOCATION: *45 miles/72km south of Dublin; the course is 2/3 mile/1km south of Arklow town on the coast*
COURSE: *18 holes, 6472yd/5884m, par 71, SSS 70*
GREEN FEES: *€€€€*
FACILITIES: *Changing rooms and showers, catering, bar, trolley hire, buggy hire*
VISITORS: *Welcome by arrangement*

Located on low-lying dunes sandwiched between the town and the sea, Arklow – once a hidden gem as far as purveyors of links terrain were concerned – is increasingly popular with visitors. Dublin golfers seeking a short break within easy distance of the capital have discovered its charms, as have visitors from Wales and England, who can make the short ferry trip to either Dun Laoghaire or Rosslare.

The course has benefited greatly from irrigation work, with the result that the greens are now among the very best to be found in the country.

Although a little short, Arklow remains a really good challenge, especially so if the wind blows, and the last three holes demand a player's full and devoted attention. After the relatively short par 4s that precede it, this stretch turns out to have a real sting in the tail. Indeed, anyone who only has time for a short break to these parts could do worse than combine a couple of days golfing at Arklow and nearby Woodenbridge; the two courses superbly capture the ambience of an Irish golfing holiday.

Arklow is a traditional links course with dunes, rough hollows and wicked little streams. Full of character and with a warm welcome at the 19th, the course requires concentration but won't prove to be too physically draining.

8 Woodenbridge

Woodenbridge Golf Club, Vale of Avoca, County Wicklow
TEL: *+353 (0)402-35202* **FAX:** *+353 (0)402-35202*
EMAIL: *wgc@eircom.net*
LOCATION: *5 miles/8km north-west of Arklow, along the R747*
COURSE: *18 holes, 6437yd/5852m, par 71, SSS 70*
GREEN FEES: *€€€€€*
FACILITIES: *Changing rooms and showers, catering, bar, trolley hire, buggy hire*
VISITORS: *Welcome, except Thursdays and Saturdays – booking advisable*

Thomas Moore immortalized the Vale of Avoca in his poetry: 'There is not in this wide world a valley so sweet; as the vale in whose bosom the bright waters meet.' By all accounts, the 'Meeting of the Waters' lies just upstream from Woodenbridge, a course – recently upgraded from nine holes to 18 – that has an exceptionally pretty, but precarious, location on the County Wicklow landscape.

Woodenbridge has shown its resilience by surviving the ravages of the natural world. The course has been hit twice in modern times by the effect of hurricanes, in 1965 and 1986, and there are photographs on the wall of the clubhouse to prove it.

A more vivid reminder came in November 2000, however, when 4 inches (10cm) of rain in a 24-hour spell and a high tide in Arklow caused the course to be flooded. Typically, the members put their hands in their pockets to finance the course's resurrection. By raising the riverbank by 3 feet (1m) near the most susceptible 8th fairway, they hope to have seen the end of raging waters.

With no trees of any note on the course, it is the water – where the rivers Avoca and Aughrim meet – that ironically helps provide the course's main defence. The water comes into play on several holes, and some 90 bunkers ensure sensible course management. The 18th is a fine finishing hole, a par 5 that requires a drive over the river.

⑨ The European

The European Golf Club, Brittas Bay, County
Wicklow
TEL: +353 (0)404-47415 **FAX:** +353 (0)404-
47449 **EMAIL:** info@theeuropeanclub.com
LOCATION: 8 miles/12.8km south of Wicklow and
5 miles/8km north of Arklow; take the turn for Brittas
Bay off the N11 at Jack White's Inn
COURSE: 18 (plus two additional) holes, 7149yd/
6499m, par 71, SSS 73
GREEN FEES: €€€€€€+
FACILITIES: Changing rooms and showers, catering,
trolley hire, buggy hire
VISITORS: Welcome – booking advisable

THE EUROPEAN

HOLE	YD	M	PAR	HOLE	YD	M	PAR
1	392	356	4	10	417	379	4
2	160	146	3	11	389	354	4
3	499	454	5	12	459	417	4
4	452	410	4	13	596	542	5
5	409	372	4	14	195	177	3
6	187	170	3	15	401	364	4
7	470	428	4	16	415	377	4
8	415	377	4	17	421	383	4
9	427	388	4	18	445	405	4
OUT	3411	3101	35	IN	3738	3398	36

7149YD • 6499M • PAR 71

If you think that the name of this course is a tad grandiose, then play it – and stay quiet. For The European is indeed a breathtaking experience, carved as it is out of quite magnificent dunesland on the Wicklow coast. Although only created in the 1990s, you'd honestly swear that it had been around for more than a hundred years.

The dream of Pat Ruddy – writer, golf-course architect and all-round golfing connoisseur – The European manoeuvres its way through majestic linksland and offers a test, especially on a windy day, that is tougher than most. It also has its own idiosyncrasies.

Rather than 18 holes, Ruddy has built an extra two – 7a and 12a – 'simply because we enjoy the game enough to play extra', while old railway sleepers are used in the faces of a number of bunkers. There is also clever use of water: the signature 7th hole has a river running up its right side, while a pond and reeds guard the left of the fairway.

When Nick Faldo visited the links, he remarked that 'great natural golfing land is exploited to the full by the repeated use of elevation and direction changes'. He is not the only world-class golfer to have been impressed. Indeed, many legendary players agreed to sign their names to particular holes. So it is that Sam Snead's signature is on the 4th; Arnold Palmer's is on the 7th; Tom Watson's on the 17th; and Byron Nelson's on the 18th.

The better the golfer you are, the more you will enjoy this spectacular course. Yet if you know your limitations, accept that you don't have to play off the back tees and use good course management, then there is every chance that a round of golf here will be a most enjoyable experience.

Typical of the majestic dunes of Brittas Bay, the 3rd hole at The European tumbles down a valley towards the sea.

The 1st hole, an uphill par 4, gives a hint of what is ahead, but the next two holes are relatively gentle before the course toughens up dramatically.

From the 4th on, there is little respite, with one dramatic and testing hole following another. There is none tougher than the 7th, a monstrous par 4 measuring 470yd/428m off the back stakes. For those playing it for the first time, it is a daunting hole. Yet the designer has used some features as optical illusions so that you actually have more fairway and bail-out areas to play with than initially appears.

This stroke index one 7th hole is the start of six difficult par 4s on the championship course, each one different and each with its own challenge. The only theme that runs through is to try and keep on the fairways, because the rough in these parts is as tigerish as it gets. The 12th, which finishes this stretch, has a green that is 127yd/115m long and is the first that runs alongside the coastline. Meanwhile, the 13th is a par 5 in the best links tradition.

The finishing holes are each memorable in their own right: the 15th has a cliff-top green; the 16th is a dogleg par 4 that, typical of this course, gets the player to use brain as well as brawn, while the magnificent 17th – with a tee shot from an elevated tee to a valley below – is simply breathtaking. The 18th hole used to have a lake in front of the green, but that has been altered in recent times to bring a more links-like feel to the finish. The lake has been replaced by a serpentine stream, which runs in front of the green and back up the fairway. It's a hole full of character – exactly what a round of golf here is all about.

10 Seafield

*Seafield Golf and Country Club, Ballymoney,
County Wexford*
TEL: *+353 (0)55-24837*
LOCATION: *5 miles/8km north-east of Gorey; approach
along the R742 and then follow signposts for Ballymoney*
COURSE: *18 holes, 6447yd/5861m, par 72, SSS 72*
GREEN FEES: *€€€€*
FACILITIES: *Changing rooms and showers, catering, bar,
trolley hire, buggy hire*
VISITORS: *Welcome*

At just 6447yd/5861m, Seafield, which only opened in 2002, is not particularly long. Yet this cliff-top course has a special appeal – it has been designed in three distinct segments to give the visiting golfer a taste of parkland, heathland and seaside golf.

The first few holes take you through mature woodland, while the second section, with the imposing Tara Hill as a backdrop, is heathland. The last third of the course enjoys a seaside effect, and none more spectacularly than the view that accompanies the player off the 17th tee box. After being hidden from view by a hedgerow on the first part of the walk down the fairway, the sea hits you again with stunning impact on approaching the double-green that is shared with the short 10th hole.

The opening holes serve as a gentle introduction. The 1st measures just 325yd/295m, with the approach to a green nestled into the hillside. However, it doesn't take long for the test to get tougher. The 6th, a par 4 of 460yd/418m, requires a drive that must first carry a lake and then thread itself between fairway bunkers and the out-of-bounds that lingers on the left.

There are two magnificent short holes on the homeward run: the 11th, which measures 180yd/163m, has a tee box perched just yards from the cliff top, and the 16th, which is played into the backdrop of the Irish Sea. However, it is the water in front that is the danger and, in many ways, the 16th could emerge as the course's signature hole.

*Railway sleepers feature in the water hazards at Seafield.
This is the approach to the 2nd green.*

11 Courtown

Courtown Golf Club, Kiltennel, Gorey, County Wexford
TEL: +353 (0)55-25166 FAX: +353 (0)55-25553
EMAIL: courtown@iol.ie
WEBSITE: www.courtowngolfclub.com
LOCATION: Leave the N11 at Gorey and follow the R742 to Courtown Harbour; the golf club is signposted
COURSE: 18 holes, 6465yd/5878m, par 71, SSS 71
GREEN FEES: €€€
FACILITIES: Changing rooms and showers, catering, bar, trolley hire, buggy hire
VISITORS: Welcome by arrangement – restrictions on Tuesdays and at weekends

Far enough removed from the fairground attractions in Courtown Harbour to offer some peace to a hassled golfer is the idyllic setting of Courtown Golf Club. A course that runs within 110yd/100m of the coast, it is, nonetheless, a quintessential parkland course. Situated on part of the old Courtown estate, there are thousands of mature trees lining the course, and a more hospitable club it would be difficult to find.

The course itself is pretty good, too. The 4th hole has wonderful views of the Irish Sea (and indeed wouldn't be out of place on any championship course), while the long dogleg par 5 9th hole, which measures all of 568yd/517m, shows that it is still possible to provide length on a course that, by modern standards, is not unduly long.

However, the four par 3s are truly special, and none more so than the 18th, which not only has a pond to put fear into the hearts of golfers as they negotiate the final hole, but also an out-of-bounds area to the left in front of the clubhouse.

12 Coollattin

Coollattin Golf Club, Shillelagh, County Wicklow
TEL: +353 (0)55-29125 FAX: +353 (0)55-29125
LOCATION: 12 miles/19km south-west of Aughrim
COURSE: 18 holes, 6184yd/5622m, par 70, SSS 69
GREEN FEES: €€€
FACILITIES: Changing rooms and showers, catering, bar, trolley hire, buggy hire
VISITORS: Welcome on weekdays

It doesn't matter what low road or high road you must negotiate to find Coollattin, located near the village of Shillelagh in the Wicklow mountains, this is a place worth discovering. From the moment you swing through the gateway into the estate on which the golf course is laid out, you will know that you have unearthed a golfing facility that has few peers in terms of natural beauty.

Over 60 different species of trees adorn a course that has recently been upgraded to 18 holes. Apart from the trees, there is also an abundance of flowers, azaleas et al, which Peter McEvoy, who designed the extra nine holes, remarked 'are more at home here than they are at Augusta'.

The new holes blend in beautifully with the old ones. For example, the green on what is now the 8th hole is one of the oldest on the course, but such was its quality that McEvoy felt no need for change. Probably the most special hole of all is the short 12th. This is designed within a walled garden, but its angelic appearance disguises a potentially hellish experience for the golfer – bunkers protect the elevated green and the close proximity of the walls to the rear simply adds to the devilment.

Courtown offers a charming finishing hole, a par 3 with a tee shot over a lake flush with reeds.

⑬ *Rosslare*

Rosslare Golf Club, Rosslare Strand, County Wexford
TEL: *+353 (0)53-32202* **FAX:** *+353 (0)53-32260*
EMAIL: *rgolfclb@iol.ie*
WEBSITE: *www.rosslaregolfclub.ie*
LOCATION: *6 miles/9.5km from Rosslare ferry terminal; 10 miles/16km south of Wexford town*
COURSE: *30 holes, 6760yd/6145m, par 72, SSS 72*
GREEN FEES: *€€€€*
FACILITIES: *Changing rooms and showers, catering, bar, pro shop, trolley hire, buggy hire*
VISITORS: *Welcome – booking advisable*

The links at Rosslare – located as it is on a sandy peninsula – is about as exposed to the elements as it is possible to get.

Unfortunately, the course has paid a price for its location. Coastal erosion along much of its 1½ miles/2.5km of shoreline has forced the club's management to invest heavily in rock-revetment work in its endless struggle with the forces of nature. Thankfully, the club finally seems to be winning the battle against erosion. Meanwhile, the other natural element, that of wind, especially on a course that has little or no trees, merely creates an even greater challenge for those who enjoy their links golf. There have also been considerable improvements made to the course, with a number of new greens and tees being constructed in recent years.

It is possible to enjoy links golf here on relatively flat links terrain, with the onus on accuracy off the tee. The 10th is a long par 4 with a blind second shot, and each of the par 3s is memorable. However, it is the finishing few holes along the coast that have the greatest appeal of all.

Rosslare Golf Club's attraction has been further boosted by the addition of a new 12-hole links down the road from the Old Course. The only hope is that the club continues to win the battle with erosion.

The proximity of the sea at Rosslare Golf Club guarantees a testing wind that accentuates the challenge of links golf.

14 St Helen's Bay

St Helen's Bay Golf and Country Club, Rosslare Harbour, County Wexford
TEL: *+353 (0)53-33234* **FAX:** *+353 (0)53-33803*
EMAIL: *sthelens@iol.ie*
WEBSITE: *www.sthelensbay.com*
LOCATION: *2 miles/3.2km south of Rosslare Harbour, off the N25 on the road to Kilrane*
COURSE: *18 holes, 6700yd/6091m, par 72, SSS 72*
GREEN FEES: €€€
FACILITIES: *Changing rooms and showers, catering, bar, club hire, trolley hire, buggy hire, on-site accommodation*
VISITORS: *Welcome*

This is a unique course, designed by Ryder Cup player Philip Walton, hero of Europe's win at Oak Hill in 1995, and who, in his course design debut, has catered quite magnificently for holiday golfers.

Although located by the sea, in this case the St George's Channel, it is only the last five holes at St Helen's Bay that can be described as resembling links; elsewhere, with the presence of over 6,000 trees, it is effectively a parkland course. The course is immaculately maintained, and on-site holiday villas and an excellent clubhouse make it well worth a stop-off for more reasons than just the golf.

The first few holes play gently uphill, affording some nice views of the Wexford coast and the surrounding countryside.

The so-called 'Wall of Famine' stone walls, dating back to the potato famine in the mid-1800s when over two million Irish people either died or emigrated, come into play on three holes (the 1st, 9th and 10th). A tower house near the 12th hole dates from the 13th century.

Such features add a certain historical allure to the place but, in terms of a golfing challenge, it is the finishing two holes that are the most demanding: the 17th is a par 3 of 211yd/192m adjacent to the coastline, while the 18th is a classic short par 4 that places the onus very much on precision off the tee.

According to meteorologists, there is more sunshine and less rain at St Helen's Bay than at any other course in Ireland.

REGIONAL DIRECTORY

Where to Stay

Wicklow Although it is possible to use some of the hotels in the south of Dublin as a base for the magnificent courses in north Wicklow, it is far more enjoyable to escape the hustle and bustle of the city for some country living. **Charlesland Golf Club** (+353 (0) 1-2876764) has a hotel that combines good cuisine with leisure facilities. Situated close to the picturesque Glen of the Downs, the **Glenview Hotel** (+353 (0)1-2873399) has horse-riding, golf, shooting and hill-walking within a five-minute radius and boasts its own leisure centre. For those who like to combine good eating with a good view, its Woodlands restaurant is located overlooking the glen. If you want to be pampered, then **Tinakilly Country House and Restaurant** (+353 (0)404-69274), with its four-poster beds and room views that overlook the Irish Sea, offers just that... and, with award-winning cuisine of local fish and Wicklow lamb, there is no need to venture any further for culinary delights. Also located in Rathnew is the family-run **Hunter's Hotel** (+353 (0)404-40106), which is one of Ireland's oldest coaching inns and boasts a fine restaurant. **The Blainroe Hotel** (+353 (0)404-67500) is an ideal base for a golfing break, located just 3 miles/4.8km south of Wicklow Town beside Blainroe Golf Club. **Ballyknocken House** (+353 (0)404-44627) in Ashford is a lovely farmhouse with charming bedrooms and great breakfasts to get the day going. One of the more innovative places to stay while on a holiday is the **Moneylands Farm** (+353 (0)402-32259) near Arklow, a family-run self-catering courtyard of stone-built coach houses, which features an indoor swimming pool, tennis courts and virtual golf simulators. **Lawless's Hotel and Aughrim Holiday Village** (+353 (0)402-36384) in the Wicklow foothills has a range of hotel rooms and self-catering apartments. If you want a golfer's personal touch, then the proprietors of **Thomond House** (+353 (0)404-67940) in Wicklow Town – which has 14 courses within a 30 minutes' drive – will even arrange your golf itinerary for you.

Wexford The **Marlfield House Hotel** (+353 (0)55-21124) is set in 35 hectares of woodlands just outside Gorey and within a few minutes' drive of Courtown Golf Club and Seafield Golf and Country Club; it has won numerous national and international awards for its food. **The Murphy-Floods Hotel** (+353 (0)54-33413) in Enniscorthy overlooks the town's 6th-century market square and, as an added incentive for golfing visitors, offers package rates for golf breaks. Few locations enjoy as splendid a location as the **Ferrycarrig Hotel** (+353 (0)53-20999), which is set on the banks of the River Slaney. Situated in close proximity to Wexford's tourist and golfing attractions, **The Cedar Lodge Hotel** (+353 (0)51-428386) is 13 miles/22km from Wexford Town in Newbain. A hotel with a superb reputation for visiting golfers is the family-run **Kelly's Resort Hotel** (+353 (0)53-32114), which also offers a wide range of leisure pursuits and entertainment for those who fancy a respite from golf. **Drinagh Court Hotel** (+353 (0)53-43295) is on the Rosslare Road and is an ideal base for a golf holiday or for societies – it also features the really pleasant Farmers Kitchen bar and restaurant. **Clarion Brand House Hotel** (+353 (0)51-421703) in New Ross is a lovely manor house set in landscaped gardens overlooking the River Barrow.

Where to Eat

Wicklow The vast majority of golf clubs also have excellent restaurants, but if you want to escape a golfing environment, then there is a wide range of eating houses available offering everything from Chinese to Italian, as well as traditional Irish cuisine. Bray, which is a good base for any golfing holiday on the east coast, has a number of good restaurants including **Sanam Tandoori** (+353 (0)1-2865337) and the **Sunnybank Bistro** (+353 (0)1-2040380). **The Strawberry Tree Restaurant** (+353 (0)402-36444) is conveniently located close to Woodenbridge and has a reputation for sublime organic and wild game cuisine. For good traditional food at good prices, the **Beehive** (+353 (0)404-469745) on the Dublin–Wexford road at Coolbeg Cross is hard to beat. **Murphy's** (+353 (0)402-32781) in Arklow is a nice, comfortable restaurant that has a wide range of good value food including grilled sole, roast lamb and fillet steak, all cooked in the traditional manner. The **Coach Inn** (+353 (0)281-8157) in Roundwood has a very good restaurant and, after dinner, there is likely to be some traditional music in its lively bar.

Wexford The **Courtyard** (+353 (0)54-66531) in Ferns, near Enniscorthy, has a bistro-style restaurant that is particularly noted for its wonderful steaks. For a taste of modern Irish cooking and delicious seafood dishes, the **Footprints Restaurant** (+353 (0)53-43444) at the Whitford House Hotel serves excellent bar food until late in the evening. **Dunbrody House Restaurant** (+353 (0)51-389600) has a stylish restaurant and is a must for those who wish to sample the best of Irish cuisine in a relaxing environment. **The Oak Tavern** (+353 (0)53-20922) in Ferrycarrig offers the warmest of welcomes and the best of traditional cooking.

What to Do

Wicklow All roads, literally, lead to the 6th-century monastic settlement of **Glendalough**. Set in a deep glacial valley with high mountains surrounding two lakes, this settlement – founded by St Kevin and a major focal point for early Christianity in Ireland – has seven churches and a round tower. It is a magnet for tourists, as much for the tranquil walks around the lakes as for the chance to delve back into history. An interpretative centre outlines the geographical and historical story behind Glendalough. Another popular attraction is the waterfall at **Powerscourt House and Gardens**, location of the highest waterfall in Ireland. The gardens on this estate – which feature steep terraces, fountains and a backdrop of the Sugarloaf mountain – are among the most visited in the country. **Avoca**, one of the most picturesque villages anywhere, is well known to television viewers as 'Ballykissangel', and is also home to the one of the country's oldest woollen mills. Two miles/3km north of Avoca on the river of the same name is the **'Meeting of the Waters'**, as immortalized by the poet Thomas More. Ireland's history is brimming with tales of resistance to invasions and resurrections; the tour of **Wicklow Gaol** takes about an hour and is a reminder of days past when it was used to imprison thousands of people from the 1798 Rebellion before they were transported to Australia or New Zealand.

Wexford An area known as the Slobs lies just 2 miles/3km north of Wexford Town. This land has been reclaimed from the sea as the natural setting for the **Wexford Wildlife Reserve**. In the winter, the reserve houses about half of the world's population of white-fronted geese, approximately 10,000 in all, which fly here from Greenland. Meanwhile, another throwback to Ireland's history comes alive at the **Irish Heritage Park** at Ferrycarrig, just off the N11, where visitors can sample Irish culture and heritage stretching back 9,000 years with replicated homesteads, graves and ringforts. Each October, also, Wexford plays host to its internationally famous **Opera Festival**, which lasts for 17 days and attracts singers from all over Europe. The **National 1798 Centre** in Enniscorthy is a family-friendly centre that uses a multimedia presentation to tell the tale of the 1798 Rebellion and its aftermath.

Tourist Information Centres

Wicklow Tourist Office, Rialto House, Fitzwilliam Square, Wicklow Town (+353 (0)404-69117)
Wexford Tourist Office Office, Crescent Quay, Wexford Town (+353 (0)53-23111)
Rosslare Tourist Office, Terminal Building, Rosslare Harbour (+353 (0)53-33232)

Crannogs such as these in the Irish Heritage Park in Ferrycarrig provided safe dwelling places in time of danger.

Chapter 3

The South Coast & Cork City

Waterford, the gateway to the south coast of Ireland, is an impressive city that immediately grips anyone visiting for the first time. A range of differently-styled golf courses within its environs serves to remind the visitor that this thriving place has more than its famous crystal to offer.

Of course, Waterford crystal is celebrated all around the world. The first glass factory was set up in the city back in 1783 and it now enjoys an international reputation for producing the ultimate in beautifully hand-crafted crystal. Waterford crystal has also forged strong links with golf. The Solheim Cup, for example, which is the women's equivalent of the Ryder Cup and is played every two years between the United States and Europe,

features a trophy that was painstakingly handcrafted in the finest tradition of the city's master glass craftsmen.

Moreover, the trophies for the Murphy's Irish Open and the Smurfit European Open are also specially crafted pieces of Waterford crystal. As all club golfers in Ireland have discovered, be they male or female, their infatuation with golf isn't complete until at least one piece of Waterford crystal has been claimed in club competition and carried home with pride.

Waterford itself is a historic city that was first conquered by the Vikings and later by the Normans, during which time King Henry II of England bestowed royal patronage on it. These days, it is one of the largest urban areas in Ireland. However, the city has a selection of fine parkland courses on its doorstep, and there are few better places to start a visit to these parts than with a short ferry trip across the

Left: Cobh Harbour, the last port of call for the Titanic *on its fateful voyage. Above: Hurling, the national sport of Ireland, enjoys a rich tradition in Waterford and Cork.*

river to the course at Waterford Castle. Indeed, the boat trip is the only means of access to the island course, which was designed by former Ryder Cup player Des Smyth.

Most hotels in this area are very golfer friendly and will even arrange tee times for you. Combined with the numerous good pubs and restaurants, this makes Waterford a perfect base for visiting golfers.

Apart from Waterford Castle, there are two other championship courses close to the city centre. Faithlegg, which has played host to the Ladies Irish Open on the European Women's Tour, and Tramore, an outstanding course close to the sea but very much of the parkland variety, are both about a 15-minute drive away.

Cork Golf Club, known as 'Little Island', boasts the trademark features of the designer Dr Alister Mackenzie.

The scenic drive westward along the coast towards Dungarvan should be taken at a leisurely pace. The road takes in some spectacular cliff-top views, and a little detour on the way out of Tramore to see the Iron Man, a massive iron replica of an 18th-century sailor, is well worth the time. Dungarvan – with three championship courses in the town – has established a reputation of its own as something of a golfing haven.

The courses featured in this chapter begin in Waterford before moving to County Cork, the largest county in Ireland, with an area of 2880 square miles/7460sq. km. East Cork is far removed from the rugged beauty of west Cork, but it still has its own charm. On the outskirts of Cork City, two of the country's finest parkland courses, Fota Island and Cork Golf Club (commonly known as Little Island), can be found.

Don't be surprised to find something akin to friendly arrogance among Cork people. It has nothing to do with the Blarney Stone, where tradition requires that anyone searching for the gift of the gab should kiss a limestone block set in the historic Blarney Castle. Cork people don't need to stoop to such measures: they are born with such a trait; it is the rest of us who have to acquire it! No, their self-assuredness comes from a belief that they come from the 'real' capital of Ireland, or so they will tell you.

There is a long tradition of golf in and around Cork City, but the most spectacular game of all can be found at The Old Head of Kinsale, where many of the holes run dangerously close to cliffs. Unfortunately, at over €200 per round, with the high recommendation that you take a caddie as well, it is the most expensive game of golf in Ireland.

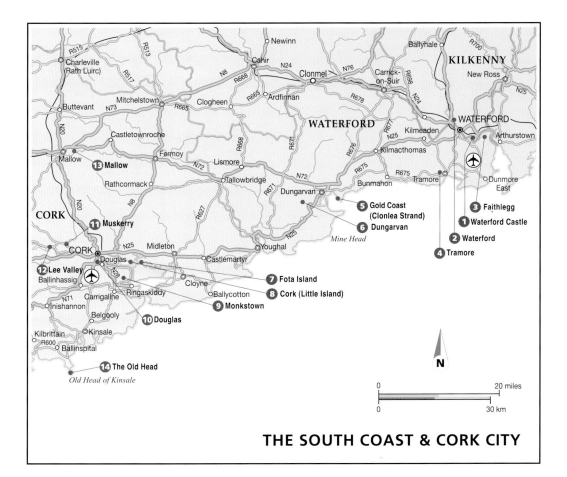

THE SOUTH COAST & CORK CITY

Planning an Itinerary

One of the most remarkable aspects of this part of Ireland is that it doesn't boast any links courses. This shouldn't deter anyone from making a golfing pilgrimage here, however. The existing parkland courses have much to offer – and the beauty and diversity of the landscape surrounding Waterford and Cork City is such that it is possible to stay in a single area, be it Waterford, Dungarvan or Cork City itself, and still enjoy a variety of courses without having to travel too far.

In Waterford City, for example, it is possible to stay and play at Waterford Castle and Faithlegg; in the Dungarvan area, there are three fine courses – Gold Coast (or Clonlea Strand as it is also known), Dungarvan and West Waterford; and in Cork you are literally spoiled for choice. Fota Island, indeed, was voted 'Best Golf Course' by the Irish Golf Tour Operators' Association in 2002.

If your schedule takes you to Fota Island, then be sure to leave at least a few hours free to visit nearby Cobh Harbour. Whales have been known to frolic in the harbour but, for maritime lovers, Cobh's history has even more to offer as the last port of call for the ill-fated *Titanic*. The local heritage centre provides plenty of information about the ship and the role that the port played in the emigration of countless Irish people to America.

🏌 *Waterford Castle*

Waterford Castle Golf and Country Club, The Island,
Ballinakill, County Waterford
TEL: *+353 (0)51-871633* **FAX:** *+353(0)51-871634*
EMAIL: *golf@waterfordcastle.com*
WEBSITE: *www.waterfordcastle.com*
LOCATION: *2 miles/3.2km from Waterford City,
on the Dunmore East road; the car ferry to the island is
signposted and the ferry journey lasts about five minutes*
COURSE: *18 holes, 6854yd/6231m, par 72, SSS 73*
GREEN FEES: €€€€
FACILITIES: *Changing rooms and showers, catering,
bar, trolley hire, buggy hire, driving range, on-site
accommodation*
VISITORS: *Welcome – booking advisable*

*The only way to reach Waterford Castle, located on an
island in the Suir estuary, is by a 10-minute ferry journey.*

Located on a 310-acre island in the River
Suir's estuary, and with a short ferry ride
the only means of access, the golf course at
Waterford Castle is a truly unique experience.
Players are requested to arrive for their tee
times about 40 minutes in advance to allow for
the ferry crossing. If the boat trip builds up the
anticipation, then the course, designed by Des
Smyth, doesn't disappoint in any way.

Although there is a wide variety of mature
trees on the course, they are not excessive
and, in fact, the astute placing of bunkers and
water features present greater hazards. Water
comes into play on the 2nd, 3rd, 4th and 16th
holes – and there is a replica of the Swilken
Bridge between the 2nd and 3rd to add to the
atmosphere – which certainly increases the
demands placed on the player.

The 3rd is a fine hole, a par 4 of
409yd/372m, which requires a drive over one
lake to a fairway with trees on either side.
Then, the approach is played to a green that is
nestled beside the second lake.

The 9th, meanwhile, is a tough hole that
doglegs left to right. A good tee shot is needed
if there is to be any chance of securing
par, while the green is well protected by
bunkers. The 12th is another lovely but
demanding hole, with trees and bunkers
increasing the challenge.

🏌 *Waterford*

Waterford Golf Club, Newrath, Waterford City
TEL: *+353(0)51-876748* **FAX:** *+353 (0)51-853405*
LOCATION: *The course is 1 mile/1.6km from the city
centre, on the northern side; approach Waterford on the
N9 from Dublin; alternatively, you will find it just off
the N25 from Rosslare*
COURSE: *18 holes, 6294yd/5722m, par 71, SSS 70*
GREEN FEES: €€€
FACILITIES: *Changing rooms and showers, catering,
bar, trolley hire, buggy hire*
VISITORS: *Welcome*

Two of Scotland's most famous golf
architects, Willie Park Jnr and James
Braid, actually had a hand in the formation of
this fine parkland course. With mature trees
and gorse lining the fairways, Waterford is a
good test for players of all levels, with a
premium placed on accuracy off the tee.

Its signature hole is kept until last. The 18th
is a very good par 4 of 404yd/368m. Built on
a height, with views of the countryside, you
are required to divert your attentions away
from the sightseeing to hit a drive from an
elevated tee along a narrow downhill fairway.
Assuming that this task has been safely
completed, the approach shot is to a green that
has earned Waterford a reputation for having
some of the finest putting surfaces around.

3 *Faithlegg*

Faithlegg Hotel and Golf Club, Faithlegg House, County Waterford
TEL: *+353 (0)51-382241* **FAX:** *+353 (0)51-382664*
LOCATION: *6 miles/9.6km from Waterford City, near Cheekpoint*
COURSE: *18 holes, 6674yd/6067m, par 72, SSS 72*
GREEN FEES: *€€€€*
FACILITIES: *Changing rooms and showers, catering, bar, pro shop, trolley hire, buggy hire, club hire, on-site accommodation*
VISITORS: *Welcome*

You can find Faithlegg just a short drive from Waterford City, along the River Suir estuary. Faithlegg is an excellent parkland course set in mature woodlands. The course, designed by Patrick Merrigan, opened for play in 1993.

Invariably, the course is in good condition. Off the back stakes, however, it can be very testing, with a significant number of doglegs that makes accuracy essential, while trees in close proximity to the fairways add to the difficulties faced by any player.

It proved to be a wonderful test for the top women players on the European Tour when it played host to the Irish Open. Certainly, with a hotel overlooking the 18th green and a clubhouse that docs very good catering, it is a club that has added greatly to this region.

There are three lovely par 3s on the outward run, but, in truth, the very best holes are left to one of the toughest finishing stretches around. The 16th is a par 3 of 175yd/160m; large trees form on either side to create a claustrophobic effect, and the green is guarded by a large bunker in front. This hole certainly sharpens the mind for what lies ahead, for the 17th – a par of 435yd/395m that doglegs right – is a real test. With trees left and right, the emphasis here is on a good, long drive with perhaps a slight fade. Yet on the finishing hole, a draw is probably the preferred shot. There is no doubt that the course demands creativity if it is to be conquered.

The 13th hole at Faithlegg is typical of the mix of gently rolling terrain and mature woodland found on the course.

4 *Tramore*

Tramore Golf Club, Newtown Hill, Tramore, County Waterford
TEL: *+353 (0)51-386170* **FAX:** *+353 (0)51-390961*
EMAIL: *tragolf@iol.ie*
WEBSITE: *www.tramoregolfclub.com*
LOCATION: *7 miles / 11km south of Waterford City, on the coast road*
COURSE: *18 holes, 6660yd / 6055m, par 72, SSS 72*
GREEN FEES: *€€€€*
FACILITIES: *Changing rooms and showers, catering, bar, pro shop, trolley hire, club hire*
VISITORS: *Welcome – booking is advisable*

Tramore, from the Irish meaning big strand, is one of the most popular holiday destinations in the south-east. For golfers, it also has considerable drawing power.

The original seaside course at Tramore was submerged in sea-water, but the move to higher ground – at the appropriately named Newtown Hill – has given this extremely welcoming County Waterford resort a fine test of golf, albeit of a parkland nature.

An interesting link with the past remains to this day in the form of the club's crest – an emblem depicting a sailing transport ship, the *Seahorse* – which foundered off the Tramore coast in 1816 with the loss of over 400 lives.

Tramore has played host to the Irish men's and women's amateur championships and, although the early holes might tempt players to open their shoulders, the fairways narrow and the trees encroach ever more as the round progresses, so length must be tempered with care.

There is great variety in the holes. The 4th is a dogleg par 4 that requires precision off the tee; the 10th is a little par 3 that is far harder than it appears, while the par 4 17th hole has been the ruin of many players who find themselves within sight of the clubhouse. The 18th, which is a par 5 of 493yd/449m, encapsulates much of the appeal of Tramore. There is out-of-bounds all the way down the right-hand side but, to add to the difficulty, a strategically placed fairway bunker on the left puts the onus on the player to be brave and accurate with the drive.

The 18th green at Tramore – a course offering immaculate tree-lined fairways and splendid greens.

5 Gold Coast (Clonea Strand)

Gold Coast Golf Club, Dungarvan, County Waterford
TEL: +353 (0)58-44055 **FAX:** +353 (0)58-44055
EMAIL: info@clonea.com **WEBSITE:** www.clonea.com
LOCATION: 3 miles/5km east of Dungarvan; the course is signposted off the R675 Tramore road
COURSE: 18 holes, 6792yd/6175m, par 72, SSS 72
GREEN FEES: €€€
FACILITIES: Changing rooms and showers, catering, bar, trolley hire, buggy hire
VISITORS: Welcome – booking advisable

The stretch of holes by the lighthouse, with views overlooking Dungarvan Bay and the Celtic Sea, captures the essence of Gold Coast Golf Club. On any given day, a line of sailing boats is likely to be in the waterway, a sight that – if it is possible – only improves the experience of playing this delightful course.

The 7th, a par 3 of 165yd/150m, looks out towards Ballyvoyle Head, and criss-crosses the 9th fairway, a hole that is played back towards the lighthouse. This is an open part of the course, whereas on other sections maturing trees come into play. It is the water holes, though, that provide most of the attraction. Although there is a good walk from the 14th green to the 15th tee box, it is well worth it as it brings you back to the coast for a couple of really nice holes.

The 16th is a par 5 that requires accuracy more than real length. The toughest hole on the course is the 17th, a par 4 of 470yd/430m that has trees on either side of the fairway and a green protected by bunkers.

Many of Gold Coast's more challenging holes run along Dungarvan Bay. This is the par 5 16th hole.

6 Dungarvan

Dungarvan Golf Club, Knocknagranagh, Dungarvan, County Waterford
TEL: +353 (0)58-43310 **FAX:** +353 (0)58-44113
EMAIL: dungarvangolf@cablesurf.com
WEBSITE: www.cablesurf.com/dungarvangolf
LOCATION: 2½ miles/4km east of Dungarvan, on the N25 Rosslare road
COURSE: 18 holes, 6747yd/6134m, par 72, SSS 73
GREEN FEES: €€€€
FACILITIES: Changing rooms and showers, catering, bar, pro shop, trolley hire, buggy hire
VISITORS: Welcome – booking required at weekends

With mountains as one backdrop, and the sea as another, Dungarvan's location is difficult to beat. There are sufficient good holes on the maturing course – designed to USGA specifications – to ensure a round of golf that will make you aware of the importance of course management.

There are seven man-made lakes on the layout, which certainly increase the challenge, and the back nine, with outer and inner loops, is especially interesting.

The 14th, a par 4 of 425yd/386m, is a demanding hole with trouble all the way up the left. It requires a long, well-positioned drive to a well-protected green.

The finishing stretch of holes is interesting, comprising the shortest par 4 on the course – the 15th – which measures 365yd/332m. This is followed by a short par 3, then one of the longest par 4s on the course and, finally, a par 5 that gives you a chance to get back at the course.

Fota Island

Fota Island Golf Club, Fota Island, County Cork
TEL: *+353 (0)21-4883700* **FAX:** *+353 (0)21-4883713*
EMAIL: *reservations@fotaisland.ie*
WEBSITE: *www.fotaisland.com*
LOCATION: *9 miles/14.5km east of Cork City, along the N25 road to Midleton; the course is signposted*
COURSE: *18 holes, 6927yd/6298m, par 71, SSS 73*
GREEN FEES: *€€€€€€+*
FACILITIES: *Changing rooms and showers, catering, bar, pro shop, trolley hire, buggy hire, club hire*
VISITORS: *Welcome – booking essential*

FOTA ISLAND

HOLE	YD	M	PAR	HOLE	YD	M	PAR
1	409	372	4	10	500	455	5
2	461	419	4	11	168	153	3
3	165	150	3	12	428	389	4
4	548	498	5	13	208	189	3
5	544	494	5	14	417	379	4
6	376	342	4	15	476	433	4
7	179	162	3	16	417	379	4
8	478	435	4	17	222	202	3
9	424	386	4	18	507	461	5
OUT	3584	3258	36	IN	3343	3040	35

6927YD • 6298M • PAR 71

It is rare that a course receives near universal praise from virtually all of the players on the European Tour, but such was the case at Fota Island when the Murphy's Irish Open was first played there in the summer of 2001. 'This course has really come to the forefront of golf in Europe now. I think it is a fabulous course, a bit of Mount Juliet and a bit of Loch Lomond,' remarked Colin Montgomerie.

Such praise was in no way overstated. Located on an island in the River Lee estuary, the course was originally designed by Peter McEvoy and Christy O'Connor Jnr. The course was redesigned by Jeff Howes in 1999 to bring the extensive water and magnificent trees on the parkland terrain more into play. Owned by the same people who developed Mount Juliet, Fota is immaculately maintained

The pond behind the 18th green at Fota Island has been a magnet for many a ball on this risk and reward par 5.

and has evolved into one of the country's top parkland courses.

Whales are well known to frolic in the estuary and players shouldn't be surprised to see white-handed gibbons stray onto the course from the wildlife park that runs adjacent to the fifth fairway. All of the above provides a hint of the special location of a course that, in itself, doesn't disappoint. It is a fine test of golf and, from the 1st hole, requires your utmost attention.

The 8th, a wicked par 4 of 478yd/435m, is an extremely tough hole, with a water hazard to the left of the green for good measure. It is the homeward run, and especially the stretch from the 10th to the 13th down by the estuary, however, that most appeals. The 12th is a splendid par 4, with water on the left and a wall to the right that could impede your approach to the elevated green if you are overly cautious.

Then, there is the final hole. The 18th is a par 5 measuring 507yd/461m and is a true risk hole. Although huge trees on either side of the fairway put the onus on the drive off the tee, the reward for a good drive is the opportunity to reach the green in two. However, be warned – water comes menacingly into play, and only the brave, or those totally on top of their game, will be tempted.

8 Cork (Little Island)

Cork Golf Club, Little Island, County Cork
TEL: *+353 (0)21-4353451* **FAX:** *+353 (0)21-4353410*
LOCATION: *5 miles/8km east of Cork City along the N25; the course is signposted.*
COURSE: *6738yd/6119m, par 72, SSS 72*
GREEN FEES: *€€€€€€*
FACILITIES: *Changing rooms and showers, catering, bar, pro shop, trolley hire, buggy hire, club hire*
VISITORS: *Welcome – booking essential*

Although the development of the Fota Island course nearby may have stolen some of its thunder, Cork – or Little Island as it is more commonly known – has the edge in terms of tradition. For one, Dr Alister Mackenzie designed this fine parkland course and, for another, it was the home club of the legendary, big-hitting Jimmy Bruen, a famous Irish golfer.

Mackenzie's influence is strikingly apparent everywhere. Little Island has large, tiered greens and is a wonderfully technical course that requires the player to think the whole way round.

Positioning off the tee is of paramount importance – the bunkers are all strategically placed – and, when you eventually get to the greens, the putting surfaces can be quite difficult to read.

Water is not a key factor, but there are some sneaky ditches around the course, and the tee shot on the 4th hole does necessitate a carry of over 180yd/165m in order to clear the shoreline.

Little Island has always been well-maintained, and this continues to be the case. It is a very pretty course that really bares its teeth over the finishing stretch, a closing run of five successive par 4s that demand extra care on every shot.

The 14th, a long par 4 of 436yd/397m, brings you back towards the clubhouse for the final run of holes that will either make or destroy your card.

9 Monkstown

Monkstown Golf Club, Parkgarriff, Monkstown, County Cork
TEL: *+353 (0)21-4841376*
FAX: *+353 (0)21-4841722*
LOCATION: *7 miles/11km south-east of Cork City; it is signposted off the R610*
COURSE: *18 holes, 6235yd/5669m, par 70, SSS 69*
GREEN FEES: *€€€*
FACILITIES: *Changing rooms and showers, catering, bar, pro shop, trolley hire, buggy hire, club hire*
VISITORS: *Welcome – there are restrictions at weekends and it is advisable to book in advance*

You could almost be stepping back in time at Monkstown; not only does a 17th-century castle grace the grounds of the course, but the castle was actually used as a clubhouse until a new building was constructed in 1994. Such progress fully reflects Monkstown's desire to be considered as one of the top golfing facilities in the Cork area.

Although not a long course by modern standards, Monkstown remains a good test, with sufficient variety to test a player's shot-making abilities. Indeed, the 3rd hole, the first of two par 5s on the course, measures all of 550yd/500m, and is on a part of the course that has stunning views overlooking Cork Harbour.

There's also a water feature that comes into play on four holes, and some old trees to add to the golfing challenge. Nowhere is this more true than on the two finishing holes. The 17th, in particular, is a testing hole of 431yd/392m that demands supreme accuracy off the tee and again with the approach shot.

While the penultimate hole is the stroke index one, and unquestionably the toughest on the course, the final hole – with more strategically placed bunkers (there are over 80 on the course) – is no soft touch. It is a par 4 of 414yd/377m and ensures that any lapse in concentration before you reach the sanctuary of the clubhouse will prove costly!

10 Douglas

Douglas Golf Club, Douglas, County Cork
TEL: +353 (0)21-4895297
FAX: +353 (0)21-4895297
EMAIL: admin@douglasgolfclub.ie
WEBSITE: www.douglasgolfclub.ie
LOCATION: 3 miles/4.8km south of Cork City, off the N28
COURSE: 18 holes, 6569yd/5972m, par 72, SSS 71
GREEN FEES: €€€€
FACILITIES: Changing rooms and showers, catering, bar, pro shop, trolley hire, club hire
VISITORS: Welcome – there are restrictions at weekends and it is advisable to book in advance

A traditional parkland course with enormous appeal, Douglas has much to offer the visiting golfer. Although a number of the early holes flirt with the out-of-bounds of the practice ground, the demand for accuracy also holds for later holes when strategic bunkering and trees become the hazards that most concern.

In particular, there are some fine par 4s on this course. The 5th hole sets the tone: the drive must be well positioned or one of the fairway bunkers will undoubtedly claim the ball. Furthermore, the approach to an elevated green with an out-of-bounds to the right and a large bunker on the left must be well struck indeed.

As you enter the homeward run at Douglas, the 14th is a particularly testing hole. It requires the golfer to hit a solid tee shot to a rising fairway that is dotted with bunkers, while the approach is to a sloping green that has yet more sand protection.

11 Muskerry

Muskerry Golf Club, Carrigohane, County Cork
TEL: +353 (0)21-4385297
FAX: +353 (0)21-4385297
LOCATION: 7 miles/11km north-west of Cork, near Blarney
COURSE: 18 holes, 6363yd/5786m, par 71, SSS 71
GREEN FEES: €€€
FACILITIES: Changing rooms and showers, catering, bar, pro shop, trolley hire, club hire
VISITORS: Welcome, but necessary to book in advance

Time has been kind to Muskerry, for this is a course that has matured wonderfully well, with woodlands, hills and rivers all combining to present a rewarding experience. First impressions count, and expectations upon making your way up the driveway are greatly raised by the sight of a lovely short hole – the 6th – which demands a tee shot over the River Shournagh to an elevated green.

The hand of the course's designer, Dr Alister Mackenzie, is evident throughout. After a relatively gentle opening few holes on flat terrain, the course takes off from the 6th, the signature hole. The loop of holes from the 10th to the 13th offer superb views of the surrounding countryside. The finishing stretch of holes is testing, and good club selection is vital.

The river comes into play again on the 18th. This time, the demand is initially on a good drive to a fairway that has the river on one side and mature trees on the other. The second shot to this 389-yd/354-m par 4 is required to carry the Shournagh to a green protected by bunkers.

Not for the faint-hearted, the 6th hole at Muskerry demands a tee shot over the River Shournagh to an elevated green.

12 Lee Valley

Lee Valley Golf Club, Ovens, County Cork
TEL: *+353 (0)21-7331721* **FAX:** *+353 (0)21-7331758*
EMAIL: *leevalleygolfclub@eircom.net*
WEBSITE: *www.leevalleygc.ie*
LOCATION: *10 miles/16km west of Cork, on the Killarney road, exiting at Ovens; the course is signposted*
COURSE: *18 holes, 6725yd/6115m, par 72, SSS 72*
GREEN FEES: *€€€€*
FACILITIES: *Changing rooms and showers, catering, bar, pro shop, trolley hire, buggy hire, club hire*
VISITORS: *Welcome – booking essential for weekends*

When this course opened for play in the early 1990s, none other than Ryder Cup foes Christy O'Connor Jnr, who designed the course, and Fred Couples performed the official ceremony. The demands of Lee Valley, which is invariably in good condition, come as a pleasant surprise to visiting golfers, for it is a challenging, yet thoroughly enjoyable, test.

The course is located above the village of Ovens and overlooks the Lee Valley. It winds its way through man-made mounds and mature trees, with a large number of dogleg holes, and also includes several distinctive water hazards. The terrain is undulating, but not unbearably so, and the testing of a player's course management begins on the opening hole, which veers sharply left. Mischievously, a water hazard awaits any shot that over-shoots the elbow of the fairway.

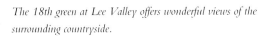
The 18th green at Lee Valley offers wonderful views of the surrounding countryside.

This is a gem of a course, and I was instantly taken with it. The 5th hole is an intimidating par 4 of 475yd/432m. It contrasts superbly with the 9th, another par 4 (but this time just 315yd/286m) that requires a straight tee shot to a narrow fairway and then an approach to a three-tier green nestled amidst woodland. Delightful!

There are many fine holes on the homeward run, a good number with water hazards, but the toughest is probably the 17th. If the drive is pushed in any way, the dense woodland will make it difficult to find the ball, while out-of-bounds lurks down the left.

13 Mallow

Mallow Golf Club, Ballyellis, Mallow, County Cork
TEL: *+353 (0)22-21145* **FAX:** *+353 (0)22-42501*
LOCATION: *1 mile/1.6km south-west of Mallow, on the Killavullen road*
COURSE: *18 holes, 6556yd/5960m, par 72, SSS 72*
GREEN FEES: *€€€*
FACILITIES: *Changing rooms and showers, catering, bar, pro shop, trolley hire, buggy hire, club hire*
VISITORS: *Welcome – restrictions at weekends; pre-booking advisable*

This progressive club has an excellent programme for developing young talent. Moreover, Mallow's fine, tree-lined, parkland layout lends itself perfectly to the demands of instilling length and accuracy into the minds of young golfers. Nowhere is this more obvious than on the 7th hole – a par 4 measuring 454yd/413m – that requires a solid tee shot to find the fairway, then, depending on the wind, an approach shot that may need anything from a three-wood to a mid-iron. A large bunker short left and another guarding the right only emphasize the hole's difficulties.

14 The Old Head

Old Head of Kinsale Golf Links, Kinsale, County Cork
TEL: *+353 (0)21-778444* **FAX:** *+353 (0)21-778022*
LOCATION: *20 miles/32km south of Cork; from
Kinsale, follow routes R600 and R640 to Old Head;
the course is signposted*
COURSE: *18 holes, 7215yd/6559m, par 72, SSS 73*
GREEN FEES: *€€€€€€ +*
FACILITIES: *Changing rooms and showers, catering, bar,
pro shop, trolley hire, club hire*
VISITORS: *Welcome – but booking is essential, and it is
recommended that golfers use a caddie*

THE OLD HEAD

HOLE	YD	M	PAR	HOLE	YD	M	PAR
1	446	405	4	10	518	471	5
2	406	369	4	11	98	180	3
3	180	164	3	12	564	513	5
4	427	388	4	13	258	235	3
5	430	391	4	14	452	411	4
6	495	450	5	15	342	311	4
7	188	171	3	16	195	177	3
8	549	499	5	17	632	574	5
9	475	432	4	18	460	418	4
OUT	3596	3269	36	IN	3619	3290	36

7215YD • 6559M • PAR 72

Nowhere on this earth is there a more spectacularly located course than the one that is found atop the Old Head of Kinsale. If you suffer from vertigo, stay away! For this rocky promontory, which juts out into the breaking waters where the Atlantic Ocean and the Celtic Sea invisibly meet, possesses a course, more heathland than links in nature, that simply takes the breath away.

Many of the tee boxes, and indeed the greens, lie perilously close to the edge of cliffs that drop some 300 feet (90m) to the waters below. As the starter, a man with a winning smile but a severe message informs you on the 1st tee box: 'If your ball disappears over the cliffs, don't bother looking for it. Reload, continue playing, and enjoy your game.' The score card further warns players and caddies not to attempt to retrieve balls from the hazards at the 2nd, 3rd, 4th, 7th, 12th, 15th, 16th, 17th and 18th holes, all of which cling to the cliff top. Indeed, legend has it that the four course designers – Patrick

GAELIC GAMES

Although the golf courses in Ireland have a magnetic attraction and make it difficult for a visiting golfer to do anything else other than play as much golf as is humanly possible, it is worthwhile trying to find time to attend either a Gaelic football or hurling match.

These are the national sports of Ireland and they attract huge and passionate crowds during the playing season, which stretches mainly from early May until the last Sunday in September, when the All-Ireland Football Final is played at Croke Park in Dublin. Both Gaelic football and hurling have 15 players on each team and, like rugby, use H-shaped goalposts. The pitch, however, is significantly bigger than that used for either soccer or rugby.

Gaelic football is a robust game: the ball is round, like a soccer ball, but players are allowed to catch and kick, similar in fact to Australian Rules. Running with the ball is allowed only by 'soloing', which involves kicking the ball from foot-to-hand in one motion. Hand-passing and kick-passing are also permitted. Play is fast and furious, with plenty of scores, and county loyalties create a passion that is arguably unrivalled in sport anywhere in the world.

If anything, hurling is an even more skilful game. Players use 'hurleys' – sticks fashioned from ash – to propel a small leather ball, about the same size as a baseball and known as a 'sliotar'. Hurling is reputed to be the fastest field sport in the world – faster even than lacrosse. Anyone interested in sport will be utterly fascinated by the exhilarating spectacle. A game lasts for 70 minutes, and is most definitely a 'must see' on any visitor's itinerary.

Merrigan, Ron Kirby, Joe Carr and Eddie Hackett – attempted 41 routings before they were all satisfied that the right one had been discovered.

Shortly after its completion, Carr, a three-times British Amateur champion, remarked, 'The Old Head, as a golf links, will in my estimation rate with the great golf courses of the world. Its location, its scenic beauty and spectacular terrain remind me of Cypress Point and Pebble Beach… it has the potential of being the eighth wonder of the world, in golfing terms.'

There are quite a number of blind tee shots, which certainly won't please everyone. The use of free-standing limestone pieces – used by the ancient Celts and called 'Stones of Accord' – will, however, guide you into hitting your ball into the right positions.

The spectacular location undoubtedly gives the Old Head – the most expensive round of golf in Ireland – its greatest appeal. Although the course doesn't possess the same run of great hole after great hole that, say, Portmarnock, Royal County Down and Ballybunion offer, there are some magnificent holes all the same. Anyway, with such

The old lighthouse can be used as a guide when driving off the par 4 4th hole, which runs along a cliff top.

breathtaking scenery all around, you deserve some respite from concentrating on every single shot.

The first introduction to the cliffs comes as early as the 2nd hole – the first of six holes located on the left-hand side of the access road to the lighthouse. The course then winds its way back around to the 7th, a par 3 of 188yd/171m with a green perched on the edge, before you cross back over the road towards a setting that becomes ever more awesome as the round progresses.

Make sure that your camera is in your bag for a shot from the 12th tee, where you must hit blindly along the cliff top to a fairway (trust your caddie's advice on this one), and then decide whether to lay up or be brave and foolish and attempt to find the small green in two.

The 14th hole is considered the toughest on the course. However, it is the final run of four holes alongside the cliff, which brings you back to the clubhouse, that is likely to remain as your abiding image of The Old Head of Kinsale.

REGIONAL DIRECTORY

Where to Stay

Waterford Dating back to the 11th century, the five-star **Waterford Castle Golf and Country Club** (+353 (0)51-878203) is just 3 miles/5km from the city centre. Access is by a chain-linked car ferry as the complex is set on a 310-acre island. In Waterford City itself, there are numerous good hotels. **Jury's Hotel** (+353 (0)51-832111) has a prime location overlooking the River Suir. The **Tower Hotel** (+353 (0)51-875801), the largest hotel in the south-east, has good leisure facilities and is part of the same group that owns **Faithlegg House Hotel** (+353 (0)51-382000), whose course has played host to the Ladies Irish Open. The **Bridge Hotel** (+353 (0)51-877222) and **Dooley's Hotel** (+353 (0)51-873531) offer guests preferential green fees on local courses. Both hotels are situated along the quays close to the landmark Reginald's Tower, constructed by the Vikings in 1003AD. **The Belfry Hotel** (+353 (0)51-844800) is in the centre of Waterford City and is a good base for golfers who wish to play a number of courses in the region. **Woodlands Hotel** (+353 (0)51-304574) is within striking distance of all of the city's courses and is also perfectly located to enjoy Dunmore, one of the most picturesque villages in this part of the country. The **Glenshelane Forest Park** (+353 (0)58-52131) offers luxury log cabins in the beautiful Blackwater Valley.

Cork **The Midleton Park Hotel** (+353 (0)21-631767) is ideally located in east Cork, not far from Fota Island and within striking distance of Cork City. **The Maryborough House Hotel** (+353 (0)21-4365555) has bedrooms overlooking orchards and gardens and is well located for shopping. **Hayfield Manor** (+353 (0)21-315600) on College Road in Cork is an elegant 19th-century mansion with five-star hotel status and a state-of-the-art leisure centre. **The Kingsley Hotel** (+353 (0)21-4800555) at Victoria Cross in Cork City has a private library with coal fire, a leisure centre and even a helipad for high flyers. **Fernhill Golf and Country Club** (+353 (0)21-4372226) in Carrigaline is a 10-minute drive from Cork City and Cork Airport and has rooms overlooking its own private golf course. **The Moorings** (+353 (0)21-4772376) is a superbly appointed guest house in Kinsale overlooking the harbour – and the owners can even arrange tee times, with preferential green fees, for their guests. **Kieran's Folkhouse Inn** (+353 (0)21-4772382) in Kinsale is a charming 250-year-old country inn and a past winner of the 'Irish Inn of the Year'. **Dunmore House Hotel** (+353 (0)23-33352) in

Clonakilty is family-owned and managed and has its own golf course adjacent to the hotel. **The Westlodge Hotel** (+353 (0)27-50438) in Bantry is ideally located for exploring the scenery as well as the hidden coves and beaches of west Cork.

Where to Eat

Waterford The restaurant at the **Granville Hotel** (+353 (0)51-8555111) serves a wide range of dishes using local produce. **Richmond House** (+353 (0)58-54278) in Cappoquin has a reputation for serving fine food. **Una's Restaurant** (+353 (0)51-358888) in Ivory's Hotel close to the Waterford Crystal factory offers a surprisingly good range of high-quality cuisine. **The Ship Restaurant** (+353 (0)51-383144) in Dunmore East is a creeper-clad Victorian building and specializes in seafood.

Cork **Aherne's Seafood Bar** (+353 (0)24-92424) in Youghal has open turf fires and a warm welcome and is renowned for its fresh seafood. Located in the Waters Edge Hotel in Cobh, **Jacob's Ladder Restaurant** (+353 (0)21-4815566) presents locally produced ingredients in some truly sumptuous dishes. **Ballymaloe House** (+353 (0)21-4652531) in Midleton serves food that is largely produced on the home farm and is very good. **Eco Restaurant** (+353 (0)21-892522) in Douglas has an excellent choice of poultry, meat, fish and vegetables and even includes some Oriental and Scandinavian dishes. **Blairs Inn** (+353 (0)21-381470) is a typical Irish pub set back from the main road in a secluded riverside position and has earned high praise for its cuisine, which gives international dishes an Irish twist. **The Blue Haven** (+353 (0)21-4772209) in the gourmet town of Kinsale has won many awards – including 'Best Seafood Bar in Ireland' – and, along with superb food, offers a cosy atmosphere. **Longueville House** (+353 (0)22-47156) is on an estate with the River Blackwater running through and offers produce from the farm, garden and river.

What to Do

Waterford If you're in Waterford, then a visit to the **Waterford Crystal Visitor Centre** is a must. The tour of this famous factory enables you to watch first-hand as masterblowers create shapes at temperatures of 1,400°, while the master craftsmen then create the intricate cuts that are the hallmark of the crystal. The visitor centre also offers an audio-visual presentation. Waterford also offers a number of walking tours that give you a valuable insight into this historic city. John Roberts designed **Christ Church Cathedral** – originally a Viking foundation – in the 18th century, while the Franciscans founded the French Church in the early 13th century. The Granary houses the

Waterford Museum of Treasures; it features an extensive range of artefacts extending back over a thousand years, which are brought to life in a multimedia presentation. Meanwhile, to the west of the city and some 5 miles/8km north of Tramore, off the L26 road, are the portal tombs of **Knockeen and Gaulstown**. Indeed, Waterford is a county with many prehistoric sights and, while the Comeragh and Knockmealdown mountains provide a lovely backdrop on the drive to the west of the county, it is worthwhile to search out the numerous ancient sites, castles and round towers in the Dungarvan area. In **Dungarvan**, there are also guided tours of historical areas.

Cork Youghal, pronounced 'yawl', from the Gaelic *Eochaill* meaning yew tree, lies at the mouth of the River Blackwater. Its most famous citizen was Sir Walter Raleigh, and it is possible to gain an insight into this town's rich past at the **Youghal Visitor Centre** and then, perhaps, take one of the guided walking tours. A tour of a different type can be taken at the **Jameson Heritage Centre** in Midleton, which relates the story of Irish whiskey. **Fota Wildlife Park** lies adjacent to the Fota Island Golf Club – which has played host to the Murphy's Irish Open – and has over 90 species of wildlife from five continents on its 70 acres. There is a wide range of facilities for young and old, and, if you feel up to it, you can even adopt an animal. **Cobh** is a town with a rich maritime history. As the country's principal port, it became associated with a stream of emigrants leaving Ireland for the 'New World'. Indeed, over 2.5 million people sailed from Cobh to America between 1845 and 1860. Cobh, then known as Queenstown, was the *Titanic's* last port of call before its ill-fated transatlantic journey. **The Cobh Heritage Centre and Railway Station** provides a multimedia experience relating the town's maritime history and also the role it played in Irish emigration. No visit to Cork, meanwhile, is complete without taking in **Blarney Castle** and the famous **Blarney Stone**. To kiss the stone, you are required to lie on your back and then – with someone holding your ankles – lean further back and kiss the limestone block. Your reward for these efforts? The gift of the gab – or eloquent speech, if you prefer to think of it that way!

Tourist Information Centres
Waterford Tourist Office, The Quay, Waterford City (+353 (0)51-875823)
Tramore Tourist Office, Railway Square, Tramore, County Waterford (+353 (0)51-381572)
Youghal Heritage Centre, Market Square, East Cork (+353 (0)24-20170)
Cobh Tourism, The Old Yacht Club, Cobh Harbour, County Cork (+353 (0)21-4813301)
Cork Tourism, Grand Parade, Cork City (+353 (0)21-4255700)

Some of the most famous trophies in golf – including the Solheim Cup – are created by master craftsmen at the Waterford Crystal factory.

Chapter 4

Kerry & the South-West

For most golfing visitors to Ireland, all roads eventually lead to the south-west, with its imposing mountains, mystical lakes and, probably most compelling of all, its seaside links courses. These links, caressed as they are by the Gulf Stream, have a deserved reputation for being among the very best in the world.

No matter what route you take to enter County Kerry – known to one and all as The Kingdom – once you arrive

here, you are made to feel very much at home by the locals.

Whether it is Ballybunion or Tralee in the north of the county, Killarney at its epicentre or Waterville, a jewel of a course located on the rugged and beautiful coastline known as the Ring of

Left: King John's Castle, situated on the banks of the River Shannon, in Limerick City. Above: A typical thatched cottage at Adare, County Limerick.

Kerry, you will certainly discover some sort of golfer's paradise. Indeed, Kerry, a county bordered by Limerick and Cork to the east but indelibly associated with the Atlantic Ocean that runs all along its west coast, has become something of a Mecca for many top US golfers in the run-up to the British Open each year. Tiger Woods, David Duval and Mark O'Meara have all visited these shores to fine-tune their links games before attempting to win the claret jug, and Tom Watson was captain of Ballybunion Golf Club in its Millennium year. Moreover, a statue to commemorate the late Payne Stewart's affinity with Waterville is a poignant reminder of how much the two-times US Open champion loved to visit this area, and of how he was welcomed as one of their own by the local people.

Apart from golf, there is much to endear Kerry to visitors, not least because

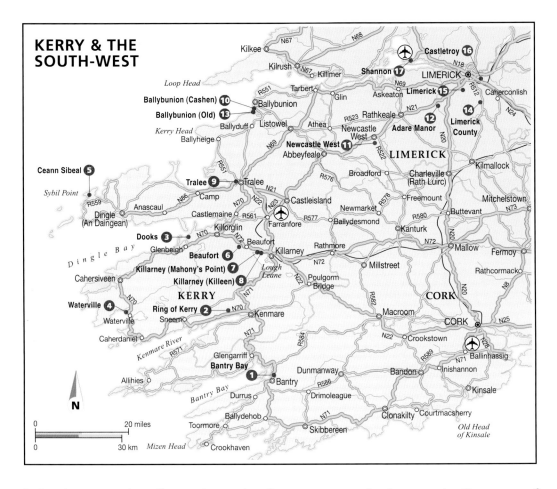

KERRY & THE SOUTH-WEST

it has its own microclimate (a result of the warm waters of the Gulf Stream) and subtropical plant life. It is unquestionably one of the most scenic areas in the country. The magically named MacGillycuddy Reeks – which boast Carrauntoohil, the highest peak in Ireland – dominate the landscape, while the lakes of Killarney (there are three of them, each dotted with islands) give new meaning to the phrase 'picture postcard'. Killarney itself is a bustling town full of good bars, restaurants and hotels and, with a number of top golf courses on its doorstep, is the ideal base for a golfing holiday. Killarney is also the traditional starting point, or finishing point if you

commence the journey in Kenmare, of the Ring of Kerry. Regardless of which direction you are going, visiting Kerry and taking in the magnificent scenery is a wonderful experience. It's probably best to travel by coach – not so much for safety, although there are numerous cliff-top roads to negotiate, but so that you can take your eyes off the road and enjoy the splendid view.

Planning an Itinerary
The choice of golf courses in Kerry alone, quite apart from the attractions further along the mouth of the River Shannon in the Limerick area, is immense. Although it is essential in most

parts of Ireland to have access to some mode of road transport, it is truer here than elsewhere. To discover and enjoy fully the golfing delights of The Kingdom, you will need the flexibility that a car or van offers.

You will also have to pre-book times on most courses. Don't tempt fate and arrive unannounced expecting to get out on to a course – the demand for tee times in the south-west is such that you are more than likely to be disappointed. Most hotels and guest-houses will be able to arrange times with local courses, and the golf-tour operator SWING (+353 (0)66-7125733) can organize times on all of the top courses.

Kerry has long been a magnet for golfers from all over the globe, with Ballybunion, Tralee, Waterville and Killarney the main attractions. There are other wonderful courses, though – Dooks, Ring of Kerry, Beaufort, Ceann

Sibeal and Castlegregory to name but a few – that have helped make this part of Ireland real golfing country.

While Limerick does not even attempt to boast of possessing similar golf terrain, certainly not with regard to links, there are a number of courses around the River Shannon's principal city to ensure that a stay to the north of Kerry is not without its own charms. Indeed, it is possible to follow in the footsteps of Tiger Woods at Limerick Golf Club (where, in 2000, the world number one player shot a course record 62 in a charity tournament). Also, the course at Adare Hotel and Golf Resort, designed by Robert Trent Jones Snr, is one of the top parkland tracks in the country. In addition, there is a well-appointed municipal facility at Rathbane in Limerick City.

Scenic beauty at the Lakes of Killarney, County Kerry, with the MacGillycuddy Reeks mountains as a backdrop.

Bantry Bay

Bantry Bay Golf Club, Donemark, Bantry, County Cork
TEL: *+353 (0)27-50579* **FAX:** *+353 (0)27-50579*
EMAIL: *info@bantrygolf.com*
WEBSITE: *www.bantrygolf.com*
LOCATION: *2 miles/3.2km north of Bantry, off the N71 to Glengarriff*
COURSE: *18 holes, 6501yd/5910m, par 71, SSS 72*
GREEN FEES: *€€*
FACILITIES: *Changing rooms and showers, catering, bar, trolley hire, buggy hire, club hire, chipping/putting area*
VISITORS: *Welcome*

Since its expansion to 18 holes, Bantry Bay has developed into probably the top parkland course in west Cork. Situated in an area of great natural beauty, with the mountains of the Beara peninsula to the north and Sheep's Head Peninsula to the south, it certainly manages to reflect the subtle charms of this part of the world.

'The architect of this course was not me, but Mother Nature – I just gave her a helping hand,' said Christy O'Connor Jnr, the designer who upgraded the original nine-hole design of Eddie Hackett to a full 18-hole course.

After a relatively easy start, as if to lull the golfer into a false sense of security, a number of par 4 holes shatter any illusions that this is an easy stroll with the main objective being to enjoy the scenery. The 4th is a tough hole

With views of the Caha mountains and Kenmare Bay, the hillside course at Ring of Kerry is stunningly located.

with an accurate approach shot required, but it is the 6th hole, measuring 418yd/380m with out-of-bounds left and an approach between two lakes to a severely sloping green, that really shakes you up.

There is another approach over water to the 8th, before a series of really good holes on the homeward journey. The 12th, a 448-yd/408-m par 4, is probably the most difficult hole on the course. There is out-of-bounds down the left with a lake and large bunker guarding the green, making both length and precision essential.

Ring of Kerry

Ring of Kerry Golf Club, Templenoe, Kenmare, County Kerry
TEL: *+353 (0)64-42000* **FAX:** *+353 (0)64-42533*
EMAIL: *ringofkerrygolf@eircom.net*
WEBSITE: *www.ringofkerry.com*
LOCATION: *4 miles/6.4km west of Kenmare, off the N70 to Sneem*
COURSE: *18 holes, 6807yd/6189m, par 71, SSS 73*
GREEN FEES: *€€€€€€*
FACILITIES: *Changing rooms and showers, catering, bar, trolley hire, buggy hire, club hire, chipping/putting area*
VISITORS: *Welcome – booking is advised*

The ingenuity of man and the grace of God contrived to produce a rather special golfing product at the Ring of Kerry, a course near the village of Templenoe that offers breathtaking views of Kenmare Bay and the Caha Mountains.

If you stand on the 4th fairway, and peer over a wall into a field not 55yd/50m away that consists of nothing but bog and rocks, heather and gorse, the impact of what has been achieved at the Ring of Kerry course hits home. In many ways, it is a modern-day miracle, helped in no small way by technological advances. Extensive earth moving to remove the rocks and bogs was necessary so that the fairways, as well as the greens, could be entirely sand-based.

During the course's construction, up to 70 truckloads of sand a day were brought from a nearby quarry until over 120,000 tonnes (seeded with a rye and fescue mix) had been transported onto the fairways. The result is a spectacular course with a superb clubhouse, situated on lush grassland that is totally at odds with what surrounds the course.

Take note, though: this is a physically demanding course for anyone attempting to walk it, and electric carts are advised. There are many fine holes throughout, although the back nine has more established trees and offers greater maturity overall. The 11th is a mammoth par 5 that requires a drive over a ravine, while the finishing hole is a 199-yd/180-m par 3 to an undulating green.

Dooks

Dooks Golf Club, Glenbeigh, County Kerry
TEL: *+353 (0)66-9768205*
FAX: *+353 (0)66-9768476* **EMAIL:** *office@dooks.com*
WEBSITE: *www.dooks.com*
LOCATION: *5 miles/8km west of Killorglin, off the N70 coastal road to Glenbeigh*
COURSE: *18 holes, 6010yd/5463m, par 70, SSS 68*
GREEN FEES: €€€
FACILITIES: *Changing rooms and showers, catering, bar, trolley hire, chipping/putting area*
VISITORS: *Welcome, but it is necessary to book in advance*

Over a hundred years has passed since the soldiers of the Royal Horse Artillery, attending compulsory training at the nearby Glenbeigh artillery range, first stumbled upon the dunes at Dooks and, recognizing it as prime golfing terrain, introduced the game to the area. Visiting the course, one senses that very little has changed since that time, for this is genuine linksland with a reliance on natural elements.

Set out on three sets of sand dunes at the head of Dingle Bay, the course is sited in an area of great natural beauty. In the immediate foreground are the sand dune peninsulas of Rossbeigh and Inch and, just a few miles away, the whitewashed houses of Cromane fishing village provide a different sort of eye-catching beauty.

There was a time when Dooks was very much a hidden gem, but word has since spread of its beauty and tranquillity, however, and nowadays it is most definitely on the golfing trail. Advance booking is essential for anyone hoping to savour the delights of this links. Despite its shortness in length, it provides a superb test as it places demands on accuracy and shot-making skills in a wind invariably coming in off the Atlantic.

The 1st and the 10th holes are unusual for the course in that they are longish par 4s, each reaching out to over 400yd/365m. It is the short 13th, at 150yd/138m, though, that captures the spirit of Dooks – its green has fallen precisely where nature intended.

The 13th hole at Dooks, a true links course close by the shoreline of Dingle Bay.

Waterville

Waterville Golf Club, Waterville, County Kerry
TEL: *+353 (0)66-9474102*
FAX: *+353 (0)66-9474482* **EMAIL:** *wvgolf@iol.ie*
WEBSITE: *www.watervillegolf.com*
LOCATION: *1 mile/1.6km north of Waterville, on the N70 to Cahersiveen*
COURSE: *18 holes, 7225yd/6570m, par 72, SSS 74*
GREEN FEES: *€€€€€€ +*
FACILITIES: *Changing rooms and showers, catering, bar, pro shop, trolley hire, buggy hire, club hire, practice area*
VISITORS: *Booking essential*

WATERVILLE

HOLE	YD	M	PAR	HOLE	YD	M	PAR
1	430	391	4	10	475	432	4
2	469	426	4	11	506	460	5
3	417	379	4	12	200	182	3
4	179	163	3	13	518	471	5
5	595	541	5	14	456	415	4
6	387	352	4	15	407	370	4
7	178	162	3	16	350	318	4
8	435	395	4	17	196	179	3
9	445	405	4	18	582	529	5
OUT	3535	3214	35	IN	3690	3356	37

7225YD • 6570M • PAR 72

It is said that one of life's greatest pleasures is not in actually playing the course at Waterville, but in getting there. Unless you travel by helicopter, the only way to the course is via the stunningly beautiful Ring of Kerry – a road that takes in some of the most breathtaking scenery in all of Europe. Moreover, the good news is that the magical appeal of this part of Ireland doesn't end upon reaching a links that has become a place of pilgrimage for some of the world's leading players.

With the MacGillycuddy's Reeks as a spectacular mountain backdrop and the Atlantic Ocean as another, Waterville – the design creation of Eddie Hackett, Ireland's most noted golf-course architect of the 20th century – is a rather special course. Its presence amongst the world's great courses, however, owes much to the late Irish-American Jack

Set in gently rolling sand-hills, the 13th at Waterville offers panoramic views of the landscape on the Iveragh peninsula.

Mulcahy, whose money and dreams in the 1970s transformed a wasting nine-hole course into the great links that it is today.

A lasting monument to the inspiration behind Waterville is that the par 3 17th is known as Mulcahy's Peak. As the name suggests, the tee is on a peak – a towering dune – and you are required to find a green over yet more dunes that lies almost 200yd/180m away.

In truth, there is one outstanding hole after another. All of the par 3s are superb; indeed Tom Watson once declared, 'Waterville possesses the best par 3 holes I have ever encountered on the same golf course.' No hole is more impressive than the 12th, known as the 'Mass Hole', which is played across a deep gorge.

While Hackett was building the new course, local contractors informed him that they were reluctant to do any earth moving in that particular hollow because Mass was once celebrated there in what were known as the Penal Times in Ireland. During this dark period, local inhabitants observed their religion in this concealed area for fear of persecution. The result of this history is a totally natural hole across the gorge to a plateau green that has no bunkers.

Given Waterville's location on one of the country's most south-westerly peninsulas, the wind that whips in off the Atlantic Ocean is a constant factor. However, the real appeal of the course is, quite simply, that it is so natural. Often, the greens are hard to see – masked, as they regularly are, by dunes – but such obstacles only add to the overall challenge of the course. Club selection and shot-making creativity are crucial elements here.

The opening nine holes unwind over fairly flat country. Unlike many traditional links courses, there are no blind shots, and perhaps only the 16th could really claim to be a dogleg.

This is indeed a long, tough course. It has been described in its time, by more than one golfing professional, as a 'beautiful monster' and, in golfing parlance at least, compliments don't come much higher than that. Christy O'Connor Snr once nominated the 2nd hole, now known as 'Christy's Choice', as one of his favourite holes in Irish golf. Further testimony to the high regard in which the course is held is that Mark O'Meara and Tiger Woods are among the players who have used it as a golfing retreat in preparation for their British Open title quests.

Ceann Sibeal

Ceann Sibeal Golf Club, Ballyferriter, near Dingle,
County Kerry
TEL: *+353 (0)66-9156255* **FAX:** *+353 (0)66-*
9156409 **EMAIL:** *dinglegc@iol.ie*
WEBSITE: *www.dingle-golf.com*
LOCATION: *9 miles/14km north-west of Dingle, off the*
R559; the course is signposted
COURSE: *18 holes, 6696yd/6088m, par 72, SSS 71*
GREEN FEES: *€€€€*
FACILITIES: *Changing rooms and showers, catering, bar,*
pro shop, trolley hire, buggy hire, chipping/putting area
VISITORS: *Welcome – booking advisable*

Deep in the heartland of the Irish-speaking area of County Kerry lies Ceann Sibeal – or Sybil Head, to give the course its English form – the westernmost golf course in Ireland. Ceann Sibeal is yet another of the links courses dotted around this particular coastline like a necklace of jewels.

'It was a delight to play such a natural links in such a beautiful place,' enthused Ronan Rafferty, who once topped the European Tour's Order of Merit, after playing the course. Any visitor is sure to concur with these sentiments. Ceann Sibeal is a marvellous

Ceann Sibeal, situated on the tip of the Dingle peninsula,
is Ireland's westernmost course.

traditional links that manoeuvres its way through low-lying dune hills and features a winding burn that twists through the course, coming into play on about 10 holes.

The views add to the entire experience. Ceann Sibeal overlooks Dingle Bay, the Blasket Islands and Mount Brandon and is on a peninsula that is steeped in history – the area abounds in archaeological treasures dating back to the Stone Age. However, the real stamp of approval is that this links, originally laid out in 1969 by Eddie Hackett and completed in 1992 by Christy O'Connor Jr, looks as if it has always been here.

It is not as tough as other Kerry courses, such as Waterville, Tralee or Ballybunion, but it doesn't need to be. Part of its charm is that it presents a challenge that requires sensible play in a traditional environment, while also offering a good variety of holes with the par 3s ranging from the 201-yd/182-m 2nd to the 156-yd/141-m 12th. Given that these two holes are in opposite directions, however, and with the wind a factor, there are days when the shorter hole requires the bigger club. That is the beauty of seaside golf.

 ## Beaufort

Beaufort Golf Club, Killarney, County Kerry
TEL: *+353 (0)64-44440* **FAX:** *+353 (0)64-44752*
EMAIL: *beaufortgc@tinet.ie*
WEBSITE: *www.globalgolf.com*
LOCATION: *7 miles/11km west of Killarney, on the*
Killorglin road
COURSE: *18 holes, 6625yd/6023m, par 71, SSS 72*
GREEN FEES: *€€€€*
FACILITIES: *Changing rooms and showers, catering,*
bar, pro shop, trolley hire, buggy hire, practice area
VISITORS: *Welcome – booking advisable*

No matter where you go in Killarney, beauty is never too far away. It is little wonder, then, that course architect Dr Arthur Spring, who spent a number of years on the

European Seniors Tour, was so taken by the special ambience he discovered at Beaufort, where fairy rings and the ruins of an old castle are ready-made features.

The course is set in the mature parkland of the Churchtown Estate and is a demanding, but fair, test of a golfer's skills. Its magical atmosphere is helped immeasurably by the spectacular Macgillycuddy's Reeks mountain range in the background. The designer is to be congratulated, however, for making the most of what nature provided, and the large contoured greens ensure that the blade cannot be cold for long if a good score is to be on the cards.

Killarney (Mahony's Point)

Killarney Golf and Fishing Club, Mahony's Point, Killarney, County Kerry
TEL: *+353 (0)64-31034* **FAX:** *+353(0)64-33064*
EMAIL: *reservations@killarney-golf.com*
WEBSITE: *www.killarney-golf.com*
LOCATION: *2 miles/3.2km west of Killarney, on the Killorglin road*
COURSE: *18 holes, 6781yd/6164m, par 72, SSS 72*
GREEN FEES:
FACILITIES: *Changing rooms and showers, catering, bar, pro shop, trolley hire, buggy hire, practice area, leisure facilities*
VISITORS: *Welcome – booking essential*

The wit of the Kerry people, whether at the counter of a bar or on a golf course, is legendary. So, when they tell you that Killarney, arguably the greatest tourist attraction in the country, is 'the end product of what the good Lord can do when He is in a good mood,' there can be no arguing.

The Lakes of Killarney and the magnificent MacGillycuddy's Reeks combine to create a spellbinding image that has graced many a picture postcard. Nowhere is this more obvious than on the 18th hole of the Mahony's Point course: ostensibly the No. 2 course of three 18-hole layouts, but probably the best parkland short hole in the country.

This par 3 measuring 196yd/179m is a hole that makes grown men tremble at the knees as they approach the tee box. The waters of the lake lap the shoreline on the right – extending from the tee to a green that is also guarded by giant pine trees – while the added hazards of bunkers and rhododendron bushes add to the final test on a course designed by Sir Guy Campbell and Henry Longhurst in 1938. Gene Sarazen, in fact, described it as 'one of the most memorable holes in golf'.

Unbelievable as it may sound, the 18th hole isn't actually the hardest to be found on Mahony's Point. That honour goes to the 11th hole, a monstrous par 4 of 468yd/426m, which is a slight right-to-left dogleg requiring both length and accuracy.

The MacGillycuddy's Reeks are an imposing backdrop to the stunning lakeside 18th hole at Mahony's Point.

Killarney (Killeen)

*Killarney Golf and Fishing Club, Mahony's Point,
Killarney, County Kerry*
TEL: *+353 (0)64-31034* FAX: *+353 (0)64-33064*
EMAIL: *reservations@killarney-golf.com*
WEBSITE: *www.killarney-golf.com*
LOCATION: *2 miles/3.2km west of Killarney, on the
Killorglin road*
COURSE: *18 holes, 7123yd/6474m, par 72, SSS 72*
GREEN FEES: *€€€€€*
FACILITIES: *Changing rooms and showers, catering,
bar, pro shop, trolley hire, buggy hire, practice area,
leisure facilities*
VISITORS: *Welcome – booking essential*

*The finishing hole at Killeen is a dogleg par 4, with a
water hazard in play to the left.*

Killeen is arguably the brightest jewel in Killarney's crown. Its closing holes may not be as spectacular in terms of scenery as those at neighbouring Mahony's Point, but, as a test of golf, there are few parkland courses that offer such a demanding and incessant variety of good holes.

When the Irish Open was played by the splendid Lakes of Killarney in both 1990 and 1991, it was the Killeen course that was chosen to test out the world stars. It was also the venue for the Curtis Cup match between Britain and Ireland's top amateur women and those from the United States.

Since then, a third course designed by Donald Steel has been built. Called Lackabane, and constructed on more elevated ground than its two predecessors, its arrival has made Killarney a 54-hole complex of the highest standard.

Killeen simply gets better and better with age. The greens are among the best to be found in the country. To reach them, a player needs to retain concentration throughout, an especially difficult task considering the sort of scenery that surrounds the course.

The level of difficulty is increased the further you go back on the tee box – the fairways look narrow and there is a premium on driving accuracy. Accurate driving is not the only requisite. The fairways are dotted with beautifully maintained bunkers and, as you'd expect on a course that caresses a lake, there are many water features.

The 1st hole is a case in point. The drive and the approach must be kept left or the beach, which is in play, acts like a magnet. The tee shot from the 6th tee box to what is effectively an island green – surrounded as it is by a burn – some 202yd/184m away is not for the faint-hearted. Designed by Eddie Hackett and Dr Billy O'Sullivan, the Killeen course serves as an enduring legacy to the memories of both men.

9 Tralee

Tralee Golf Club, Barrow, Tralee, County Kerry
TEL: *+353 (0)66-7136379* **FAX:** *+353 (0)66-
7136008* **EMAIL:** *info@traleegolfclub.com*
WEBSITE: *www.traleegolfclub.com*
LOCATION: *7 miles/11km north-west of Tralee, off the
R558; the course is signposted*
COURSE: *18 holes, 7187yd/6533m, par 71, SSS 73*
GREEN FEES: *€€€€€ +*
FACILITIES: *Changing rooms and showers, catering,
bar, pro shop, trolley hire, club hire, practice area*
VISITORS: *Welcome – booking advisable*

If legend is to be believed, then word of
Tralee – before there was ever a golf
course, it must be said – travelled across the
Atlantic to the New World long before
Christopher Columbus discovered such a
place. According to the lore, St Brendan the
Navigator, who hailed from these parts, sailed
the seas and was the first to discover the
Americas. It seems his spirit of adventure is
well and truly alive today. Brendan is depicted
on Tralee Golf Club's crest – and the saint
surely guided club officials when they asked
Arnold Palmer to design his first course in
Europe at Tralee.

Although the salt-spray from the Atlantic
initially led to some problems with the greens,
that set-back has been rectified. Tralee, a
demanding course that will leave you
physically drained but contented at the end of
play, has since earned itself a justifiable
reputation for being amongst the top links
courses in the whole of Ireland.

The Barrow course, as it is known,
occupies rugged terrain, particularly so on the
back nine. The first nine holes give you a
glimpse of two very different periods of
history. Below the 3rd green you will find a
cave that was used extensively in the making
of the movie *Ryan's Daughter*, while the 4th
hole is called Cuchullain's Table because the
ancient Irish hero was reputed to have feasted
there with his army.

The homeward run takes in towering
duneland and is genuinely spectacular. When
Jeff Sluman played here in preparation for a
British Open, he alleged that he had finally
'found a hole even Tiger can't reach in two'.
He was referring to the 570-yd/518-m 11th
hole – known as Palmer's Peak – where
a wall comes into play for any pushed
approach shots.

As with all true links courses, the wind is
very much a factor when playing Tralee. All
in all, a truly magnificent round of golf with
no respite until the uphill finishing hole has
been climbed.

*Created in towering dunes by designer Arnold Palmer,
Tralee is a serious test of a golfer's ability. This is the 13th.*

Ballybunion (Cashen)

Ballybunion Golf Club, Ballybunion, County Kerry
TEL: *+353 (0)68-27146* **FAX:** *+353 (0)68-27387*
EMAIL: *bbgolfc@iol.ie*
WEBSITE: *www.ballybuniongolfclub.ie*
LOCATION: *⅔ miles/1km south of Ballybunion; the course is signposted*
COURSE: *18 holes, 6296yd/5724m, par 72, SSS 73*
GREEN FEES: €€€€€
FACILITIES: *Changing rooms and showers, catering, bar, pro shop, caddies, practice area*
VISITORS: *Welcome – booking essential*

Even if the Cashen links were not in the shadow of Ballybunion's Old Course, it would still be a cause for pilgrimage. Cashen is set in a spectacular seaside location with massive dunes; indeed, on first seeing the land, the designer Robert Trent Jones Jnr declared that it was 'the finest piece of linksland in the world'.

THE IRISH LANGUAGE

Officially, there are two languages in Ireland: Irish, or 'Gaeilge' (Gaelic), and English. Irish is a very musical language and is very easy on the ear, but it has little connection with the English tongue and is totally incomprehensible to anyone who doesn't actually speak it. English is by far the more widely spoken language, but it is certainly useful to know some words when it comes to toilet/rest room doors. *Fir* is the Irish word for men, and *Mna* is the Irish word for women. So, take care!

Although Irish is compulsory in schools in the Republic, and increasingly common in classrooms in Northern Ireland, most people converse in English. However, there are a number of areas – Connemara in the west, Donegal in the north-west and the Gaeltacht areas of west Kerry and Waterford – where it is the first spoken language. If you are driving in these areas, it is advisable to have a good road map as, very often, the road signs – usually bilingual – are in Irish only.

Rather than merely imitating its famous neighbour, Trent Jones chose to give the Cashen course a character of its own. From the start, as you fire your first drive down the narrow 1st fairway with high banks on either side, this course demands accuracy off the tee. By the day's end, you'll have used every club in the bag and, unless extremely lucky, lost a number of balls into the bargain.

The par 5s are, quite rightly, considered the feature holes of the Cashen course. Each one is spectacular in its own right, but there is no more natural hole than the 10th, a par 4 of just 332yd/301m, which majestically proves the point that a classic short hole can cause as much distress and wonder as any three-shot hole.

Perched on a sandy cliff top beside the Atlantic, the 16th green on the Cashen course enjoys an exalted position.

Newcastle West

Newcastle West Golf Club, Ardagh, County Limerick
TEL: +353 (0)69-76500 **FAX:** +353 (0)69-76511
LOCATION: 3 miles/4.8km west of Rathkeale, off the
N21 near the village of Ardagh
COURSE: 18 holes, 6502yd/5911m, par 71, SSS 72
GREEN FEES: €€
FACILITIES: Changing rooms and showers, catering,
bar, pro shop, trolley hire, club hire, practice area
VISITORS: Welcome

The equine influence is immediately apparent at Newcastle West, a maturing course that has been developed on an old stud farm. Indeed, the former stables have been converted into locker rooms downstairs and a bar and restaurant upstairs.

A decision to move from the outskirts of Newcastle West to the village of Ardagh – famous in Ireland as the place where the Ardagh Chalice, a national treasure now on view in the National Museum in Dublin, was found – was taken in 1994.

On undulating terrain, blessed by free-draining land and mature trees, the new course has developed well and offers a welcome stop-off for travellers going from Shannon Airport to the links courses of Kerry.

The 1st hole is a relatively easy par 5, but the influence of water is apparent as early as the 6th – a par 3 of 187yd/180m that demands a carry all the way to the green. The 12th is an extremely tough par 4 with out-of-bounds left and trees on the right awaiting any weak tee shot; the 14th is a fine par 5 that sweeps to the left and requires both precision and length.

Adare Manor

Adare Manor Hotel and Golf Resort, Adare, County
Limerick
TEL: +353 (0)61-396566
LOCATION: 11 miles/17km south-west of Limerick,
off the Killarney road; 22 miles/35km from Shannon
Airport
COURSE: 18 holes, 7138yd/6489m, par 72, SSS 73
GREEN FEES: €€€€€€+
FACILITIES: Changing rooms and showers, catering,
bar, pro shop, trolley hire, buggy hire, club hire, practice
area, leisure facilities, on-site accommodation
VISITORS: Welcome – booking advisable

There's something bewitching about the grandeur of Adare Manor Hotel and Golf Resort, which opened for play in 1995. Not only is it a five-star hotel, but it also has a championship course designed by Robert Trent Jones Snr.

Built by the banks of the River Maigue, which comes into play spectacularly on the 18th, this parkland course has distinctive features, including a Lebanese cedar tree near the final green – reputed to be the oldest in Europe – and historic ruins on its grounds. It also has the course architect's trademark clover-leaf bunkers, plenty of water hazards and subtly undulating greens.

The front nine holes are dominated by a huge 14-acre lake, seen at its best on the 7th hole (a par 5 of 537yd/488m). There are two smaller lakes on the homeward run: to the right of the 14th green and between the tee and the green at the short 16th. All four final holes are superb, but the pièce de résistance is the 18th – a par 5 of 544yd/494m that crosses the River Maigue.

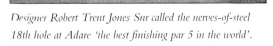

Designer Robert Trent Jones Snr called the nerves-of-steel 18th hole at Adare 'the best finishing par 5 in the world'.

Ballybunion (Old)

Ballybunion Golf Club, Ballybunion, County Kerry
TEL: +353 (0)68-27146 **FAX:** +353 (0)68-27387
EMAIL: bbgolf@iol.ie
WEBSITE: www.ballybuniongolfclub.ie
LOCATION: ⅔ miles/1km south of Ballybunion;
the course is signposted
COURSE: 18 holes, 6638yd/6036m, par 71, SSS 72
GREEN FEES: €€€€€€+
FACILITIES: Changing rooms and showers, catering,
bar, pro shop, caddies, practice area
VISITORS: Welcome – booking essential

BALLYBUNION (OLD)

HOLE	YD	M	PAR	HOLE	YD	M	PAR
1	396	360	4	10	362	329	4
2	439	399	4	11	454	413	4
3	221	201	3	12	200	182	3
4	529	481	5	13	482	438	5
5	529	481	5	14	136	124	3
6	381	346	4	15	212	193	3
7	425	386	4	16	493	449	5
8	154	140	3	17	392	356	4
9	455	414	4	18	378	344	4
OUT	3529	3208	36	IN	3109	2828	35

6638YD • 6036M • PAR 71

The irony isn't lost on anybody who stands on the 1st tee at Ballybunion's Old Course and notices that the first hazard is the graveyard to the right. Many a half-pushed tee shot has found its way into a parcel of land studded with headstones and Celtic crosses. Yet, if there were a golfing heaven on earth, then this piece of links in north Kerry would lay a strong claim to being it.

Tom Watson, who was the club's Millennium Captain in 2000, considers it to be the 'best and most beautiful test of links golf anywhere in the world'. This is a far cry from the opinion of the newspaper correspondent in the 1890s who described it as 'a rabbit warren below the village, where a golfer requires limitless patience and an inexhaustible supply of golf balls'; he's most likely turning in his grave now that the Old Course is earning its just acclaim.

When the wind blows, as it often does, there is no tougher course than Ballybunion (Old). In comparison with what lies ahead, the opening few holes are nothing very spectacular, but from the 6th hole on there is one magnificent hole after another and, for many, the bottom line is sheer survival.

For a number of years in the 1970s, survival was very much the only concern of those who loved the old links. Coastal erosion threatened the course's very existence and it was only after a worldwide 'Friends of Ballybunion' campaign had been launched that sufficient revenue was raised for the erection of sea-gabions (large boulders encased in wire mesh) to halt the menace.

'The contours, on the fairways and the greens, are what make it a great golf course – there are uphill and downhill and sidehill shots … there is a wild look to the place, the long grass covering the dunes that pitch and roll throughout the course making it very intimidating,' insisted Watson, whose association with Ballybunion helped no end in broadening the course's appeal. Yet,

every word that Watson has uttered about the Old Course comes from the heart. It is no marketing ploy, and the locals have adopted the American as a favoured son.

The demands of the course are enormous, with every club in the bag sure to be utilized, but this is its greatest attraction. The course is quite possibly the ultimate test for any player, of any standard. Indeed, when the Irish Open was played here in 2000, the professionals hollered so loudly after the Pro-Am about the course's difficulty that late decisions were made to cut back the rough and to water the greens.

Unfortunately for Ballybunion, the wind, uncharacteristically, failed to blow for the four days of the actual championship (won by Sweden's Patrik Sjoland), and the professionals didn't get to experience the real links in tournament play.

The 11th hole at Ballybunion involves an approach shot from a narrow fairway over a chasm to a small green.

On most days, however, this links is the supreme test. Anyone who plays the course will have a favourite hole – perhaps the dogleg 6th that brings the course closest to the village; maybe the superb par 3 15th of 212yd/193m from an elevated tee over wild dunes to a viciously difficult green; or the 7th, a wonderful dogleg that requires an error-free drive over tall dunes to find the fairway. My own favourite is the 11th, a magnificent par 4 of 454yd/413m, which straddles the coast.

Ballybunion Old is what links golf is all about, and the course, along with the hospitality in the gigantic clubhouse that overlooks the 18th green, draws golfers to it like a magnet.

14   Limerick County

Limerick County Golf and Country Club, Ballyneety,
County Limerick
TEL: *+353 (0)61-351881* FAX: *+353 (0)61-351384*
EMAIL: *lcgolf@iol.ie*
WEBSITE: *www.limerickcounty.com*
LOCATION: *5 miles/8km south of Limerick City, off
the Kilmallock road*
COURSE: *18 holes, 6788yd/6171m, par 72, SSS 74*
GREEN FEES: *€€€*
FACILITIES: *Changing rooms and showers, catering,
bar, pro shop, trolley hire, buggy hire, club hire, golf
academy, on-site accommodation*
VISITORS: *Welcome – booking advisable*

A fine parkland course on undulating terrain, Limerick County has become one of the more popular courses on Shannonside. Built to the highest USGA specifications, the course is on land that once formed part of the Croker Estate, the ancestral home of the notorious 'Boss' Croker of New York. On his deathbed, Croker was promised a fairer land on the other side... to which he replied, 'I doubt it'. Croker didn't get to play golf here, but Limerick County – or Ballyneety, as it is often called – has developed into a course that offers very good variety and demands all-round shot-making skills.

The course at Limerick County has a number of water features. None are too extravagant, but they all make approach shots particularly important.

Designed in two loops over the rolling landscape, the course continues to mature. Probably the toughest hole on the outward run is the 5th, a par 4 of 446yd/405m, which takes you to the furthest point from the fine clubhouse that dominates the course.

The last of the three par 5s is the 11th, which is followed by a short par 4. The 12th is a hole full of character, with water in play on either side of the fairway. The 18th is an extremely tough finishing hole, a par 4 of 447yd/406m, which frequently decides who wins the side bet.

15   Limerick

Limerick Golf Club, Ballyclough, County Limerick
TEL: *+353 (0)61-415146* FAX: *+353 (0)61-319219*
EMAIL: *lgc@eircom.net* WEBSITE: *www.limerickgc.com*
LOCATION: *3 miles/4.8km south of Limerick City,
off the Killarney road; the course is signposted*
COURSE: *18 holes, 6525yd/5932m, par 72, SSS 71*
GREEN FEES: *€€€€*
FACILITIES: *Changing rooms and showers, catering,
bar, pro shop, trolley hire, club hire, practice area*
VISITORS: *Welcome mid-week*

With a club that can trace its roots back to its foundation in 1891 – and a course that was partially designed by Dr Alister Mackenzie – it would seem that nothing more could surprise Ballyclough's golfers. Yet in the summer of 2000, Tiger Woods and several other top professionals, including David Duval and Mark O'Meara, came to this mature parkland course on the outskirts of Limerick for the JP McManus International tournament and raised an incredible €19 million for local charities.

Not only that, but in the process Woods shot a course record 62, and if the course is good enough for him, it is surely good enough for the rest of us. He subsequently returned to Limerick Golf Club, where Honorary Life Membership was conferred upon him. Woods in turn presented the club with the flag from the 18th green at St Andrews, the scene of his British Open triumph in 2000 when he completed his career Grand Slam of the majors.

There are some good holes at Limerick, most notably the long par 4 3rd, which is 469yd/427m, and the par 3 14th, with an out-of-bounds on the left and a devilishly difficult green.

However, it is the thought that you are following in the footsteps of the incomparable Tiger Woods that will probably prove every bit as big an attraction as the qualities of the course itself.

16 Castletroy

Castletroy Golf Club, Castletroy, County Limerick
TEL: *+353 (0)61-335753* **FAX:** *+353 (0)61-335373*
EMAIL: *cgc@iol.ie*
LOCATION: *2 miles/3.2km from Limerick, on the N7 Dublin road*
COURSE: *18 holes, 6382yd/5802m, par 71, SSS 71*
GREEN FEES: €€€
FACILITIES: *Changing rooms and showers, catering, bar, pro shop, trolley hire, practice area*
VISITORS: *Weekday mornings – restrictions at other times*

A very busy city course, with a big membership, Castletroy is blessed with an abundance of mature trees. With the added complication of out-of-bounds on the left of the first two holes, anyone setting out to play this course does so fully aware that their mind must be focused if suitable reward is to be garnered from the round.

Always in superb playing condition, and host venue to a number of the country's top amateur championships in its time, Castletroy offers a number of extremely testing holes to be negotiated. The best of the 18 holes come on the homeward run. The par 5 10th, measuring 503yd/458m, has a stream guarding the green that can prove fatal to those trying to reach it in two. Although it is only a short hole, the 13th has a wonderful panoramic view. The toughest hole is unquestionably the 15th, a par 4 of 447yd/406m, which demands length and a good deal more – woe betide those who don't keep it straight.

17 Shannon

Shannon Golf Club, Shannon, County Clare
TEL: *+353 (0)61-471849* **FAX:** *+353 (0)61-471507*
EMAIL: *shannongolfclub@eircom.net*
LOCATION: *⅔ miles/1km from Shannon Airport*
COURSE: *18 holes, 6874yd/6249m, par 72, SSS 74*
GREEN FEES: €€€€
FACILITIES: *Changing rooms and showers, catering, bar, pro shop, trolley hire, club hire, practice area*
VISITORS: *Welcome – booking advisable*

For many visitors from the United States, Shannon is probably one of the first courses that will be glimpsed, albeit through the window of a plane. The course, nestled at the mouth of the River Shannon and just north of Limerick City, is adjacent to one of Ireland's major international airports.

Shannon has a good parkland layout with plenty of interesting holes. With mature trees and several water features coming into play, visitors would be well-advised not to let their guard slip.

Indeed, the opening few holes are quite tough, particularly the 433-yd/394-m 3rd hole, and the first real respite doesn't come until the 5th.

One of Shannon's peculiarities is that the front nine features three par 5s, but there is only one – the 18th – on the homeward journey. The best holes are probably the short ones, and the course's signature hole is the 17th, a par 3 of 224yd/203m, with much of the carry being over a small inlet of the Shannon estuary.

Mature trees and numerous water hazards come into frequent play at Shannon Golf Club.

REGIONAL DIRECTORY

Where to Stay

Kerry One of the best hotels in Ireland, the **Sheen Falls Lodge** (+353 (0)64-41600) in Kenmare is located in 300 acres of woodland, with a crystal-clear waterfall beside the hotel. It is a magnificent base for golfers touring the Ring of Kerry courses. **The Butler Arms Hotel** (+353 (0)66-9474144) overlooks the Atlantic Ocean in Waterville and has a reputation for being one of the best family-run hotels. **Hotel Ard na Sidhe** (+353 (0)66-9769282) is an 18th-century Victorian manor overlooking Caragh Lake, and it has won several prizes in the National Gardens competitions. If the choice for golf is good in Killarney, then the same applies to the wide variety of accommodation on offer. **The Aghadoe Heights Hotel** (+353 (0)64-31766) by the Lakes of Killarney, the **Castlerosse Hotel** (+353 (0)64-31144), the **Hotel Europe** (+353 (0)64-319000), the **International Hotel** (+353 (0)64-31816) and the **Arbutus Hotel** (+353 (0)64-31037) are all perfect bases. **The Lake Hotel Killarney** (+353 (0)64-31035) is another excellent hotel and offers upgrades to suites that boast Jacuzzis and four-poster beds. It even offers Roman and medieval theme rooms. **Hotel Dunloe Castle** (+353 (0)64-44111) is a five-star hotel situated in lush parklands 5 miles/8km from Killarney and overlooking the famous Gap of Dunloe. There are self-catering cottages at the **Forest Lake Cottages** (+353 (0)64-31554) for groups or families who prefer a little more flexibility. **Brenners Hotel** (+353 (0)66-9151638) in Dingle offers old-world charm, while the five-star **Emlagh House** (+353 (0)66-9152345), also in Dingle, is ideal for those who prefer a night or two away from bigger hotels. **Milltown House** (+353 (0)66-9151372) overlooks Dingle Bay and has its own herb and flower garden, promising guests one of the most colourful breakfasts in Ireland. **The Westward Court** (+353 (0)66-80081) in Tralee is perfectly located as a base for the local Barrow course, or for the courses in north Kerry.

Limerick Not only is it a perfect base for a break to the south-west, but the **Dunraven Arms Hotel** (+353 (0)61-396633) has a fully equipped leisure centre and swimming pool to ease away some of the aches and pains after a day's golfing. **Woodlands House Hotel** (+353 (0)61-605100) is set in 44 wooded acres and includes the award-winning Brennan Room Restaurant, while the **Adare Manor Hotel** (+353 (0)61-396566) overlooks the championship course designed by Robert Trent Jones Snr. **The South Court Hotel** (0+353 (0)65-23000) offers easy access to Kerry and the entire Shannon region, and each of its suites has been developed with the help of an international stress consultant. Other good hotels in the Limerick city area are the **Jury's Hotel** (+353 (0)61-327777), the **Castletroy Park Hotel** (+353 (0)61-335566) and the **Limerick Inn** (+353 (0)61-326666) on the Ennis Road.

Where to Eat

Kerry The restaurant at the **Park Hotel** (+353 (0)64-41200) in Kenmare is extremely popular, offering top-quality food in a luxury environment. A family-run town house, **Foleys** (+353 (0)64-31217) in Killarney not only has excellent accommodation, but its award-winning seafood and steak restaurant uses the very best of local produce. **Ballygreen Country House** (+353 (0)64-35035) offers the serenity of a river walk in a wooded glen, plus the attractions of outstanding food, and afterwards, perhaps, a chat about golf in the pub. **Harty-Costello Townhouse** (+353 (0)68-27129) in Ballybunion was one of the favoured eateries for players competing in the Murphy's Irish Open in 2000.

Limerick The restaurant at the **Courtenay Lodge** (+353 (0)69-62244) in Newcastle West has a full à la carte menu to tempt golfers after a day on the course, while the **Rathkeale House** (+353 (0)69-63330) has a fine restaurant in which to unwind. **The Wild Geese** (+353 (0)61-396451) is a terrific restaurant in a magnificent row of thatched cottages in Adare. **The Peppercorn** (+353 (0)61-355999) is located on the main Limerick–Cork road in the village of Patrickswell and offers fine food and friendly service in an intimate restaurant. **The Mustard Seed** at Echo Lodge (+353 (0)69-68508) in Ballingarry offers the best in Irish cooking, using herbs and vegetables gathered daily from its own gardens. **Gregan's Castle** (+353 (0)68-34112) in Glin offers excellent country-house cuisine, and uses fresh fruit and vegetables from the beautifully kept walled kitchen garden.

What to Do

West Cork In this part of the world, the best things in life – the scenery, that is – won't cost you a single euro. No matter which byway or road you choose to take, one view outmatches the other and, in truth, there are few more spectacular sights anywhere in Europe. In addition to the scenery, there is much to occupy the mind and body. The **Schull Planetarium** in west Cork offers a 45-minute trip through the stars. When your star-gazing is done, a trip back to nature to see the beauties of **Garninish Island** in Bantry Bay at first hand is a must on any itinerary. Also known as Ilnacullin, this island, accessed by small ferry boats and water-buses, is known to horticulturists and lovers of trees and shrubs the world over as an island garden of rare distinction. **The Mizen Head Signal Station Visitor Centre**, which requires a walk over a suspension bridge, offers spectacular views of the Atlantic from Ireland's most south-westerly point. It is often described as the edge of Europe.

Kerry Once you cross from Cork into Kerry, the beauty is literally breathtaking. The **Lakes of Killarney** and the **Ring of Kerry** are musts on anyone's travel plans, but it is also worth taking a trip up to the **Gap of Dunloe** as well. For those who would like to gain an insight into Irish history, then a trip to **Derrynane House**, the ancestral home of Daniel O'Connell, politician and statesman, is essential. It is possible to view a video about O'Connell's life in the room where he lived and worked. The **Blasket Centre** in Dún Chaoin on the tip of the Dingle Peninsula celebrates the history and cultural traditions of the Blasket Islanders. The **Great Blasket Island** was abandoned in 1953, but visitors can make day trips from Dingle and Dún Chaoin to the island. The **Dingle Oceanworld** provides background on the sea creatures found in the waters around these shores, which benefit from the warm-water Gulf Stream that originates off the Mexican coast. If

The discreet entrance to Beaufort Golf Club in Killarney, County Kerry.

you're lucky, you may even get to see the Dingle dolphin, Fungie, who is a big tourist attraction in the bay. **The Skellig Experience–Skellig Heritage Centre** is located on Valentia Island and relates the history of the Skellig Rocks, which lie off the Kerry coast. The rocks are renowned for their scenery, seabird colonies and early-Christian monastic settlements dating back 1400 years, and the centre has an 80-seat auditorium and features an audio-visual tour. **The Museum of Irish Transport** in Killarney has a display of vintage cars, bikes and fire engines, and features a Silver Stream (1907), complete with original blueprints and data. Once in Killarney, you can't leave

without taking a trip in one of the town's famous jaunting cars. A number of boat cruises are available on the majestic lakes, and offer a full commentary on the flora, fauna and historical heritage of the area. Priceless archaeological treasures and modern interpretative media stand side by side in the **Kerry The Kingdom** story at the Ashe Memorial Hall in Tralee, which uses slide presentations, scale models and audio and visual displays to tell the story of the county. The **Blennerville Windmill** is a five-storey structure that gives you the chance to see the restored milling business in action once again. There is also an emigration exhibition.

Limerick The village of **Adare** in County Limerick is one of the nicest in Ireland, with a succession of thatched cottages – a number of which have been turned into craft shops and restaurants. **Adare Manor**, a 19th-century mansion that has been converted into a luxury hotel with its own championship course, is also here; it features oak staircases and a carved fireplace by Pugin. **Desmond Castle** is a 13th-century fortified keep built on the site of an ancient ringfort. Limerick is a historical city and, as such, its main tourist attractions are **King John's Castle** – with its battlement walkways and five drum towers – and **St Mary's Cathedral**, with its pre-Reformation stone altar. The modern Limerick doesn't bear any resemblance to the one portrayed by Frank McCourt in his novel *Angela's Ashes,* but **Castle Lane** is an authentic scene of bygone years.

Tourist Information Centres
Kenmare Heritage Centre, Kenmare, County Kerry (+353 (0)64-41233)
Killarney Tourist Office, Beech Road, Killarney (+353 (0)64-31633)
Adare Heritage Centre, Adare, County Limerick (+353 (0)61-396255)
Limerick Tourism, Arthurs Quay, Limerick City (+353 (0)61-317522)

Chapter 5

The West of Ireland

The land west of the River Shannon bears little resemblance to the bleak and desolate image conveyed by Oliver Cromwell who, when leading an armed force from England in the 17th century, condemned the native Irish to 'hell, or to Connacht'. Indeed, this region is among the most picturesque and − in industrial terms at least − the most progressive in Ireland.

Technically, Clare, where many visitors from the US first set foot in the 'Emerald Isle' at Shannon Airport, belongs in the province of Munster. It espouses all that is best about the west of Ireland, however, from traditional music to good food and drink to magnificent golf courses! County Clare is also ideally located, with the Connacht

counties of Galway and Mayo lying further up the western seaboard.

County Clare also has a great deal to offer as far as golf courses are concerned. Lahinch, which has been remodelled in recent years to restore Dr Alister Mackenzie's original design, has long been one of the jewels in the crown of Irish golf. It has also been a favoured stopping-off point for American golfer Phil Mickelson, an honourary member of the club, for a number of years.

More recently, another links course, Doonbeg, some 20 miles/ 32km south of Lahinch, has also opened, making west Clare more of a golfing hotspot than ever. Despite its modern birth, Doonbeg − set in towering duneland and designed by Australian golfer Greg Norman − is actually a throwback to the old, traditional design of links courses, with a number of tee shots from elevated tees driving over nearby greens.

Left: Atlantic sunset over the Aran Islands, off the coast at Doolin, County Clare. Above: Kylemore Abbey in Connemara, County Galway.

More golfing treasures exist further up the western seaboard. Connemara in Galway, Carne in Mayo and Enniscrone in Sligo are among the most challenging and demanding links to be found anywhere, especially on days when the wind whips in off the Atlantic Ocean. They also represent very good value for money.

The west of Ireland also possesses a number of superb parkland courses, none better than Westport, which is located in the shadows of Croagh Patrick, where pilgrims annually climb the mountain in their bare feet in dedication to St Patrick, the patron saint of Ireland.

The main urban centre on the western seaboard is Galway City, one of the fastest-growing cities in Europe and the fourth largest city in Ireland (behind Dublin, Belfast and Cork). Galway City is also known as a cultural hotspot, with art and theatre playing an important part in the lives of the population. It also has plenty of fine golf courses, either within its environs or just a short road trip away.

One of the newer developments is Galway Bay Golf Club, which was designed by European Ryder Cup player Christy O'Connor Jnr, a native of the area. His uncle, Christy Snr, played in 10 Ryder Cup matches and, back in 1970, was awarded the freedom of the city in recognition of his heroics on fairways and greens all over the globe.

Planning an Itinerary

One piece of advice for anyone savouring the delights of golfing in the west of Ireland is, 'don't rush'. It is worth taking the time to soak up the special ambience of the west, and to experience something of the area's culture.

From west Clare to Galway and through the Gaelic-speaking areas of Connemara – a vast tract of land that begins just west of Galway city and extends to Killary Harbour in the north of the county, and which possesses beautiful and dramatic scenery – and on into Mayo, you will find pubs where Irish music, song and dance provide a beguiling insight into the Irish character.

As ever, though, the importance of transport in negotiating a route from one course to another cannot be over-emphasized. It is possible to conduct a golfing tour of the west – stretching from the mouth of the River Shannon all the way up to the north Mayo coast – but you will require time, and plenty of it, to do it properly. For those with time to spare, however, you are unlikely to find more rewarding challenges anywhere.

Connemara's rich landscape is located in an area known as the Gaeltacht, where Gaelic remains the first language.

THE WEST OF IRELAND

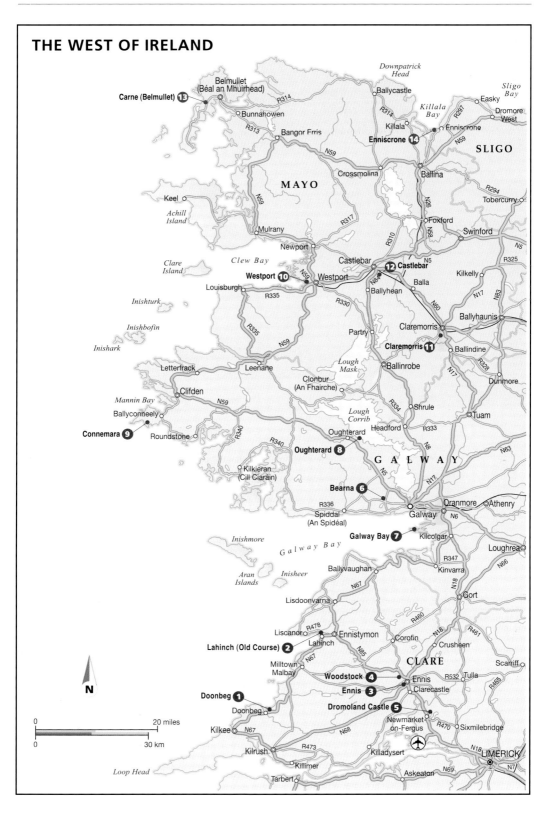

Downpatrick
Head

Sligo
Bay

Belmullet
(Béal an Mhuirhead)

Carne (Belmullet) **13**

Ballycastle

Easky

R314

Dromore
West

Bunnahowen

R314

Killala
Bay

Enniscrone

R297

Killala

R313

Bangor Frris

Enniscrone **14**

N59

SLIGO

N59

Ballina

N59

Crossmolina

R294

MAYO

Tobercurry

Keel

Achill
Island

N26

Foxford

Swinford

N5

Mulrany

R317

R310

N58

Clare
Island

Clew Bay

Newport

Castlebar

N5

R325

Westport **10**

N59

Westport

Castlebar **12** Castlebar

Kilkelly

Louisburgh

R335

Ballyhean

Balla

N17

R83

Inishturk

R330

N60

Ballyhaunis

Inishbofin

R335

Partry

Claremorris

Inishark

N59

Claremorris **11**

Ballindine

R328

Letterfrack

Leenane

Lough
Mask

Ballinrobe

N17

Dunmore

Clonbur
(An Fhairche)

Clifden

N59

R334

Shrule

Mannin Bay

Lough
Corrib

Tuam

Ballyconneely

R340

Oughterard

Headford

R333

Connemara **9**

Roundstone

R340

Oughterard **8**

N6

N63

GALWAY

Kilkieran
(Cill Ciaráin)

N59

Bearna **6**

N17

R336

Oranmore

Athenry

Spiddal
(An Spidéal)

Galway

N6

Inishmore

Galway Bay **7**

Kilcolgar

Loughrea

Galway Bay

R347

Aran
Islands

Inisheer

Ballyvaughan

Kinvarra

N66

N67

Gort

Lisdoonvarna

N18

R460

Liscanor

R478

Ennistymon

Corofin

N18

R461

Lahinch (Old Course) **2**

Lahinch

Crusheen

Scariff

Milltown
Malbay

N67

N85

CLARE

Woodstock **4**

Ennis

R532

Tulla

R465

Doonbeg **1**

Ennis **3**

Clarecastle

Doonbeg

Dromoland Castle **5**

Newmarket
on-Fergus

R470

Sixmilebridge

Kilkee

N67

N68

N18

Kilrush

R473

Killadysert

LIMERICK

Killimer

N69

N7

Loop Head

Tarbert

Askeaton

N

0   20 miles

0   30 km

🏌 *Doonbeg*

Doonbeg Golf Links, Doonbeg, County Clare
TEL: *+353 (0)65-9055246* **FAX:** *+353 (0)65-9055247* **EMAIL:** *doonbeggolfclub@eircom.net*
WEBSITE: *www.doonbeggolfclub.com*
LOCATION: *About 40 miles/64km from Shannon Airport, on the N67 main coastal road, near the village of Doonbeg; the course is signposted*
COURSE: *18 holes, 6835yd/6214m, par 72, SSS 72*
GREEN FEES: *€€€€€€+*
FACILITIES: *Changing rooms and showers, catering, shop, practice area, buggy hire, trolley hire*
VISITORS: *Welcome – booking essential*

The Doonbeg links have been declared a 'Special Area of Conservation' due to the discovery of a rare snail.

The road to Doonbeg, a little village in the remotest part of County Clare, is a winding one, but the final destination more than compensates for the driving conditions along the way. When the great Australian golfer Greg Norman was asked to create a new links course in 1997, he travelled to Doonbeg not by road, but by helicopter. His reaction to what he encountered, though, is likely to be the same as that of the mere mortals who must negotiate the route by roadway. Norman was stunned – as you are sure to be.

Indeed, Norman was later heard to remark, 'If I spent the rest of my life building courses, I don't think I would find a comparable site anywhere... this is spectacular, land made by God.' That he took a hands-on approach in the course's development (making over 15 visits) and effectively created an old-style traditional links is an indication of just how captivated the 'Great White Shark' was by the project.

Doonbeg's development was not completed without its share of problems. The discovery of an endangered snail – *vertigo angustior* – on the land created delays, and it was only after the area in which it was found had been designated a Special Area of Conservation that the course's shape could evolve. It finally opened for play in the spring

of 2002, almost five years after Norman had first set foot on the dunes.

This spectacular stretch of virgin dunes alongside the Atlantic Ocean was first considered as a possible site for a golf course by officers of the Scottish Black Watch Guard – who were stationed in Limerick way back in 1892 – but the lack of a railroad link deterred them. Over a century later, however, its belated transformation into a fine links course has been completed. The wonder is that it doesn't look like a new course, but rather one that was created a hundred years ago.

There are throwbacks to old-style design. Norman wasn't afraid to put tee boxes on elevated sites overlooking the green of the previous hole, requiring players to drive over the putting surface. Also, he wasn't afraid to include blind tee shots, knowing that the fairways were sufficiently generous and that the dunes up ahead provided definition to indicate where the shots should be aimed.

Some may complain about the course's severity, and about the requirement to cross

The 14th is only 100yd/91m from tee-to-green but usually plays into the teeth of an Atlantic wind.

the first fairway on the way from the 17th green to the 18th tee. All in all, however, this is a course that further accentuates Ireland's reputation for having some of the finest links courses in the world. The wild grasses around the fringes of the deep bunkers are reminiscent of those at Royal County Down and, if anything, the duneland is even more spectacular than that at Ballybunion.

Everyone will have their own particular favourite hole – and the choices are many, for one great hole is followed by another. The 8th, a par 5, could yet prove to be the hardest hole on the course; or, perhaps, it could be the 15th, which is played entirely along an ocean ridge to a green that is located at the bottom of a natural amphitheatre of high dunes.

Certainly the most picturesque hole is the 14th, a short hole of no more than 100yd/91m to an elevated green, with the wild Atlantic as an imposing backdrop.

2 Lahinch (Old Course)

Lahinch Golf Club, Lahinch, County Clare
TEL: +353 (0)65-7081003
FAX: +353 (0)65-7081592
LOCATION: 2 miles/3.2km west of Ennistymon
COURSE: 36 holes (2 courses), Old: 6882yd/6256m, par 71, SSS 73
GREEN FEES: €€€€€€ +
FACILITIES: Changing rooms and showers, full catering, bar, pro shop, practice area, club hire, buggy hire, trolley hire
VISITORS: Welcome – booking essential

LAHINCH OLD COURSE

HOLE	YD	M	PAR	HOLE	YD	M	PAR
1	381	346	4	10	441	401	4
2	506	460	5	11	170	155	3
3	420	382	4	12	577	525	5
4	472	429	4	13	279	254	4
5	154	140	3	14	451	410	4
6	424	385	4	15	466	424	4
7	411	374	4	16	197	179	3
8	163	148	3	17	436	395	4
9	400	364	4	18	534	485	5
OUT	3331	3028	36	IN	3551	3228	36

6882YD • 6256M • PAR 72

Lahinch may have its quirks – blind tee shots and approach shots among them – but nowhere else in the country does a links roll up so close to a town as it does here. Recent remodelling of the course to return it even closer to its natural state, as it was when Dr Alister Mackenzie improved on the original work of Old Tom Morris, has only served to make it even greater.

Lahinch, a traditional out-and-back course with small undulating greens, is home to the annual amateur South of Ireland championship. It has easily captivated the hearts of some of the game's great players; when Phil Mickelson came here in advance of the US's Walker Cup match at Portmarnock in 1991, he professed Lahinch to be his favourite links course of all.

What is so captivating? The ambience of the place, a favoured haunt of Limerick people at weekends, immediately wins your heart. As you take the high road from Ennistymon, the first glimpse of the sea and then the course is confirmation that a stress-free zone is near at hand. With the Cliffs of Moher just up the coast and the get-away-from-it-all coastal village of Doolin not much further on, there is plenty to see away from the course.

No serious golfer will want to escape from the links, though. In fact, there are two links courses at Lahinch: the Old Course (the championship links) and the Castle, located across the road at the back of an army training camp and an altogether more leisurely proposition.

Recent upgrading of the Old Course, under the supervision of British golf architect Martin Hawtree, has seen the construction of a high mound to separate the 14th and 15th holes, which previously shared the one fairway. The move was prompted by safety concerns, but the result is that the 14th,

previously a shortish par 5, is now an exceptionally fine par 4, which places a huge onus on a good drive to a narrow fairway.

Ask anyone what memory they take home about Lahinch and the answer will most likely involve the two back-to-back quirky holes that come early on in the round. It is unlikely that any modern-day designer would ever create their like. But the Klondyke and the Dell, as the 4th and 5th holes are known, are famed the world over.

The Klondyke is a par 5 of 472yd/429m. The drive is into a tunnel, with high dunes left and right. More often than not, even a slightly mishit tee shot will bounce off one of the banks and end up on the undulating fairway. Then the fun starts, for smack bang in the line of sight to the green (or even the lay-up shot) is a huge dune. When Old Tom designed the original course, the machinery didn't exist to move the dune and nobody has had the nerve to do so since. Of course, it is a safety concern, but the club has organized for a man to be permanently placed on top of the dune with a flag, to inform the golfer

The 7th at Lahinch, the traditional home of the annual South of Ireland amateur championship.

playing from the fairway when it is safe to hit to a green that has a stone wall behind it.

You can then make the short walk to the 5th hole, a par 3 of just 154yd/140m. It is one of the most famous short holes in golf – not for its difficulty, but because another giant dune hides the green from view. Your task is to aim at a white stone on top of the hill (the stone indicates the position of the flag) and trust that you have the right club in your hands. The green is located in a valley between the two dunes.

These two holes may be the fun element of the round, but there are many really good holes: the 6th and 7th, which are played towards the ocean; the 10th, probably the toughest on the course; the 12th, down by the estuary; and so on to the 18th, with the road running all the way up the left as a highly visible out-of-bounds. The journey through the high dunes is also likely to be recalled with the utmost fondness.

Ennis

Ennis Golf Club, Drumbiggle, Ennis, County Clare
TEL: *+353 (0)65-6824074* **FAX:** *+353 (0)65-6841848* **EMAIL:** *egc@eircom.net*
WEBSITE: *www.golfclub.ennis.ie*
LOCATION: *1 mile/1.6km from Ennis town centre; the course is signposted*
COURSE: *18 holes, 6151yd/5592m, par 71, SSS 69*
GREEN FEES: *€€*
FACILITIES: *Changing rooms and showers, full catering, bar, pro shop, tuition, practice area, buggy hire, trolley hire*
VISITORS: *Welcome*

The recent building of a state-of-the-art clubhouse has considerably lifted the appeal of Ennis for visiting golfers. The course itself, which is always in excellent condition, is ideal for holiday play and, in some ways, is a welcome respite from the tough links terrain that attracts most visitors to the west.

Ennis is a thriving town and an excellent base to visit the Cliffs of Moher and to explore the Burren, a limestone region not unlike the lunar landscape of the moon, which covers over 100 square miles/260 sq. km and boasts a marvellous array of flora and fauna. The local golf club has also produced a number of Irish amateur internationals, most notably Valerie Hassett, a multiple winner of the British Ladies Seniors' Championship.

The course is tree-lined, putting a premium on straight driving, and the challenge is further accentuated by the necessity of good approach play to tight greens. There is a comfortable run of holes at the start, but the sequence from the 5th to the 8th can be formidable. The 6th in particular, a par 4 of 460yd/419m, will make you focus the mind, and the 16th is a fine par 3 with the green protected by bunkers. The 17th is one of a number of short par 4s on the course – measuring 334yd/304m – but it proves that length is not everything when it comes to a decent golf hole. Indeed, it puts the emphasis back on club selection and course management.

Woodstock

Woodstock Golf Club, Ennis, County Clare
TEL: *+353 (0)65-6829463* **FAX:** *+353 (0)65-6820304*
EMAIL: *woodstock.ennis@eircom.net*
LOCATION: *2 miles/3.2km west of Ennis, on the Lahinch road*
COURSE: *18 holes, 6466yd/5879m, par 71, SSS 70*
GREEN FEES: *€€€*
FACILITIES: *Changing rooms and showers, full catering, bar, shop, practice area, buggy hire, trolley hire, on-site accommodation*
VISITORS: *Welcome – booking advisable*

One dependable aspect of the design work of Dr Arthur Spring is that his courses are always interesting. So it is at Woodstock, a quality course on the outskirts of Ennis that has successfully married the hotel/golf course concept. The use of different tee boxes means that it is a parkland course that can facilitate holiday golfers looking for a not-too-taxing day, and is also capable of providing a genuine test off the back stakes for the very best.

Constructed on rolling terrain with a limestone base, which makes the course playable all year round, the greatest natural hazard is the River Inch and its streams, rather than the huge man-made lake of almost three acres in dimension that has also been incorporated into the design. The presence of so much water can be pretty intimidating, but it works well here, and the result is a very good course with a number of truly memorable holes. In particular, the sequence from the 6th, a par 3 of 197yd/179m, taking in the long par 4 7th and then another short hole, wouldn't be out of place on any of Ireland's inland courses.

You will find that Woodstock is always in good condition, and the planting of over 5,000 trees – ranging from lime to ash and maple – will in time make it an even better course. Woodstock deserves more than a stop-off; the on-site hotel makes it an excellent base for a county that seems to be making up for lost time in the area of golf tourism.

 *Dromoland Castle*

Dromoland Castle, Newmarket-on-Fergus, County Clare
TEL: *+353 (0)61-368444* **FAX:** *+353 (0)61-368498*
EMAIL: *dromolandgc@eircom.net*
LOCATION: *1 mile/1.6km north of Newmarket-on-Fergus, on the N18 Ennis road*
COURSE: *18 holes, 6290yd/5719m, par 71, SSS 71*
GREEN FEES: *€€€*
FACILITIES: *Changing rooms and showers, full catering, bar, shop, tuition, practice area, buggy hire, trolley hire, leisure facilities, on-site accommodation*
VISITORS: *Welcome – booking advisable*

The five-star hotel at Dromoland Castle has always attracted the rich and famous in droves. For a golfer driving up to the magnificent edifice, the temptation to jump immediately out of the car and rush to the 1st tee box is overpowering.

Set in a 700-acre estate, Dromoland Castle's course features classic parkland terrain – rolling hills and plenty of fairway undulations – with lakes, streams and woodland as natural hazards. The River Rine is a feature on three of the holes. Such physical characteristics pose problems for handicappers of all standards, yet Dromoland Castle is a superbly maintained and appealing course in a wonderful location.

The signature hole, but by no means the toughest, is probably the par 3 7th, measuring a mere 143yd/130m from an elevated tee that affords a panoramic view of the historic castle. Indeed, the history of this area is emphasized by the presence of a fort on the land; with commanding views over the Shannon estuary, it is believed to be the largest hill-fort in the country.

Golf, in an environment fit for a king, at the magnificent tree-lined Dromoland Castle course.

 *Bearna*

Bearna Golf Club, Corboley, Bearna, County Galway
TEL: *+353 (0)91-592677* **FAX:** *+353 (0)91-592674*
EMAIL: *bearnagc@tinet.ie*
LOCATION: *5 miles/8km west of Galway, off the Spiddle road; the course is signposted from Bearna village*
COURSE: *18 holes, 6898yd/6271m, par 72, SSS 73*
GREEN FEES: *€€€*
FACILITIES: *Changing rooms and showers, full catering, bar, shop, practice area, buggy hire, trolley hire*
VISITORS: *Welcome – booking advisable*

Stand anywhere on Bearna's golf course, look at the surrounding landscape – comprised of nothing but bog, rocks, gorse and heather – and wonder at how such a creation could appear at the gateway into Connemara.

Bobby Browne, the club professional at Laytown and Bettystown on the opposite side of the country, and also a very good course designer, was specially recruited to accomplish the routing. It was his creative mind that ensured a unique course, moorland in texture, appeared amidst the bogland.

Water comes into play on 13 holes, but many elevated tees, generous fairways and sand-based greens combine to make Bearna a most enjoyable, if testing, course. There is great variety. For instance, the 6th is a par 4 of 445yd/405m and consequently puts a premium on length and accuracy. The 13th is a par 3 of just 132yd/120m, but Loch Toirmeaschta – the Forbidden Lake – guards the green. After a round, the clubhouse – which has fantastic panoramic views of the course and beyond to Galway Bay and the Aran Islands – is the perfect place to unwind.

7 Galway Bay

Galway Bay Golf Club, Oranmore, County Galway
TEL: *+353 (0)91-790503*
FAX: *+353 (0)91-792510*
EMAIL: *gbay@iol.ie* **WEBSITE:** *www.gbaygolf.com*
LOCATION: *3 miles/4.8km south of Oranmore; the course is signposted*
COURSE: *18 holes, 7190yd/6537m, par 72, SSS 73*
GREEN FEES: *€€€€€*
FACILITIES: *Changing rooms and showers, full catering, bar, shop, practice area, buggy hire, trolley hire, on-site accommodation*
VISITORS: *Welcome – booking advisable*

Galway Bay is set on the Renville Peninsula, a tract of land that juts out into the pounding waters of the Atlantic Ocean. Some of the trees down by the coastline on this course are almost horizontal, so wind-beaten are they. The wind is very much a factor on this seaside course, which is more parkland than links, but it is still a rigorous and fair test of golf, and an enjoyable one at that.

All around are mystical reminders of the past: there are small ancient circular stone huts on the shoreline behind the 16th tee; old 'ringforts' lie close to the 2nd and 10th greens; and a lead and copper mine dating back to the 15th century, renamed Leadmine Hill, serves as a backdrop to the 13th hole.

Galway Bay, which is the work of Christy O'Connor Jnr, is a course that ensures that players never let down their guard. Although the Atlantic surrounds the course on three sides, a number of man-made lakes add to the overall challenge. The 7th is a short par 3, measuring 151yd/138m, to a two-tier green, but almost all of it is over water.

The influence of water is most apparent on the 12th, a splendid hole that bends left to right. After demanding a long, straight drive, the hole puts the onus on the player to hit a precise iron over water to a green with a large bunker on the left to punish those who bail-out too much.

8 Oughterard

Oughterard Golf Club, Oughterard, County Galway
TEL: *+353 (0)91-552131*
FAX: *+353 (0)91-552733* **EMAIL:** *golfough@iol.ie*
LOCATION: *15 miles/24km north-west of Galway city, off the N59; the course, which is 2 miles/3.2km east of Oughterard, is signposted*
COURSE: *18 holes, 6528yd/5935m, par 70, SSS 70*
GREEN FEES: *€€*
FACILITIES: *Changing rooms and showers, full catering, bar, pro shop, practice area, club hire, buggy hire, trolley hire*
VISITORS: *Welcome – booking advisable*

Oughterard Golf Club is very pleasantly located at the edge of Lough Corrib, the largest lake in Connacht. With stone walls, gorse and gentle hills all around, it is one of the most natural environments for a golf course.

The fairways are lush and the greens are beautifully manicured, but the underlying earth is more akin to peat – which has led to the clever creation of three natural bog lakes by digging into the ground around the 9th, 10th and 11th holes. Water comes into play on six holes in all.

The stone walls are an integral part of the charm of Oughterard, known as the 'Gateway to Connemara'. There are large numbers of mature trees on the course – ash, beech and birch – which can play havoc with a promising scorecard should the wheels start to come off. Patrick Merrigan's new design for the course uses the trees to frame the greens, and this works wonderfully well.

The 8th is a slight double dogleg. Anyone tempted to cut the first corner should be warned that much trouble lurks, including out-of-bounds, so the sensible ploy is to take this 488-yd/444-m hole as a genuine par 5.

However, it is the par 3s – four of them in all, and all very different from each other – that encapsulate Oughterard's appeal and make this course a must for anyone visiting the west.

9 Connemara

Connemara Golf Club, Ballyconneely, County Galway
TEL: +353 (0)95-23502 FAX: +353 (0)95-23662
EMAIL: links@iol.ie
WEBSITE: www.golfclubireland.com/connemara
LOCATION: 8 miles/12.8km south west of Clifden,
4 miles/6.4km west of the village of Ballyconneely
COURSE: 27 holes, 7272yd/6611m, par 72, SSS 75
GREEN FEES: €€€
FACILITIES: Changing rooms and showers, full catering,
bar, pro shop, practice area, club hire, buggy hire, trolley hire
VISITORS: Welcome – booking essential

Carved out of the most magnificent links terrain along the coast, Connemara has many admirers. The completion of a new nine holes should enhance the course's appeal.

In time, the new holes will combine with the back nine of the old course to make for a championship course of the highest order, as all 18 holes will be played through high duneland with one difficult hole after another. The front nine on the original course are constructed on relatively flat terrain, leading many poeople to believe that the real Connemara doesn't get going until the tee-off on the 8th.

The 3rd at Connemara, typical of the spectacular terrain to be found on the Ballyconneely links.

10 Westport

Westport Golf Club, Carrowholly, Westport, County Mayo
TEL: +353 (0)98-28262 FAX: +353 (0)98-27217
EMAIL: wpgolf@iol.ie
LOCATION: 2 miles/3.2km west of Westport town; the course is signposted
COURSE: 18 holes, 7086yd/6446m, par 73, SSS 74
GREEN FEES: €€€
FACILITIES: Changing rooms and showers, full catering, bar, pro shop, practice area, club hire, buggy hire, trolley hire
VISITORS: Welcome – booking advisable

Although Westport was deemed a good enough course to play host to a number of Irish amateur championships, recent upgrading work has considerably toughened the challenge.

The work is most obvious on the 18th hole. In its prior existence, it was a relatively ordinary par 5, with big hitters liable to find its green in two. Now it has been lengthened to 550yd/500m and, for good measure, a pond guards the green.

The most celebrated hole remains the 15th, however. This is a par 5 of 580yd/527m that requires long and accurate shots to be played alongside the shoreline of Clew Bay – any mishit shot will prove costly.

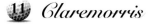

Claremorris

Claremorris Golf Club, Claremorris, County Mayo
TEL: *+353 (0)94-71527*
EMAIL: *claremorrisgc@ebookireland.com*
WEBSITE: *www.ebookireland.com*
LOCATION: *2 miles/3.2km south of Claremorris, on the N17 Galway road; the course is signposted*
COURSE: *18 holes, 6930yd/6300m, par 73, SSS 72*
GREEN FEES: *€€*
FACILITIES: *Changing rooms and showers, full catering, bar, practice area, buggy hire, trolley hire*
VISITORS: *Welcome – booking advisable and there are restrictions at weekends*

Slowly but surely, many of the old nine-hole courses have had to move with the times and upgrade to 18 holes. Few courses could claim to have made the transition as smoothly, or as successfully, as Claremorris. The new course, designed by Tom Craddock, opened for play in 1999 and has added considerably to the quality of parkland courses in the west.

The rolling terrain and many mature trees – ash and sycamore among them – help to give the course its great character. It is the presence of water features, with the River Robe traversing the course, however, that most accentuate the challenge.

The feature hole is the 14th, a par 4 of just 352yd/320m. The green is surrounded by water and nothing more than a precise approach shot will bring any sort of joy.

This signature hole is followed by yet another classic short par 4 – the 15th, a hole of 360yd/330m – and two par 5s, which are left until near the end on the homeward run. The long 16th and 18th holes provide a late opportunity to open the shoulders, while sandwiched in between is a difficult par 4 – the 17th measures 418yd/380m – that can often make or break a card.

Overall, Claremorris is a good parkland test, and with its undulating greens and friendly clubhouse atmosphere it will entice you to return again and again.

Castlebar

Castlebar Golf Club, Rocklands, Castlebar, County Mayo
TEL: *+353 (0)94-21649* **FAX:** *+353 (0)94-26088*
EMAIL: *castlebargolf@eircom.ie*
LOCATION: *2 miles/3.2km outside Castlebar, on the N84 Ballinrobe road*
COURSE: *18 holes, 6492yd/5902m, par 71, SSS 72*
GREEN FEES: *€€€*
FACILITIES: *Changing rooms and showers, full catering, bar, practice area, trolley hire*
VISITORS: *Welcome – booking advisable*

A recent remodelling of this course by Peter McEvoy has brought Castlebar into the top echelon of parkland courses. The club operates a soft-spikes only policy, and this has paid dividends with greens – all built to top USGA specifications – which are perfectly manicured and lightning fast. Indeed, the tee boxes are so good that some other clubs would fancy having them for greens!

There are five par 3 holes on the course, and the attractions of the short holes are obvious from early on in the round. You have barely had time to flex your muscles than you are required to hit a tee shot of some 218yd/199m to the 2nd green. Then the 6th hole – another par 3 of 188yd/171m – requires a precise iron shot to a green that is surrounded by water on three sides.

In upgrading the course, McEvoy created three new water features and added some 40 bunkers to the course. The par 3s all leave a good impression, none more so than the pretty 16th – measuring 159yd/145m – a hole that is many people's favourite.

Probably, the most memorable hole is the 17th, as much for its physical demands as for the shot-making required. It is a mammoth par 4 of 464yd/422m, with the second shot made more difficult by the presence of a valley in front of the green. The par 5 finishing hole is another excellent hole, with water to the back and left of the green.

13 Carne (Belmullet)

Carne Golf Links, Belmullet, County Mayo
TEL: +353 (0)97-82292 **FAX:** +353 (0)97-81477
EMAIL: belmulletgolfclub@eircom.net
WEBSITE: www.belmulletgolfclub.ie
LOCATION: 3 miles/4.8km south-west of Belmullet town; the course is signposted
COURSE: 18 holes, 6730yd/6119m, par 72, SSS 71
GREEN FEES: €€€
FACILITIES: Changing rooms and showers, full catering, bar, practice area, club hire, buggy hire, trolley hire
VISITORS: Welcome – booking advisable

The most exposed, and probably the most isolated, course in the country is also one of the best. Carne links – also called Belmullet – is the last great creation of Eddie Hackett.

Carne, on the north-west coast of County Mayo, is a fitting swansong to Hackett's legacy. Not only is it a supreme test; it also captures the true ambience of Irish golf. Unless you go to Carne on an unusually calm day, the course will quickly teach you how to cope with the wind. Regardless of the weather, you will be able to enjoy spirit-lifting views of Blacksod Bay and the Inis Geidhe and Inis Gluaire islands, which have a place in Irish folklore.

The dunes are quite literally towering – which is good in one sense, as they offer some protection from the wind – and there are many blind holes. This is exactly how Hackett wanted it. Rather than use earth-moving machinery, he decided to leave the dunes as they were. Once you accept such blind shots, your game will become all about shot-making, course management and good accurate drives.

There is a contrast between the two nines. One thing that remains true throughout the course, however, is the need to place your tee shot as accurately as possible; otherwise the prospects of a blind approach shot to the greens increase accordingly.

The par 4 11th hole is a dogleg in the classic tradition, played around a giant dune. Meanwhile, the 17th is an exceptional hole that will have you scratching your head and wondering how on earth Carne was kept a secret from everyone until this golf course appeared. It is worth making the effort to play at Carne at least once in your life.

The 13th hole at Carne, a spectacular links course in County Mayo located by the Atlantic Ocean.

14 Enniscrone

Enniscrone Golf Club, Enniscrone, County Sligo
TEL: *+353 (0)96-36297* **FAX:** *+353 (0)96-366657*
EMAIL: *enniscronegolf@eircom.net*
WEBSITE: *www.homepage.tinet.ie/~enniscronegolf/*
LOCATION: *0.6 miles/1km south of Enniscrone, on the Ballina road*
COURSE: *27 holes, 6835yd/6214m, par 73, SSS 72*
GREEN FEES: *€€€€*
FACILITIES: *Changing rooms and showers, full catering, bar, pro shop, tuition, practice area, buggy hire, trolley hire*
VISITORS: *Welcome – restrictions on Sunday and booking is advisable*

ENNISCRONE

HOLE	YD	M	PAR	HOLE	YD	M	PAR
1	403	366	4	10	374	340	4
2	505	459	5	11	170	155	3
3	190	173	3	12	345	314	4
4	550	500	5	13	350	318	4
5	440	400	4	14	500	455	5
6	395	359	4	15	440	400	4
7	534	485	5	16	525	477	5
8	170	155	3	17	149	135	3
9	395	359	4	18	400	364	4
OUT	3582	3256	37	IN	3253	2958	36

6835 YD • 6214 M • PAR 73

It isn't quite fair to say that Enniscrone has come of age, given that it has always been considered an excellent links. Additional holes set amidst some of the highest dunes in Europe – which opened for play in 2001 – have transformed Enniscrone, however, from a very good links into a great links.

The British golf architect Donald Steel designed the new six holes at Enniscrone. These have been incorporated into 12 holes from the old course, the work of Eddie Hackett.

The result is a championship course of genuine character. The six old holes (effectively the long but rather boring sequence that started the old lay-up) have been bequeathed a new life as part of a nine-hole course that is ideal for holiday golfers, or for those looking to play a few holes in the evening.

Enniscrone, the last outpost on Sligo's western coastline before it merges with Mayo, is a lovely place. There is always a warm welcome, the seaweed baths give new life back to old joints and the sunsets are so vivid that the golf club was left with no other option than to make the club crest a sunset.

The old course had a rather brutish start, a couple of long and characterless par 5s. The same cannot be said of the revised course layout, for the 1st is now what used to be the old 16th hole. It is, quite feasibly, the hardest opening hole in Irish golf. The clubhouse is to the right and so, too, is out-of-bounds. Depending on the

wind, the tee shot demands a shot that will either clear the right dogleg (too hard and tiger rough awaits on the other side of the fairway) or bring you to the elbow. The hard work is not done yet, however, for the small green is perched on top of a hill and is approached through a narrow entrance, with dunes left and right.

Once your work is done, there is a sharp turn to the left and you are onto the first of the new holes. From the tee it appears that there is not much fairway, but the dunes define the hole and, in truth, there is a substantial landing area. That is true for most of the holes; the hard part is convincing yourself on the tee that it is so.

The new and the old holes have blended together marvellously well, and the resulting challenge is relentless but most enjoyable. Many of the old holes remain as challenging as they were before the course was extended, and the views over the Moy Estuary and Killala Bay from some of the high tee boxes are breathtaking.

Enniscrone's 1st – a dogleg par 4 with an uphill approach to the green – is probably the toughest start in Irish golf.

It is reputed that when St Patrick first came here to spread the word, he was forced back across the estuary by the locals. However, other unwelcome visitors suffered even more dire consequences than St Patrick. The biggest dune on the course, situated beside the par 5 14th fairway, is called Cnoc nag Corp – 'The Hill of the Bodies' – because it allegedly contains the corpses of vanquished Viking invaders.

Fortunately, you'll find that visitors these days are a lot more welcome in these parts, although the journey onward from the 14th doesn't abate. The sea is on your left all the way home and the 15th – a 440yd/400m par 4 – demands a long and accurate drive. The par 5 16th completes the holes through the massive dunes before you rejoin the 17th – a par 3 that holds no room for error off the elevated tee – and the 18th, which has a blind drive over the crest of the hill.

REGIONAL DIRECTORY

Where to Stay

Clare Situated about 10 minutes' drive from Shannon International Airport is **Thomond House** (+353 (0)61-368304) in Newmarket-on-Fergus, which has tennis and clay shooting to augment the tourist and golfing attractions. **Dromoland Castle** (+353 (0)61-368144) is one of Europe's leading five-star resorts and has a wide range of activities on its 1500-acre estate. **The Woodstock Hotel** (+353 (0)65-6846600) in Ennis has full leisure facilities, golf on site and children's entertainment. **The Greenbrier Inn** (+353 (0)65-7081247) in Lahinch is within walking distance of the famous links and offers a fine gourmet breakfast. **Moy House** (+353 (0)65-7082800) in Lahinch overlooks some of the best surfing beaches in the country.

Galway **The Quality Hotel** (+353 (0)91-792244) in Oranmore offers good facilities at good prices and is only a few minutes' drive away from the Galway Bay golf course. **Park House Hotel** (+353 (0)91-546924) is located in the heart of Galway City and includes an award-winning restaurant. **Jamesons Hotel** (+353 (0)91-528666) is in Salthill, five minutes from the city centre, and has rooms with views over Galway Bay. So, too, does the **Galway Bay Hotel** (+353 (0)91-520520), which is a little further down the promenade. **The Connemara Coast Hotel** (+353 (0)91-592065) in Furbo has the course in Bearna nearby, while the **Connemara Gateway Hotel** (+353 (0)91-552328) in Oughterard is also a good base for golfing trips. **The Boat Inn** (+353 (0)91-552196) is owned and run by a golfer, Michael Murphy, who can organize keenly priced packages incorporating Oughterard and Bearna. Golf on the nearby championship links in Ballyconneely and gourmet cuisine musical evenings are among the attractions of staying at the **Abbeyglen Castle Hotel** (+353 (0)95-22832) in Clifden. **Renvyle House Hotel** (+353 (0)95-43511) claims to serve fish only caught daily at the bottom of the garden; the hotel is nicely positioned to explore the fine links courses nestled along the Atlantic Ocean in Connemara.

Leitrim **The Landmark Hotel** (+353 (0)78-22222) in Carrick-on-Shannon has full leisure facilities and a golf course, river cruising and horse-riding amenities in the area.

Mayo **The Castlecourt Hotel** (+353 (0)98-25444) in Westport also has leisure facilities and is a good base for exploring the links and parkland courses of the county. A family-run hotel with leisure centre, the recently renovated **Downhill House Hotel** (+353 (0)96-21033) in Ballina is perfect for exploring the fine links of north Mayo and west Sligo. **Drom Caoin** (+353 (0)97-81195), a B&B near Carne links, has won a national food award. **Enniscoe House** (+353 (0)96-31112) near Crossmolina is listed as a heritage house and is located on the shores of Lough Conn.

Where to Eat

Clare **O'Brien's Restaurant** (+353 (0)65-6828127) in the Old Ground House Hotel in Ennis serves the best of local produce in a very pleasant environment. **Vittles** (+353 (0)65-9056032) is a restaurant in Halpin's Hotel in the coastal town of Kilkee; the ambience of the residence is matched by superb cuisine. **Mr Eamon's** (+353 (0)65-81050) in Lahinch is famous in this part of the world for its delicious seafood dishes.

Galway **Keanes Country Kitchen** (+353 (0)91-794075) in Oranmore serves very good Irish food at a reasonable price. Oysters are always a popular choice in the bars and restaurants of Clarinbridge, and **Paddy Burke's Restaurant** (+353 (0)91-796226) is no exception. You can enjoy stunning lake views while you nourish your palate with the fine food and wines at the **Delphi Lodge** (+353 (0)95-42222) in the heart of Connemara country. If you simply want to get away from it all, then the **Ardagh Hotel & Restaurant** (+353 (0)95-21384) will definitely suit. **Rosleague Manor** (+353 (0)95-41168) in Letterfrack is a delightfully situated Georgian house overlooking Ballinakill Bay with cuisine based on the freshest and finest of ingredients; salmon and lamb are specialities of the kitchen.

Mayo The **La Fougère Restaurant** (+353 (0)98-28600) in Knockranny House, Westport, has a fine reputation and an extremely varied menu. **Newport House** (+353 (0)98-41222) in Newport is an historic Georgian house set in its own grounds and well known for its fine food and wines. **Breaffy House Hotel** (+353 (0)65-6823759) has an award-winning Garden Restaurant; after dining, the Mulberry Bar is but a short stroll away.

What to Do

Clare At **Bunratty Folk Park** it is possible to see Irish stew and griddle bread being prepared in the traditional manner. For those nocturnal animals, a visit to the **Bunratty Castle Banquet**, which offers the opportunity to indulge in some mead, shouldn't be missed. Not far from Lahinch's magnificent golf links lie the **Cliffs of Moher**, one of the most majestic sights in the whole of Ireland. **The Clare Heritage and Genealogical**

Centre in Corrofin offers an insight to 300 years of local history, including an on-the-spot genealogical service for those interested in tracing their roots. The **de Valera Museum and Library** in Ennis has a number of exhibits relating to some of Ireland's most famous leaders, including Eamon de Valera and Charles Stewart Parnell. **The Burren**, a vast tract of limestone that resembles the landscape of the moon's surface and is home to a vast array of flora, enriches the Clare landscape and is a must for the tourist to the area.

Galway **The Galway Crystal Heritage Centre** on the Dublin Road offers an introduction to local boat-building methods, a demonstration of glassworking skills by master craftsmen and a history of Galway families. You can see the casting of bronzes and the production of hand-painted bone china at the **Royal Tara** factory. The **Church of St Nicholas** is the city's most significant medieval building. It was constructed in 1320 and used as a stable by Oliver Cromwell. Christopher Columbus also prayed at the church on one of his visits to Galway. **Turoe Pet Farm and Leisure Park** incorporates the Turoe Stone, a rare national monument dating back to the 2nd or 1st century BC. To the east of the county, you will find the **Battle of Aughrim Interpretative Centre** in Aughrim, which explains the battle between William of Orange and King James II in 1691. **Connemara National Park** is a conservation area of great splendour, including the Twelve Pins mountains and the Glanmore valley. The visitor centre even provides its own on-site botanist who, during high season, conducts a two-hour guided walk through mountains, bogs and grasslands. Large sections of **Kylemore Abbey and Walled Gardens** are open to the public. This area not only offers great natural beauty, but also magnificent craftworks – and the **Ceardlann an Spidéil** is a group of small shops where woodworkers, sculptors, potters, weavers and jewellers produce their wares. For anyone with a day or two to spare, a boat trip to the **Aran Islands** will undoubtedly capture your heart. **The Aran Heritage Centre**, which is found in Cill Rónáin, offers a wonderful introduction to the culture of all three islands.

Mayo **The Louisburgh Folk and Heritage Centre** will teach you all that you need to know about the O'Malleys, a famous clan from the area; for children, the high point is likely to be the true-life story of Gráinne Ní Mháille, also known as the Pirate Queen. **Westport House** is another good place to bring the kids, featuring as it does a small zoo, mini-golf course and paddle boats. **Knock**, where, in 1879, some people claimed to have seen visions of the Virgin Mary, is another must-see; the **Knock Folk Museum** is an interpretative centre that supplies background information on the apparition. Still on a religious theme, a climb up **Craogh Patrick**, a traditional walk of pilgrimage, will give you enormous bragging rights upon your return home. **The Foxford Woollen Mills** offers a guided tour that will transport you back to the 1890s, while the **Céide Fields** in north Mayo will take you back even further, offering as they do an opportunity to view a Stone Age landscape of fields and megalithic tombs. After a hard day's golfing, unwind with a seaweed bath in **Enniscrone Seaweed Baths**, Enniscrone, County Sligo.

Tourist Information Centres
Shannon Airport Information Office, Terminal Building, Shannon, County Clare (+353 (0)61-471664)
Cliffs of Moher Tourist Centre, Liscannor, County Clare (+353 (0)65-7081171)
Ireland-West Information Office, Aras Failte, Eyre Square, Galway (+353 (0)91-563081)
Westport Tourist Information Office, The Square, Westport, County Mayo (+353 (0)98-25711)

The Cliffs of Moher, just 3 miles/5km up the coast from the famed Old Course at Lahinch.

Chapter 6

The

Midlands

Once upon a time, the Midlands — that part of Ireland unlucky enough not to have any access to the sea — was considered infertile land as far as golf courses were concerned. After all, isn't Irish golf mainly about links courses? It was almost heretical to suggest that golf could exist away from the taste of saltwater and the smell of seaweed.

Serious investment by some players in the business world has helped to change such an outlook. In fact, anyone taking the N4/M4 out of Dublin — one of the main arteries out of the city — won't have to travel too far into the country-side to realize that Ireland now has a number of parkland courses to rank with the very best.

These days, the Midlands — which, for the purpose of this guide, consists of the counties of Kildare, Carlow, Kilkenny,

Tipperary, Westmeath and brief forays into the western territories of Wicklow and Meath — has a huge number of top-class courses. For the visitor, it also offers a wonderful contrast to seaside links.

As you travel west on the M4, the town of Maynooth lies to the right and so, too, does the new Carton House demesne, which features two new courses. These courses, which opened in 2002, were designed by Mark O'Meara and Colin Montgomerie. To the left, in the direction of Straffan, you will discover two more championship courses at The K Club — the host venue for the 2006 Ryder Cup matches between Europe and the United States — designed by American legend Arnold Palmer. Both Carton House and the K Club cater almost exclusively for the upper end of the golfing market.

The K Club, a supreme test of a player's ability, has played host to the Smurfit European Open since 1995, when Bernhard Langer won. The Smurfit is one

Left: The Rock of Cashel, County Tipperary, was the seat of the Kings of Munster. Above: Irish traditional dancer and musicians.

of the flagship tournaments on the PGA European Tour. Some 70 miles/112km to the south lies another magnificent parkland course, Mount Juliet in Thomastown, County Kilkenny.

Opened within a few months of each other in 1991, The K Club and Mount Juliet (the latter designed by Jack Nicklaus) will forever be mentioned in the same breath, not only because of their shared date of birth but also because they represented new standards for Irish parkland developments. The two courses have matured to represent all that is good about parkland golf in the country.

They are not alone in this respect. Traditional parkland courses, such as Carlow and Mullingar represent good value for money and are also extremely demanding and well-maintained. Tulfarris, situated alongside the man-made Blessington Lakes in the Wicklow foothills, has also earned a fine reputation since upgrading from a nine-hole facility into a full championship course. Rathsallagh, near the village of Dunlavin, is another magnificent addition to the landscape of West Wicklow.

All around, it seems, golf courses are seen as the new greening of Ireland. Further inland and to the north, Headfort (No. 2) – designed by Christy O'Connor Jnr – is another tremendous test, combining mature woodland and a healthy smattering of water.

Although the scenery in the Midlands is nowhere near as spectacular as the mountainous and rugged coastlines of the south-west, west and north-west, and

The restored telescope at Birr Castle, County Offaly, was once the largest telescope in the world.

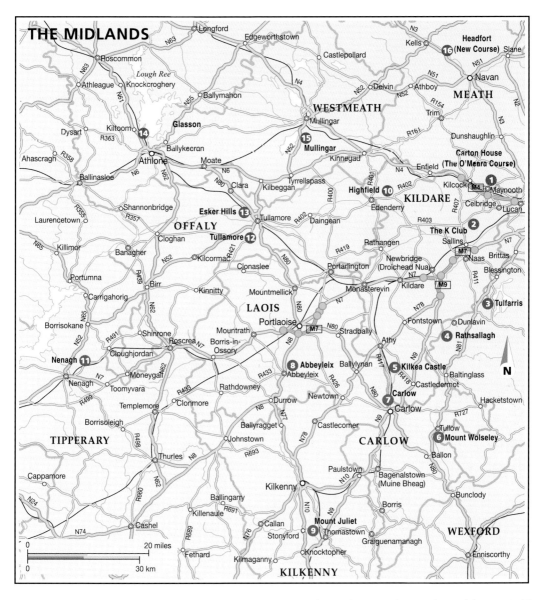

won't exactly make you catch your breath, it has its own charm, as well as numerous attractions for the visitor. The west Midlands also has the River Shannon, the country's largest waterway, as a constant and beautiful companion.

An island in Lough Ree, one of the lakes on the Shannon, is reputed to be the geographical centre of Ireland. Typical of a land where a golf course never seems to be far away, two superb courses overlook

the island from either side. Athlone Golf Club lies on the west bank (the adjacent Hodson Bay hotel holds a fun competition every year to see if anyone can drive a ball from the shore onto the island), while Glasson, situated on the east bank, is one of O'Connor Jnr's finest works.

Such fine and dramatic inland courses give a lie to the oft-repeated assertion that Irish golf is all about links courses.

Carton House (The O'Meara Course)

Carton House Golf Club, Maynooth, County Kildare
TEL: *+353 (0)1-6286271* **FAX:** *+353 (0)1-6286054*
EMAIL: *carton@iol.ie* **WEBSITE:** *www.carton.ie*
LOCATION: *14 miles/22km west of Dublin, off the M4 between Leixlip and Maynooth; the course is signposted*
COURSE: *36 holes (two courses), The O'Meara Course: 6976yd/6375m, par 72*
GREEN FEES: *€€€€€€*
FACILITIES: *Changing rooms and showers, full catering, bar, shop, practice area, buggy hire, trolley hire*
VISITORS: *Welcome – booking essential*

CARTON HOUSE
THE O'MEARA COURSE

HOLE	YD	M	PAR	HOLE	YD	M	PAR
1	383	350	4	10	421	385	4
2	558	510	5	11	405	370	4
3	208	190	3	12	367	335	4
4	361	330	4	13	175	160	3
5	558	510	5	14	558	510	5
6	153	140	3	15	175	160	3
7	443	405	4	16	558	510	5
8	383	350	4	17	427	390	4
9	449	410	4	18	394	360	4
OUT	3496	3195	36	IN	3480	3180	36

6976YD • 6375M • PAR 72

For over 250 years, the tall grey walls – all 5 miles/8km of them – that hid Carton House and its 1,000-plus acres from view have intrigued the outsiders – from those in bygone days who jaunted past one of Ireland's most exclusive estates on the outskirts of Maynooth, County Kildare, in hackney carts to, more recently, people who catch a glimpse of the rolling fields from the top of a double-decker bus.

The mystery is now over. Since its development as a prime golfing resort with two championship golf courses, Carton House has shed its mystique, while still retaining its sense of grandeur, and taken a place among the top echelon of the country's parkland courses. Two courses, one by Mark O'Meara, and the other, a style of inland links, by Colin Montgomerie, are the centrepieces of a major commercial development, which has also included the sensitive restoration of the old house.

The O'Meara Course was the first to open, in the spring of 2002. The American designer, who has strong Irish connections, has produced a masterpiece. On one of his first visits to the site, O'Meara remarked: 'This is my first European design venture, and I couldn't have asked for better in terms of terrain and topography… this little piece of property is very special.'

Carton House was built in 1739 by Richard Castles, who also created Leinster House, now the seat of the Irish Government in Dublin. Lady Emily Lennox, wife of the first Duke of Leinster, had the most influence

in landscaping the grounds. Indeed, it is richly ironic that, in the drawing room of Carton House, there is a painting by the artist William Ashford depicting Emily looking across the River Rye through woodlands. Her gaze is cast precisely on the land that is now the 14th fairway.

An interesting design feature of The O'Meara Course is that all four par 5s off the back stakes measure 558yd/510m and, yet, each of them is completely different in shape and challenge to the other.

Set in a mature parkland setting, the opening holes are quite delightful and offer tremendous variety, in both length and shape. The 7th hole, a 443yd/405m par 4, has numerous species of trees as a natural boundary up the left-hand side, and is considered sufficiently tough not to warrant any fairway bunkers. The 9th is another tough par 4, returning uphill to complete the initial loop that has so far avoided any water hazards.

However, it is the series of holes designed around the River Rye that enthrall. The 13th, a par 3 of 175yd/160m, is played from

The approach to the 14th green must cross the River Rye, which has a wonderful weir to the right of the green.

an elevated tee across the river to a green, with water on the left, and demands a precise, well-struck shot to hold the green. The 14th, a par 5 that traverses the river twice when hitting from the back tees, is a magnificent hole. As its backdrop, the green has a wonderful weir to the right; the pretty Shell Cottage is tucked into the trees on the hill behind.

The highlight of this sequence of great holes is the 15th, a par 3 of 175yd/160m. This time, virtually all of the carry is over water to a green surrounded by tall trees.

The Montgomerie Course runs on the opposite side of the River Rye to The O'Meara Course and is a completely different challenge. Built on a large area of open and undulating terrain, more reminiscent of links, and with some 130 bunkers (most of them steep-faced and cavernous), the Montgomerie course has a distinctive style that contrasts sharply with the more Americanized and parkland nature of The O'Meara Course.

The K Club (No. 1)

The Kildare Hotel and Country Club, Straffan, County Kildare
TEL: *+353 (0)1-6017300* **FAX:** *+353 (0)1-6017399*
EMAIL: *golf@kclub.ie* **WEBSITE:** *www.kclub.ie*
LOCATION: *20 miles/32km west of Dublin, via the N4/M4, exiting at Maynooth for Straffan or, alternatively, via the N7 exiting at Kill for Straffan*
COURSE: *36 holes (two courses), No. 1: 7178yd/ 6524m, par 72, SSS 76*
GREEN FEES: *€€€€€€+*
FACILITIES: *Changing rooms and showers, full catering, bar, pro shop, tuition, club hire, practice area, buggy hire, trolley hire, on-site accommodation*
VISITORS: *Welcome – booking essential*

THE K CLUB (NO. 1)

HOLE	YD	M	PAR	HOLE	YD	M	PAR
1	584	531	5	10	418	380	4
2	408	371	4	11	413	375	4
3	173	157	3	12	170	155	3
4	402	365	4	13	568	516	5
5	213	194	3	14	416	378	4
6	446	405	4	15	447	406	4
7	606	551	5	16	395	359	4
8	375	341	4	17	173	157	3
9	434	395	4	18	537	488	5
OUT	3641	3310	36	IN	3537	3214	36

7178YD • 6524M • PAR 72

Perfection, especially on a golf course, is a hard goal to attain. Yet with the golfing intuition and creativity of the legendary American player, Arnold Palmer, and the financial resources of Ireland's best-known businessman, Dr Michael Smurfit, such a standard was set – and met – in the development of The Kildare Hotel and Country Club, beside the village of Straffan.

Known simply as The K Club, it is the traditional home of the Smurfit European Open. It will also be the focal point for inter-national golf as host to the Ryder Cup match between Europe and the US in 2006.

With the country's first five-star hotel also in the grounds, and the River Liffey as a delectable diversion for fly-fishermen, it is hard to believe that The K Club is just a half-hour drive from Dublin's city centre.

'What I have done is to offer the option of an extremely testing course off the back tees, or the playing of a more modest length from

The River Liffey comes into play on three holes – this is the 7th, a par 5 played to an island green.

IRELAND & THE RYDER CUP

Ever since Fred Daly became the first Irishman to play in the Ryder Cup, the link between the competition and Irish golfers has been formidable.

Three months after he won the British Open's claret jug at Hoylake in 1947, Daly set sail on the first part of a journey that would finish in Portland, Oregon, where he was to become Ireland's first representative in the match with the United States. From an Irish viewpoint, Daly was the trendsetter –

and the Irish, now with 17 players who have played in the Ryder Cup, have grown to love the biggest team competition in professional golf.

Indeed, when the 2006 edition of the Ryder Cup is played at The K Club, the hope is that a number of Irishmen will be playing. With Darren Clarke, Padraig Harrington and Paul McGinley (all members of the 2002 team) in the top 50 of the world golf rankings, it is a very real possibility.

---

the middle to forward tees,' said Palmer, when the course opened in 1991. 'Either way, I feel I have guaranteed that the player will get enjoyment from his efforts, and that is the design concept we set out to achieve.' So pleased was Dr Smurfit with Palmer's work that he asked the American to design the second course on the other side of the Liffey.

The No. 1 course starts and finishes with two very different par 5s, and in between is a variety of holes that will examine every aspect of your game. As well as the Liffey – which comes directly into play on the 7th, 8th, 16th and 17th holes – there are many other water features. In fact, water is in play on no less than 14 holes. Mature trees and strategic bunkers add to the challenge.

On the front nine, the undisputed feature hole is the 7th, a par 5 of 606yd/551m off the back stakes, which is very much a three-shot hole (at best!) for most players. Playing off more forward tees, players can be

tempted to have a go for the island green in two, but greed demands a heavy penalty, with the Liffey usually emerging the winner. A new tee box, which has players firing over the edge of the river at the 8th, has made the challenge that much harder.

The course's signature hole is the 16th – appropriately named Michael's Favourite – which demands a long and straight drive through trees left and water right, and then a precise approach over yet more water to a wide and narrow green.

The 17th is a short par 3, but the Liffey comes into play again, and any shot pushed even marginally to the right will find a watery grave. The finishing hole is a classic par 5, offering the brave player an opportunity to find the large green in two: it was here, on the 72nd hole of the 1995 European Open, that Bernhard Langer holed an eagle putt of some 90 feet/27m to force a play-off, which he subsequently won.

Tulfarris

Tulfarris Hotel and Golf Resort, Blessington Lakes, Blessington, County Wicklow
TEL: *+353 (0)45-867600*
FAX: *+353 (0)45-867561* **EMAIL:** *info@tulfarris.com*
WEBSITE: *www.tulfarris.com*
LOCATION: *6 miles/10km from Blessington, off the N81 road to Baltinglass; the course is signposted*
COURSE: *18 holes, 7832yd/7116m, par 72, SSS 74*
GREEN FEES: €€€€€€
FACILITIES: *Changing rooms and showers, full catering, bar, shop, practice area, buggy hire, trolley hire, on-site accommodation*
VISITORS: *Welcome – booking essential*

On a fine day, and in these surroundings, it seems that there is indeed a heaven on earth. You will find Tulfarris some 6 miles/10km past the village of Blessington, in the foothills of the Wicklow mountains and adjoining the giant man-made reservoirs that serve Dublin.

This lakeside course is a credit to its designer, Patrick Merrigan. It not only captivates, but also challenges just about every aspect of a player's game. Stonework features adorn the course, and just about everything is perfect – as you'd expect from a championship course that is the centrepiece of a development that includes a four-star hotel and leisure complex.

In hosting the Irish Seniors' Open, Tulfarris has proven itself as a fine tournament venue. There are many great holes. It would be hard to find a more intimidating tee shot than the one off the 7th, a par 5 of 608yd/553m, with the drive starting out over the lake.

The back nine is a pure joy. The 11th is a challenging par 3 and, likewise, another short hole, the 16th, will survive in the memory long after the end of the round.

However, it is the 18th, a par 4 of 449yd/408m, with a marshy area to the right of the fairway, that is the show hole for a superb course.

Rathsallagh

Rathsallagh Golf Club, Dunlavin, County Wicklow
TEL: *+353 (0)45-403316* **FAX:** *+353 (0)45-403295*
EMAIL: *info@rathsallagh.com*
WEBSITE: *www.rathsallagh.com*
LOCATION: *15 miles/24km south of Naas, off the N9 near Dunlavin; the course is signposted*
COURSE: *18 holes, 6885yd/6260m, par 72, SSS 72*
GREEN FEES: €€€€€€
FACILITIES: *Changing rooms and showers, full catering, bar, pro shop, tuition, practice area, buggy hire, trolley hire, on-site accommodation*
VISITORS: *Welcome – advisable to pre-book*

Tucked neatly away on the western side of the Wicklow mountains is one of the finest courses in the country. Rathsallagh only opened in 1996, but it has quickly taken its place among the top inland courses. It is very accessible to Dublin day-trippers, as there is motorway virtually all the way from the capital, via the M7 and the M9.

A wonderfully thought-out clubhouse, with commanding views of the 9th, 10th and 18th holes, is the focal point of a golf course that offers tremendous variety. It is an undulating course, particularly on the back nine, and there is little or no let-up in the demands that shot-making places on a player.

Designed by Christy O'Connor Jnr and Peter McEvoy, there is a mix of trees, lakes, streams and bunkers that need considerable course management. The uphill par 4 9th hole, which demands a well-struck drive to the elbow of the dogleg and then a mid-iron to find a raised and undulating green, is a great way to finish the front nine. There is reason to be nervous on the 10th tee, because everyone relaxing in the clubhouse will be watching you. There are then a couple of streams to be crossed before the green is found.

There is a tremendous loop of holes on the way home, and the only golfers you will see are those either in front or behind until the 18th tee box is reached.

5 *Kilkea Castle*

*Kilkea Castle Golf Club, near Castledermot,
County Kildare*
TEL: *+353 (0)503-45555* **FAX:** *+353 (0)503-45505*
EMAIL: *kilkeagolfclub@eircom.net*
WEBSITE: *www.kilkeacastlehotelgolf.com*
LOCATION: *3²/₃ miles/6km north of Castledermot, off
the N9; the course is signposted*
COURSE: *18 holes, 6706yd/6097m, par 70, SSS 72*
GREEN FEES: *€€€€*
FACILITIES: *Changing rooms and showers, full catering,
bar, shop, practice area, buggy hire, trolley hire, on-site
accommodation and leisure facilities*
VISITORS: *Welcome – booking advisable*

As a popular venue for weddings, it is quite likely that your round of golf at Kilkea Castle – which dates back to 1180 and is the oldest continually inhabited castle in Ireland – will be played to the strains of a lone piper serenading a newly married couple into the castle's courtyard.

Be that as it may, Kilkea Castle is a very enjoyable parkland course. On the front nine, course management, rather than sheer power, is extremely important; the river has been cleverly utilized, most obviously in guarding the front of the 3rd and 4th greens and in cutting across the par 4 8th hole. However, it is the closing stretch of holes that is most talked about in the clubhouse afterwards.

The 16th is a par 3 of 190yd/173m. It must be hit all the way to the elevated green, or the River Greese will surely find a home for the ball.

The 17th is a short par 4 with wicked intent. It only measures 378yd/344m and is a dogleg, but the tee shot must clear the river and must not go through the fairway. The approach is to a long narrow green with trees on the left.

There is no let-up on the last hole, either. A large pond on the left awaits any pulled drive and forces players to go more to the right for safety – a much more difficult approach to the green. The sight of the castle behind the 18th may be sufficient to take one's mind off the tricky task at hand, even if only momentarily.

Kilkea Castle is a beautifully maintained course with some interesting holes. This is the 18th.

6 Mount Wolseley

Mount Wolseley Hotel, Golf and Country Club, Tullow, County Carlow
TEL: *+353 (0)503-52055* **FAX:** *+353 (0)503-52123* **EMAIL:** *wolseley@iol.ie*
WEBSITE: *www.golfclubireland.com/mountwolseley.htm*
LOCATION: *2 miles/3.2km south-east of Tullow, on the Ardattin road; the course is signposted*
COURSE: *18 holes, 7106yd/6459m, par 72, SSS 73*
GREEN FEES: *€€€€€*
FACILITIES: *Changing rooms and showers, full catering, bar, shop, practice area, club hire, buggy hire, trolley hire, on-site accommodation*
VISITORS: *Welcome – essential to check weekend availability in advance*

Located just 10 miles/16km from Carlow Town near the village of Tullow, Mount Wolseley is yet another fine piece of work by Christy O'Connor Jnr. The course, which is squeezed between the Slaney and Derreen rivers, runs through an old estate with many mature trees.

It is an estate with a long and, at times, troublesome history. Mount Wolseley first came into the possession of the Wolseley family, the inventors of the first designed British motor car, in 1725. The estate was

Water comes into play on no less than 11 holes at Mount Wolseley and adds considerably to the course's challenge.

torched by insurgents during the 1798 Rebellion, however. When it was rebuilt some years later, it eventually came into the hands of the Patrician Brothers. In 1994, it was bought by the Morrissey family and transformed into a luxury hotel.

The course is long and demanding, with the trees and water features adding to the overall challenge. There is water in play on 11 holes, with the 11th hole requiring a carry of 200yd/182m over a lake. Overall, Mount Wolseley is an immaculately maintained course and a fair test of a player's ability.

7 Carlow

Carlow Golf Club, Deerpark, Carlow Town, County Carlow
TEL: *+353 (0)503-31695* **FAX:** *+353 (0)503-40065*
EMAIL: *carlowgolfclub@tinet.ie*
WEBSITE: *www.carlowgolfclub.com*
LOCATION: *1¼ miles/2km north of Carlow on the N9, approximately 54 miles/86km south of Dublin*
COURSE: *18 holes, 6571yd/5974m, par 70, SSS 71*
GREEN FEES: *€€€€€*
FACILITIES: *Changing rooms and showers, full catering, bar, pro shop, tuition, practice/putting area, club hire, buggy hire, trolley hire*
VISITORS: *Welcome – contact the club in advance*

If ever an inland course has stood the test of time, then Carlow – with the intrepid hand of Tom Simpson behind its longevity in the face of modern golf-course technology – has managed to do so. It is a wonderful course, pleasing from the start, that succeeds in extracting considerable shot-making skills from the player.

Simpson was responsible for creating the links at County Louth (Baltray) and also influenced the layout on the Old Course at Ballybunion, so his pedigree is beyond reproach. At Carlow, he used the undulating terrain superbly, with numerous elevated tee boxes, several doglegs, strategic bunkering and well-shaped fairways, while also creating large, slick putting surfaces. There are also some subtle water hazards at the 2nd, 10th and 11th holes to heighten the dangers.

Probably the toughest hole on the course is the 16th, a par 4 of 435yd/396m. It is played through a tunnel-like valley and anyone who garners a par here can feel extremely pleased with themselves.

There are only two par 5s on the course, which accounts for its par of 70. The 18th, a hole that tumbles downhill to the clubhouse, is a pleasant way to finish a round on a course that is always in good condition.

IRELAND & THE HORSE

The Irish psyche is imbued with a love of all things equine from a very young age. Celtic folklore tells us magical tales of horsemen who live in Tír na nÓg – the 'Land of Eternal Youth' – and, to this day, the horse has a special place in Irish life.

Ireland is one of the world's major bloodstock centres, producing thoroughbreds and steeple-chasers that go on to entertain at racecourses all over the globe.

A number of famous horses have had a special affinity with the Irish. Arkle, perhaps the greatest racer in National Hunt history, is still remembered with great fondness, and Red Rum, who dominated the Aintree Grand National, was also bred in Ireland.

Horse racing unites two Irish passions – horses and betting. Flat racing is concentrated around the Curragh, where the classics, including the Irish Derby, are held each summer. The Irish Grand National is run at Fairyhouse at Easter time, and horse-racing festivals are also held at Leopardstown, Punchestown, Galway and Tralee. In fact, hardly a day goes by when there is not a race meeting. The flat-racing season runs from mid-March to early November. National Hunt racing over fences takes place throughout the year.

Abbeyleix

Abbeyleix Golf Club, Rathmoyle, Abbeyleix, County Laois
TEL: *+353 (0)502-31450*
EMAIL: *info@abbeyleixgolfclub.ie*
LOCATION: *2/3 miles/1km from the town centre; the course is signposted*
COURSE: *18 holes, 6365yd/5786m, par 72, SSS 70*
GREEN FEES: *€€*
FACILITIES: *Changing rooms and showers, full catering, bar, shop, practice area, buggy hire, trolley hire*
VISITORS: *Welcome*

If ever care and attention were rewarded with a fine parkland course, then it is true in the case of Abbeyleix, which has expanded and remodelled its course to a full 18 holes in recent years. This has been achieved with a new Vi-Aqua Water Treatment irrigation system, which has never before been used on a golf course. This has resulted in remarkably true greens and has transformed a two-acre marsh area in the middle of the course into a nature reserve.

Designed by Mel Flanagan, the course unfolds on classic parkland terrain. It incorporates dramatic changes of elevation and an abundance of mature trees, with the Devil's Bit mountain in Tipperary as a distant backdrop. One of the prettiest holes on the course is probably the short 3rd. This par 3 hole measures 121yd/110m and comes after two opening par 5s, so demands a player's utmost concentration with the tee shot played from an elevated tee to a green that has water to the front and trees at the rear. The toughest hole on the course is the 8th, a par 4 of 467yd/424m, which follows a right-to-left downhill sweep, but has the added danger of a ditch just short of the green.

The finishing hole, a par 4 of 426yd/387m, is extremely tough, so much so that it doesn't need bunkers. The road up the right is out-of-bounds and the difficulty is accentuated by an uphill approach.

9 Mount Juliet

Mount Juliet Golf Club, Thomastown, County Kilkenny
TEL: *+353 (0)56-73000* **FAX:** *+353 (0)56-73019*
EMAIL: *info@mountjuliet.ie*
WEBSITE: *www.mountjuliet.com*
LOCATION: *10 miles/16km south of Kilkenny, off the N10 from Kilkenny to Waterford or, alternatively, off the N9 from Thomastown to Waterford City*
COURSE: *18 holes, 7112yd/6465m, par 72, SSS 74*
GREEN FEES: *€€€€€€+*
FACILITIES: *Changing rooms and showers, full catering, bar, pro shop, academy, practice area, putting course, club hire, buggy hire, trolley hire, on-site accommodation*
VISITORS: *Welcome – booking essential*

MOUNT JULIET

HOLE	YD	M	PAR	HOLE	YD	M	PAR
1	364	331	4	10	553	503	5
2	419	381	4	11	169	153	3
3	182	166	3	12	411	374	4
4	404	367	4	13	433	394	4
5	540	491	5	14	195	177	3
6	229	209	3	15	370	336	4
7	419	381	4	16	433	393	4
8	575	523	5	17	516	469	5
9	426	388	4	18	474	430	4
OUT	3558	3236	36	IN	3554	3229	36

7112 YD • 6465 M • PAR 72

Few golfing facilities have created a better ambience, or have captured the spirit of Irish golf more succesfully, than Mount Juliet. This delightful but immensely challenging parkland course near Thomastown, in County Kilkenny, is the design work of the legendary American golfer Jack Nicklaus and is his showpiece course in Europe.

Mount Juliet has proven itself on the big stage, too. The American Express World Golf Championship, the Murphy's Irish Open and the Shell Wonderful World of Golf have all been staged on the course, which is set amidst 1,500 acres of invigorating woodlands encircling the River Nore. Intriguingly, Nicklaus chose not to use the river as a feature, for fear it could complicate drainage if earth moving was conducted too close to its banks. That is not to say that water does not play a big part – it does, especially on the homeward run.

There are obvious similarities between Mount Juliet and The K Club, given that they opened for play within weeks of each other in 1991 and both, of course, were designed by American players of some acclaim. Mount Juliet is probably the more relaxed environment, however; it also offers the additional pastimes of angling, clay target shooting, archery and horse riding within a walled estate that dates back to the 17th century.

As with most classical parkland courses, the introduction is not too strenuous – although a tree on the left-hand side of the fairway captures more than its share of tee shots – but it doesn't take too long to bite. The 2nd hole, a dogleg that swings to the right, requires a precise shot off the tee: too short or to the right and a stream lurks, and too far left will find trees. This is followed by an approach through yet more trees to a deceptive undulating green.

Tough as the 2nd hole is, the 3rd hole – a masterful par 3 with much of its 182yd/166m over water – really emphasizes the fact that the course won't be taken easily. If you're playing in a four ball, regardless of standard, don't be surprised if at least one of you is so intimidated by the water that the ball falls into its clutches. This great sequence of holes is completed by the 4th, another par 4 requiring a precise tee shot – probably with a three-wood – and a pin-point approach over water to a narrow green.

Still, Mount Juliet is there to be played. There is no trickery, and Nicklaus has allowed a sufficient number of holes to give something back – particularly the par 5s – so that there is no sense of being overpowered by the course. On and on it goes, and it is a terrific experience. It gets even better on the back nine holes.

The 12th, a slightly uphill par 4 of 411yd/374m, has matured into a lovely hole, with the green nestled among mature trees in a quiet corner of the course. It is a tranquil

setting, and very much a case of the calm before the storm. The 13th is the course's signature hole. It is a par 4 of 433yd/394m and it is imperative to get away a good drive to have any chance at all of going for the green, which has water in front, in two. If you miss the fairway, accept your punishment, lay-up and attempt to get up and down – no easy task, it must be said, on a green that slopes from the back to the front.

A sign of a really good course is that there are no weak holes, and this is the case at Mount Juliet. The use of different tee boxes means that the course is playable for anyone who has a grasp of the game – but even the most accomplished player will have trouble on the last. There is no tougher finishing hole in parkland golf than the 18th, a par 4 of 474yd/430m that somehow always appears to play into a wind. The biggest lake on the course is in play all the way up the left-hand side. The place to aim is probably just left of the big tree on the right.

The 13th hole – a par 4 of 433yd/394m – is the signature hole at Mount Juliet.

10 *Highfield*

Highfield Golf Club, Carbury, County Kildare
TEL: *+353 (0)405-31021*
FAX: *+353 (0)405-31021* **EMAIL:** *hgc@indigo.ie*
WEBSITE: *www.highfield-golf.ie*
LOCATION: *2 miles/3.2km north-east of Edenderry; the course is best approached from the N4, turning off near Enfield – it is well signposted*
COURSE: *18 holes, 6292yd/5720m, par 72, SSS 70*
GREEN FEES: *€€*
FACILITIES: *Changing rooms and showers, full catering, bar, shop, practice area, buggy hire, trolley hire*
VISITORS: *Welcome – booking required for weekends*

On land that has been in the Duggan family for over 250 years (some of it is still retained for farming and it is not uncommon to see turkeys wandering the fairway on the 1st hole), a gem of a course – designed by Alan Duggan – has materialized. Indeed, environmentalists praise it as 'a fine example of the sensitive integration of a leisure facility with the environment'.

Careful grassland management has led to the creation of greens with minimal use of chemicals. Unused areas, well away from play, have been left uncultivated. There is a network of wildlife corridors that incorporates watercourse banks, hedgerows and mature trees.

All in all, it is a place that leaves you in no doubt that you are in the heart of the countryside. There are some fine golf holes, too. The creation of new water hazards and the planting of over 1,000 hardwood trees to augment those already on the course will no doubt make it even better.

11 *Nenagh*

Nenagh Golf Club, Beechwood, Nenagh, County Tipperary
TEL: *+353 (0)67-31476* **FAX:** *+353 (0)67-34808*
LOCATION: *4¼ miles/7km north-east of Nenagh, off the N7; the course is signposted*
COURSE: *18 holes, 6609yd/6009m, par 72, SSS 72*
GREEN FEES: *€€€*
FACILITIES: *Changing rooms and showers, full catering, bar, pro shop, practice area, buggy hire, trolley hire*
VISITORS: *Welcome – advisable to book in advance*

A major course redevelopment, under the guidance of golf architect Patrick Merrigan, has transformed Nenagh from a merely enjoyable course into a really good course. The refurbishment, which introduced water features as well as upgrading greens and tees, was completed in 2001.

This parkland course is always in excellent condition, with maturing trees and a sandy subsoil – a feature that allows play to continue throughout the year. Nenagh has been developed into a true test of golfing skill that doesn't allow for any loss of concentration: the feature hole is the 6th, a par 3 of 194yd/177m, to a three-tier green that is surrounded by bunkers. Indeed, the front nine has some fine holes, including the 3rd, a par 5 that has two lakes in play down the right.

On the homeward run, the short 11th, which normally plays no more than a wedge or a nine-iron, and the 16th, which is probably the toughest hole on the course, demonstrate the attractive contrast that has been achieved here.

The numerous mature trees at Nenagh make accuracy off the tee essential to a good score.

⑫ Tullamore

Tullamore Golf Club, Brookfield, Tullamore, County Offaly
TEL: *+353 (0)506-21439* **FAX:** *+353 (0)506-41806*
LOCATION: *3 miles/5km south of Tullamore, on the Birr road*
COURSE: *18 holes, 6428yd/5814m, par 70, SSS 71*
GREEN FEES: €€€
FACILITIES: *Changing rooms and showers, full catering, bar, shop, practice area, buggy hire, trolley hire*
VISITORS: *Welcome – booking advisable*

⑬ Esker Hills

Esker Hills Golf Club, Tullamore, County Offaly
TEL: *+353 (0)506-55999* **FAX:** *+353 (0)506-55021*
EMAIL: *info@eskerhillsgolf.com*
WEBSITE: *www.eskerhillsgolf.com*
LOCATION: *3 miles/5km from Tullamore, on the Clara road; the course is signposted*
COURSE: *18 holes, 6669yd/6063m, par 71, SSS 70*
GREEN FEES: €€€
FACILITIES: *Changing rooms and showers, full catering, bar, shop, practice area, buggy hire, trolley hire*
VISITORS: *Welcome – booking advisable*

Tullamore, on the outskirts of this prosperous and progressive County Offaly town, has always been considered an interesting course. It is a superior parkland course in the heart of the Midlands, with mature trees recently augmented by additional tree-planting. James Braid had a hand in tweaking the design of this 100-year-old course in 1938, and a more recent redesign by Patrick Merrigan has given it new life.

Merrigan created seven new greens and 11 new tee boxes, but his most dramatic addition was the formation of three lakes. The old and the new blend together quite wonderfully in a lovely sylvan setting, with hardwoods – among them oak and beech trees – giving the course great character. Tullamore is fairly flat and the fairways are not too demanding. As such, only the truly wayward shot is penalized.

The 16th, a par 4 of 460yd/419m, has a green that is protected by water and trees, and is one of the toughest two-shot holes in the Midlands.

Esker Hills is created around drumlins, 10,000 year-old relics of the last Ice Age.

Nature is a wonderful thing and, when you play a round of golf at Esker Hills, you can't help but agree with such a sentiment. Some 10,000 years ago, the retreating Ice Age glaciers moulded this landscape into a series of sweeping valleys, plateaux and natural lakes. This is the environment from which Christy O'Connor Jnr created this stunning course.

Esker Hills offers a serious golfing challenge and will most reward those who are accurate, not only off the tee, but also with approach shots. Be warned, however; this is very demanding terrain and, unless you are very fit, a buggy or an electric cart is advisable.

The dogleg 1st hole, a par 5 of 491yd/446m, from an elevated tee box gives an early indication of what lies ahead. Yet as the round progresses, the hills seem to grow larger and the water comes more and more into play. The hills and a surprising number of mature trees keep you in your own private world and you will rarely see anyone playing on a different hole.

14 Glasson

Glasson Golf Club, Glasson, near Athlone, County Westmeath
TEL: *+353 (0)902-85120* **FAX:** *+353 (0)902-85444*
EMAIL: *info@glassongolf.ie*
WEBSITE: *www.glassongolf.ie*
LOCATION: *6 miles/9.6km north of Athlone; turn off the N6 east of Athlone and take the N55 Ballymahon road; the course is signposted*
COURSE: *18 holes, 7120yd/6472m, par 72, SSS 74*
GREEN FEES: *€€€€*
FACILITIES: *Changing rooms and showers, full catering, bar, pro shop, practice area, buggy hire, trolley hire*
VISITORS: *Welcome – booking advisable*

Christy O'Connor Jnr has made a significant contribution to the Irish golfing landscape, and the lakeside course at Glasson could well be his finest work of all.

O'Connor was given a remarkable site on which to weave his magic. The land overlooks Lough Ree on the River Shannon, and the course architect used extensive earth-moving on the front nine and the rolling terrain on the back to create something very special.

This undulating but not unduly physically demanding course can facilitate all handicappers. There is clever use of bunkering – evident as early as the par 3 3rd – but the beauty of the course is that the golfer is allowed time to recover and is not faced by one demanding hole after another. However, the 6th – a par 5 of 559yd/508m – has out-of-bounds left and then water awaiting any errant second shot.

The 14th starts a run of some jaw-dropping golf holes. The 14th is a par 5 where you drive from a high tee in natural woodland, with views over Killinure Bay. The fairway then bends to the right to run alongside the shoreline. The green is protected by water on both sides. The magic doesn't stop here, though, for the 15th – a par 3 of 185yd/168m – is a quite wonderful hole, with both the tee and the green jutting out into Lough Ree.

There are stunning views of Lough Ree – the geographical centre of Ireland – from Glasson. This is the 7th hole.

15 Mullingar

Mullingar Golf Club, Belvedere, Mullingar, County Westmeath
TEL: *+353 (0)44-48366* FAX: *+353 (0)44-41499*
LOCATION: *3 miles/4.8km south of Mullingar Town, on the N52 Mullingar–Tyrells pass road*
COURSE: *18 holes, 6504yd/5913m, par 72, SSS 71*
GREEN FEES: *€€€*
FACILITIES: *Changing rooms and showers, full catering, bar, pro shop, practice area, buggy hire, trolley hire*
VISITORS: *Welcome – restrictions on Wednesdays and Saturdays; booking advisable*

If there is a more welcoming or serene club than Mullingar, then it is doing a fine job of hiding its existence. Mullingar throws down the 'welcome mat' with heartfelt warmth, and the fact that it is an inland track of considerable merit – designed by five-times British Open winner James Braid – provides an additional reason to call.

Although some minor surgery has been performed to the course in recent times, it remains, by and large, much as Braid had intended. Built on the old Belvedere demesne, just outside the town and close to some very good freshwater lakes that are popular with fly-fishermen, Mullingar consists of a number of loops. It is a design ploy that successfully ensures no two holes are remotely similar.

There are a number of good holes on the front nine, particularly the two par 3s: the 2nd, which plays off an elevated tee over a valley to a raised green 189yd/172m away, and the 5th, which plays to a green that is even more raised, are rather special.

The homeward run, has even more character as it works its way through mature trees. The 16th is a par 5 that brings a ditch into play off the tee and, most probably after a good lay-up, an approach to a green that is extremely difficult to hold. More often than not, the ball is liable to come back down the hill to your feet.

16 Headfort (New Course)

Headfort Golf Club, Kells, County Meath
TEL: *+353 (0)46-40857* FAX: *+353 (0)46-49282*
LOCATION: *1 mile/1.6km outside Kells on the Navan road*
COURSE: *36 holes (two courses), New: 7135yd/6487m, par 72, SSS 75*
GREEN FEES: *€€€€*
FACILITIES: *Changing rooms and showers, full catering, bar, pro shop, tuition, practice area, buggy hire, trolley hire*
VISITORS: *Welcome – restrictions on Tuesdays; booking advisable*

The New Course at Headfort Golf Club opened in 2001 and is built on the land of the fourth Marquis of Headfort, who had the distinction of driving the first ball in competition for the Headfort Cup back in 1907. Although the Old Course has always been highly rated, and rightly so, the New Course – designed by Christy O'Connor Jnr – is magnificent. O'Connor has used both the mature trees and the River Blackwater, which comes into play on 13 holes, in his design.

The magic is delivered from the start. The 4th is the first of the short holes, with a tee shot of 183yd/167m over water to a green that is surrounded on three sides by water. The 6th is a downhill par 5 – a monstrous 567yd/516m, to a green protected by two magnificent old trees and water at the back! On the 9th, a par 4 of 414yd/377m, you are forced to cross water not once but twice. The 11th hole, a par 3, is the only one constructed on Small Island and it deserves to have the place all to itself. The 12th is a par 4 of 402yd/366m where the green protrudes out into the river. The finish, too, is exhilarating. The 17th is the last of the short holes but, again, the river sneaks in front of the green. Just when you think you have left the water behind, it is there again to torment you off the final tee box, a par 4 of 430yd/391m, with the drive required to fly reeds and marshes to a curving fairway.

REGIONAL DIRECTORY
Where to Stay
Kildare For a little self-indulgence, there are few finer places than the magnificent five-star **Kildare Hotel and Country Club** (+353 (0)1-6017200) by the River Liffey in Straffan, with two championship courses designed by Arnold Palmer on the estate. **Barberstown Castle** (+353 (0)1-6288157) is also a super place to stay and to eat. **The Harbour Hotel** (+353 (0)45-879145) in Naas is also recommended. **The Hazel Hotel** (+353 (0)45-525373) in Monasterevin is nicely located for visiting the Curragh racecourse.

West Wicklow The location of **Tulfarris Golf and Country Club** (+353 (0)45-867555) by the Blessington Lakes gives it an immediate edge, but the addition of leisure facilities, such as its championship course, gymnasium, tennis courts and swimming pool, make it as good a base as any.

Carlow **Mount Wolseley Hotel and Golf Resort** (+353 (0)503-51674) in Tullow is on a rambling estate that has been transformed into one of the finest golfing facilities in the country.

Kilkenny For a bit of family comfort, the **Glendine Inn** (+353 (0)56-21069) on the Castlecomber Road in Kilkenny City is a good spot to stay, with many fine restaurants within walking distance. **Springhill Court Hotel** (+353 (0)56-21122) is just a 10-minute walk from the heart of the medieval city, which has more than its fair share of brilliant pubs. **The Hotel Kilkenny** (+353 (0)56-62000) is a well-located hotel within walking distance of Kilkenny Castle and is a good base for the numerous courses in this part of the Midlands. **Mount Juliet Hotel** (+353 (0)56-73000) in Thomastown is one of Ireland's premier hotels and offers residents a wide range of activities, including golf, horse riding, shooting, archery and fly fishing.

Tipperary **Dundrum House Hotel** (+353 (0)62-71116) in Dundrum is close to Cashel and incorporates an 18th-century manor with a Philip Walton-designed championship golf course. **Cashel Palace Hotel** (+353 (0)62-61521) is in the heart of the historic old town of Cashel, within walking distance of the Rock of Cashel.

Offaly The **County Arms Hotel** (+353 (0)509-20791) in Birr, set in its own landscaped gardens, is within striking distance of some fine golf courses. **Kinnity Castle** (+353 (0)509-37318) near Birr is sublime; the gothic revival mansion is nestled in the foothills of the Slieve Bloom mountains and has 37 bedrooms, many with four-poster beds.

Westmeath **Crookedwood House** (+353 (0)44-72165) in Mullingar is a former parish rectory. **Mearescourt House** (+353 (0)44-55112) is a Georgian mansion set in parkland; the grounds feature many rare trees and plants.

Where to Eat
Kildare **Moyglare Manor Restaurant** (+353 (0)1-6286351) has excellent food with intimate, candlelit rooms and an exhaustive wine list.

Wicklow **Rathsallagh Country House** (+353 (0)45-403112) near the village of Dunlavin is one of the county's premier country houses.

Carlow **Ballykealey Country House and Restaurant** (+353 (0)503-59288) is approached by a winding road through beautiful woodlands and will transport you right back to the 1830s. The best part is the gothic restaurant, where fresh local produce is delivered to the table in sumptuous dishes. **Teach Dolmain** (+353 (0)503-30911) in Carlow Town is how all Irish pubs should be, with food and drink of the highest order.

Kilkenny The old-world charm of stone and timberwork sets the tone of comfort in the **Rising Sun** (+353 (0)51-898173) in Mullinavat, County Kilkenny. **Lacken House** (+353 (0)56-61085) in Kilkenny City has been setting standards of the highest kind for many years, and it is still one of the best places for fine dining.

Westmeath **Wineport Lakeshore Restaurant** (+353 (0)902-85466) in Glasson is beautifully situated on the edge of the inner lakes of Lough Ree; diners can arrive by road or water. The chef specializes in simple preparation of local produce to enhance the natural flavours of the food, while also allowing space on the menu for the latest culinary trends. **Oscars** (+353 (0)44-44909) in the middle of Mullingar is famous for its Emperor burgers, served with fried onions and garlic sauce.

Meath **The Ground Floor Restaurant** (+353 (0)46-49688) in Kells is one of the top eating places in this heritage town, and serves excellent chargrilled steaks.

What to Do
Kildare Horses, especially racing breeds, are indubitably linked with the Irish. Nowhere is this more true than on the plains of the **Curragh** in County Kildare, the traditional home of flat horse racing in Ireland. The Irish Derby, the Irish 1000 and 2000 Guineas and the Irish Oaks are held here each summer. If you're lucky enough to be in the vicinity on race day, go along. You'll have a ball! Otherwise, the **National Stud**, 1 mile/1.6km outside Kildare Town, is worth a visit. Here, you can walk the equestrian compound, visit an equine museum and see some famous stallions. The admission fee also includes entry to the **Japanese Gardens**, which date from 1910 and apparently represent a person's journey through life. While you are in the area you might also wish to see a fine example of a round tower, adjacent to St Brigid's Cathedral in Kildare Town.

Laois The magnificient neo-classical house at **Emo Court and Gardens** is one of the most stunning pieces of architecture to be found in the Midlands. The **Abbeyleix Heritage Centre** details the history of the area and also exhibits the Turkish-style carpets woven in the town in the early 1900s.

Kilkenny As castles go, **Kilkenny Castle** is a splendid and imposing building. The castle has been occupied for over 700 years and retains the lines of the medieval fortress that it was constructed to be. A number of paintings by van Dyck and Lely and four Gobelin tapestries designed by Rubens adorn its walls. **Jerpoint Abbey** in nearby Thomastown is arguably the most interesting and best-preserved Cistercian ruin in the country.

Tipperary Unquestionably the most imposing national monument in Ireland is the **Rock of Cashel** in Cashel, County Tipperary. Its history stretches back to the 4th century when it was the seat of Munster kings. Here in 978, Brian Boru was made High King of Ireland and declared it his capital. A fine 12th-century Romanesque chapel still stands on the limestone outcrop. The **Bolton Library** in Cashel contains the smallest book in the world and some silver altarpieces from the Rock's original cathedral.

Offaly At one time, for 70 years in fact, **Birr Castle** in County Offaly was home to the largest telescope in the world. Bigger telescopes have since taken over, but the historic telescope can still be admired in the castle. The opportunity to wander through the castle's magnificent gardens also shouldn't be missed. Further along the River

County Kildare is the home of horse racing and breeding in Ireland. This is a race meeting at Punchestown.

Shannon, and close to the centre of Ireland, is **Clonmacnoise**, one of the finest monastic sites in Ireland. For over 1,000 years, Clonmacnoise was a religious centre famed for its literary and artistic activity. The Vikings and later the Anglo-Normans carried out successive plundering raids and sadly all that remains now are the ruins of a cathedral, eight churches, two round towers, three high crosses, 200 grave-slabs and a 13th-century ringfort.

Westmeath Athlone Castle and Visitor Centre incorporates an audio-visual presentation of the flora and fauna and power resources of the Shannon, Ireland's longest river.

Tourist Information Centres

County Kildare Failte Office, Main St, Naas, County Kildare (+353 (0)45-898887)

Kilkenny Information Office, Shee Alms House, Rose Inn Street, Kilkenny City (+353 (0)56-51500)

Cashel Information Office, Main Street, Cashel (+353 (0)62-61333)

Birr Information Office, Castle Street, Birr, County Offaly (+353 (0)509-2011)

Clonmacnoise Information Office, Clonmacnoise, County Offaly (+353 (0)905-74134)

Athlone Tourist Office, Athlone Castle, County Westmeath (+353 (0)902-94630)

Mullingar Tourist Office, Market Square, Mullingar, County Westmeath (+353 (0)44-48650)

Kells Tourist Office, Headfort Place, Kells, County Meath (+353 (0)46-49336)

Chapter 7

The North-West & Causeway Coast

This wild, rugged and beautiful land has some of the most remote and isolated spots in Ireland. Yet, perhaps because it is a great place to get away from everything, it has also contrived to fashion itself into a sort of golfer's paradise, offering some of the finest links courses with some of the most spectacular scenery that you will ever see.

When Nick Faldo visited Ballyliffin – the northernmost course in the country, sited close to Malin Head in County Donegal – he fell so much in love with the place that he offered to buy it. Although they were deeply flattered, the club's members politely declined his offer.

Ballyliffin, which boasts two courses, the Old and Glashedy links, was once a

hidden gem. Since its discovery, however, it has earned a reputation as one of the toughest tests of links golf in the world. Despite its remoteness, it is now very much on the tourist trail. The Inishowen 100 is the northern equivalent of the Ring of Kerry, for both home-based golfers and golfers visiting from abroad.

Donegal, which has to be the ultimate destination for anyone heading to the north-west, has numerous other courses to delight and torment in equal measure. In many ways, this is golf in its most natural state – invariably, there is a howling wind coming in off the North Atlantic and, as it should be on links terrain, if you miss either the fairway or the green then you are liable to pay a heavy penalty. Make sure there are plenty of golf balls zipped into your bag!

Donegal also boasts Glenveagh National Park. Covering nearly 25,000

Left: The seemingly snow-like quartzite peak of Mount Errigal, in County Donegal. Above: The Carrick-a-Rede rope bridge on the Causeway Coast.

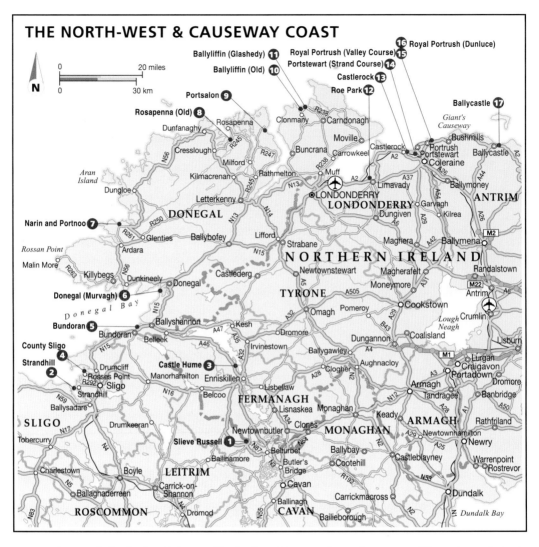

THE NORTH-WEST & CAUSEWAY COAST

acres, the park includes Mount Errigal, which is often referred to as a miniature Fujiyama because of its conical quartzite peak. On the edge of the park is Lough Gartan, which is claimed to be the birthplace of St Comcille (in AD521) and is marked by a huge cross. Close to this you will find the Flagstone of Loneliness. If you lie on the Flagstone, so tradition tells us, all your sorrows and troubles will disappear.

Separated by a border and by Lough Foyle, a famous golf course lies just 25 miles/40km to the east of County

Donegal as the crow flies, though it is more like 80 miles/128km by road through Derry City. Royal Portrush, on the north Antrim coast in Northern Ireland, played host to the 1951 British Open and, given the quality of the course, would surely have hosted many more if only the infrastructure were in place to support such a major championship.

This is a truly great course, ideally situated near to the Bushmills distillery, the oldest licensed distillery in the world. Just a little further along the coast is the awesome sight of the Giant's Causeway, which mythology tells us was used by Fionn MacCumhaill as stepping-stones to the Island of Staffa, where a particular female giant lived.

The Dunluce championship course at Royal Portrush is consistently rated in the top 15 courses in the world by *Golf* magazine, and anyone who has played the course will understand why. It places a premium on length and accuracy, and the rough – often knee high – heavily penalizes waywardness.

The north Antrim coast is littered with some fine links courses – Portstewart, Castlerock and Ballycastle – but anyone who is really serious about their golf should ensure that Royal Portrush is listed on their play list at least once in their lifetime. It is also worth having a look at Dunluce Castle, which is open to the public from April to September.

Planning an Itinerary

The sequence of courses in this chapter starts inland in County Cavan and works its way over to the coast, taking in the magnificent links courses of Sligo, Donegal and north Antrim. To reach the area, one option is to fly into the regional airport at Derry, which has greatly improved accessibility, and use a hire car for your journeys. The road network in Donegal has improved in recent years, but there are still many twisting roads, so make sure you leave plenty of time for your journey so that you can meet your tee times.

The recent arrival of a car ferry, that links the Inishowen peninsula with the Causeway Coast, cuts one and a half hours off the road journey between Ballyliffin and Portrush. It could well prove to be a very popular ferry journey.

THE GIANT'S CAUSEWAY

'When the world was moulded and fashioned out of formless chaos, this must have been the bit over – a remnant of chaos.' William Makepeace Thackeray

Thackeray's view of how the Giant's Causeway came into being is probably close to the truth – that it is a geological freak, caused by volcanic eruptions and cooling lava. But Irish legend would have you believe a more romantic version.

The real story is that it was the work of Fionn MacCumhaill, the Ulster warrior and commander of the King of Ireland's armies. Fionn fell in love with a lady giant on Staffa, an island in the Hebrides, and he built this highway of stones to bring her back to Ulster... and so was created the Giant's Causeway.

It could be true, for Fionn was capable of amazing feats of strength and could pick thorns from his heels while running. Once, during a fight with a Scottish giant, he scooped up a huge clod of earth and flung it at his rival. The earth fell into the sea, and became the Isle of Man. The hole it left filled up with water and became Lough Neagh, Ireland's largest lake. Well, that's what they say – believe it, or not!

1 Slieve Russell

Slieve Russell Hotel and Golf Resort, Ballyconnell, County Cavan
TEL: *+353 (0)49-9526444*
FAX: *+353 (0)49-9526474*
EMAIL: *slieve-golf-club@quinnhotels.com*
WEBSITE: *www.quinnhotels.com*
LOCATION: *Leave the N3 at Belturbet and take the N87 road to Ballyconnell; the resort is 2 miles/3.2km north of the town*
COURSE: *18 holes, 7093yd/6449m, par 72, SSS 74*
GREEN FEES: *€€€€€*
FACILITIES: *Changing rooms and showers, full catering, bar, pro shop, tuition, practice area, buggy hire, trolley hire, on-site accommodation*
VISITORS: *Welcome – booking advisable*

The roads in north Cavan are narrow and twisting. No matter which direction you're coming from, north or south, the impact of turning a corner and suddenly seeing the magnificent edifice of the Slieve Russell Hotel by the roadside for the first time is a sight that almost beggars belief.

The Slieve Russell golf course, located just north of the town of Ballyconnell, is equally mesmerizing for golfers. Designed by Patrick Merrigan, the course – considered the centrepiece of the hotel's leisure amenities – uses the natural drumlins in the landscape to extremely good effect. There is also the matter of two large lakes, interlocked by a stream, which lurk menacingly throughout. All in all, there are a number of very good reasons why Slieve Russell has become one of the country's premier inland courses.

After a reasonably gentle opening hole, you only have to walk to the elevated 2nd tee box to know that a demanding round lies ahead. This is a par 4, 434-yd/395-m dogleg and it brings the first sign of water. With no room for error, the tee shot is crucial. Even if the first part of the test is passed, there is still the matter of a second shot over that ubiquitous stream to a raised green. From now on you're hooked, or at least you should

be, for Merrigan's design qualities are unsurpassed.

Each short hole is terrific, but the two 'beasts' down by the lake on the homeward run – the 12th and the 13th – are the two feature holes. The 12th is a long par 4 of 442yd/402m, with the lake on the left. Go too far right, though, and trees become a factor, while the approach shot to the green is made all the more difficult.

Then there is the 13th, known as Watergate, which has proven to be the downfall of many. The par 5 curls itself around Lough Rud, and this is not a time to be brave or stupid. Play sensibly, keep to the right (all the way down the fairway) and play it as a three-shotter to a green that protrudes into the lake.

2 Strandhill

Strandhill Golf Club, Strandhill, County Sligo
TEL: *+353 (0)71-68188* **FAX:** *+353 (0)71-68188*
EMAIL: *strandhillgc@eircom.net*
LOCATION: *5 miles/8km west of Sligo Town; the course is signposted off the R292*
COURSE: *18 holes, 6067yd/5516m, par 69, SSS 68*
GREEN FEES: *€€€*
FACILITIES: *Changing rooms and showers, full catering, bar, practice area, buggy hire, trolley hire*
VISITORS: *Welcome – booking advisable*

Located on the Sligo coastline and almost squeezed between two giants of the links – Enniscrone on one side and Rosses Point on the other – Strandhill could all too easily be overlooked. It shouldn't be. Although Strandhill is considerably shorter and less demanding than its more famous neighbours, it is a lovely little links, with many traditional nuances – a number of blind shots and greens that require precise iron play.

Strandhill is surrounded by nature. There is the imposing backdrop of Knocknarea Mountain (with Queen Méabh's Cairn on top) on virtually every hole. As you play the holes along the coast, the waves of the Atlantic Ocean crash onto the beach.

One of the nicest holes on the outward run is, statistically, also the easiest. The stroke index 18 5th hole has an elevated tee set high in the dunes and is a par 5 that is played to a sunken green.

The 7th is also a very attractive hole – a par 4 of 410yd/373m, it requires a long tee shot which will then leave you with a mid-to-high iron approach to a green that has a couple of hidden bunkers guarding it.

The most unique hole on the course is the 13th, known as The Valley. It is a potentially punishing hole with a green located between two large sand dunes; accuracy is vital off the tee and with the approach shot.

This course demands and deserves your full attention – and nowhere more so than on the finishing hole, a tough par 4 that doglegs right and leaves no room for error.

Although short by modern standards, Strandhill is classic links terrain with some outstanding holes.

 ## Castle Hume

Castle Hume Golf Club, Enniskillen, County Fermanagh
TEL: *+44 (0)28-6632 7077* **FAX:** *+44 (0)28-6632 7076*
LOCATION: *4 miles/6.5km from Enniskillen, off the Belleek Road*
COURSE: *18 holes, 6525yd/5932m, par 72, SSS 71*
GREEN FEES: *££*
FACILITIES: *Changing rooms and showers, full catering, bar, pro shop, practice area, buggy hire, trolley hire*
VISITORS: *Welcome – booking advisable*

There are few more captivating locations than the Castle Hume golf course, which lies on the banks of Lough Erne, not far from Fermanagh's principal town of Enniskillen.

With lakes and mature woodland all around, the course is situated within the grounds of the old Ely Estate and is a very enjoyable test of golf. There is water on nine holes, and over 7,000 trees and strategically placed bunkers make course management a critical part of play. The 15th, a par 3 of 152yd/139m, is the signature hole: the green protrudes into Castle Hume Lake with reeds literally brushing against the putting surface.

County Sligo

County Sligo Golf Club, Rosses Point, County Sligo
TEL: *+353 (0)71-77134* **FAX:** *+353 (0)71-77460*
EMAIL: *cosligo@iol.ie*
LOCATION: *5 miles/8km north-west of Sligo Town in Rosses Point*
COURSE: *27 holes, 6647yd/6043m, par 71, SSS 72*
GREEN FEES: €€€€€
FACILITIES: *Changing rooms and showers, full catering, bar, pro shop, tuition, practice area, buggy hire, trolley hire*
VISITORS: *Welcome, although restrictions apply, and it is essential to book in advance*

There's something about Rosses Point that tugs at the heartstrings. Its appeal lies with the people as much as the course, a links in the traditional out-and-back mode that is among the country's best.

When Bernhard Langer arrived here for his first ever round on a links course, he planned to stay for a day, but he apparently ended up staying for a fortnight. Legendary players such as Walter Hagen, Bobby Locke and Henry Cotton have all visited this course in their time to play beside the Atlantic Ocean under the imposing shadow of Ben Bulben.

Invariably, the course and the elements – it is rare to have a day when there is not a fresh-to-strong wind blowing in off the sea – make this a test for the very best. In the immortal words of Cecil Ewing, a former Walker Cup player and the club's most famous son, 'When the winds blow, the only hiding place is the clubhouse.' Those

words are as true today as when they were first uttered, but County Sligo is a links course in the finest tradition. It is an old-fashioned, out-and-back design – the handiwork of Harry Colt is evident in a redesign of the late 1920s – with a wide variety of holes.

The first time I ever played here was in a dreadful gale with rain and sleet pelting into my face. As I struggled up the 18th, a figure appeared in a long overcoat with a disintegrating newspaper as ineffectual protection for his head. It was 'The Squire', God rest his soul, a journalist colleague who had abandoned play much earlier only to realize, while nursing a pint at the bar counter and lampooning those who had stayed out, that he had left his pipe behind in one of the shelter huts. The weather isn't always so bad, though, and on a sunny day there is no better place on which to play golf.

From the start, Rosses Point demands the best out of a player. The 1st and 2nd holes are both played uphill. The 3rd, is a wonderful downhill par 5 – entitled The Metalman because the hole is in the same direction as a local landmark perched out in the estuary. It is a hole that attempts to give something back after a tough opening – though not too much.

From the 5th onwards, play is in the lower part of the course, where a further nine holes have been developed in wetlands known as Bowmore. Throughout this part of the course, no two holes are the same, although an accompanying ditch becomes a familiar hazard on a number of them. The 9th is the second par 3, called Cast a Cold Eye, in honour of the poet W. B. Yeats, who is buried in Drumcliffe cemetery across the bay.

The four holes on this particular part of the course (with the looming presence of Ben Bulben becoming closer than ever) are particularly scenic, but they do require good course management. Yet once you tee-up on the 13th and hit from the elevated tee to the green below, the battle is on in earnest with only the 16th hole possibly allowing any breathing space.

The run back up along the beach is demanding, but it seems easy when faced with the prospect of driving off the 17th, a par 4 of 455yd/414m that demands a long and accurate drive. Then, the approach shot (hopefully!) is played to a raised and tilted green that is perched midway up a ridge that physically divides the course into two distinct sections. The 17th is surely one of the great holes in current Irish golf, and Rosses Point is certainly one of the great courses.

The imposing presence of 'Bare Ben Bulben's head', as the poet W. B. Yeats put it, is everywhere at Rosses Point.

5 Bundoran

Bundoran Golf Club, Bundoran, County Donegal
TEL: *+353 (0)72-41302* **FAX:** *+353 (0)72-42014*
LOCATION: *25 miles/40km north of Sligo, off the N15 coast road*
COURSE: *18 holes, 6256yd/5688m, par 70, SSS 70*
GREEN FEES: *€€€*
FACILITIES: *Changing rooms and showers, full catering, bar, shop, practice area, buggy hire, trolley hire, on-site accommodation*
VISITORS: *Welcome – restrictions on Sundays*

Harry Vardon had a part to play in Bundoran's design, which is a pretty sound reason to play the course. Another good reason for visiting is the four-star hotel that lies in the course's midst, surrounded by a mixture of links and parkland. It is an ideal base for exploring Donegal and even Rosses Point, which is only half an hour's drive away in County Sligo.

The course has a lovely setting, lying right by the North Atlantic. The wind is nearly always a factor, and there are guaranteed to be people surfing the breakers on a stretch of beach that has waves comparable to those in Hawaii and Sydney.

This is not a long course by modern standards, but the shortest courses are not always the easiest. With only two par 5s, there aren't many genuine opportunities to get back at the card.

There are some very tough holes, too. The 8th, for instance, requires a drive to the left-hand side of the fairway for the green to be threatened, although at least the view will provide some consolation if the golf is not going well. The 10th, with the first part uphill, is a difficult par 4 (measuring 403yd/367m) that again must see the drive favour the left-hand side. The 13th is a par 3 of 235yd/214m. Although there is no trouble in front, don't miss the green on the left, as it is almost impossible to get up and down from that side.

6 Donegal (Murvagh)

Donegal Golf Club, Murvagh, County Donegal
TEL: *+353 (0)73-34054* **FAX:** *+353 (0)73-34377*
EMAIL: *info@donegalgolfclub.ie*
WEBSITE: *www.donegalgolfclub.ie*
LOCATION: *6 miles/9.5km south of Donegal Town, on the N15*
COURSE: *18 holes, 7213yd/6557m, par 73, SSS 73*
GREEN FEES: *€€€€*
FACILITIES: *Changing rooms and showers, full catering, bar, pro shop, tuition, practice area, buggy hire, trolley hire*
VISITORS: *Welcome – book in advance*

Donegal's reputation is akin to that of a murderous brute, and it is certainly one of the most difficult courses in the country. It is long, and it is hard. The wind seems to blow all the time, and the greens are hard to hold. Nonetheless, the links at Murvagh – on a headland that is reached through a national forest and has the stunning Blue Stack Mountains for a backdrop – shouldn't, under any circumstances, be left off anyone's golfing itinerary.

Lying as it does in Donegal Bay, on a peninsula with the pretty village of Mount Charles across the water, Murvagh occupies a most splendid site for a golf course. The elements, gales and thunderous waves coming in off the Atlantic Ocean have not always been kind to the course, and the battle against coastal erosion is on-going. Yet it remains a wonderful, if testing, experience to go up against a links that has the capacity to bite you at any time.

This hits you as early as the 5th hole, a par 3 of 187yd/170m. The hole is known as the Valley of Tears, with just cause, for the tee shot from an elevated tee box to a plateau green is fraught with danger. There is rough in between the tee and green, and bunkers around the putting surface ready to gobble up any loosely hit shot. Later on in the round, the 16th, which measures 229yd/209m, is even more intimidating, if that is possible.

In between, there are some mighty par 4s and 5s. The sequence from the 6th to the 9th through the dunes is especially noteworthy, with the 8th measuring all of 548yd/499m; this is a test that will appeal to low-handicap players especially. However, the use of forward tees, as is the norm for visitors, eases the overall difficulty. By the time you return to the 19th, you'll be guaranteed a warm welcome and the opportunity to look out of the new clubhouse's windows at other poor souls trying to conquer the unconquerable.

Pat Ruddy recently redesigned six of the holes and the overall result has been to make the links even more imposing.

7 *Narin and Portnoo*

Narin and Portnoo Golf Club, Narin, County Donegal
TEL: *+353 (0)75-45107* **FAX:** *+353 (0)75-45107*
EMAIL: *portnoo@globalgolf.com*
WEBSITE: *www.globalgolf.com/portnoo*
LOCATION: *6 miles/9.5km north of Ardara, off the R261*
COURSE: *18 holes, 5854yd/5322m, par 69, SSS 68*
GREEN FEES: *€€*
FACILITIES: *Changing rooms and showers, full catering, bar, practice area, buggy hire, trolley hire*
VISITORS: *Welcome – advance booking is advisable at weekends*

The strong winds, and rough and fearsome bunkers, make Donegal a true challenge of links golf.

To find what is arguably the wildest links terrain in either Ireland or Britain, you must travel out to Narin and Portnoo golf course. The course, overlooking Gweebara Bay, has remained blissfully untouched by modern machinery or techniques.

Similar in many respects to the classic links layout at Prestwick in Scotland, Narin and Portnoo is a magical journey from one hole to another. Once you leave the 6th green, you head into hilly linksland at the most exposed part of the course, and it is a sheer joy. The 7th is short in length, a par 4 of 350yd/319m, but is played uphill to a green perched on the side of a ledge. The hole demands an accurate approach, as the left-to-right sweeping land guides any mishit shot into trouble.

The 10th is one of the most natural par 4s in links golf, and a flat lie on the undulating fairway is almost impossible to find. As if to justify Narin and Portnoo's reputation as a true links, the closing hole is yet another short par 4. As ever, the best philosophy is to use course management and keep the ball in play, rather than to go for a wild swing off the tee.

🏌️ 8 *Rosapenna (Old)*

Rosapenna Hotel and Golf Links, Downings, County Donegal
TEL: *+353 (0)74-55301* **FAX:** *+353 (0)74-26043*
LOCATION: *25 miles/40km north of Letterkenny; take the R245 to Carrigart, then the R248 for 1 mile/ 1.6km towards Downings*
COURSE: *36 holes (2 courses), Old: 6307yd/5734m par 70, SSS 71*
GREEN FEES: *€€€*
FACILITIES: *Changing rooms and showers, full catering, bar, shop, practice area, buggy hire, trolley hire, on-site accommodation*
VISITORS: *Welcome – booking advisable*

It is said that Old Tom Morris could scarcely believe his eyes when, on a short break in Donegal, he literally stumbled across the dunes at Rosapenna. Indeed, the linksland was so pure and natural that he felt it necessary to build only three of the 18 greens; the other 15, created by nature, were left as they were.

Rosapenna Old Course was reshaped in 1906 by two other golfing greats – James Braid and Harry Vardon – who added length

Some of the most natural linksland in the world can be found at Rosapenna.

and detailed bunkering before Eddie Hackett and Pat Ruddy made some final touches in 1993 and 2001 respectively. Rosapenna's appeal has been increased by the development of a second links, also designed by Ruddy.

The 1st hole is a short dogleg, but then the course opens up into spectacular links terrain. From the elevated tee box on the 2nd, you have a superb view of Sheephaven Bay. So begins a charming sequence of holes that takes you along the coastline. The 3rd is a long par 4 beside the shore. The 5th is a short par 4 that is almost driveable, and the 6th – a par 3 of 173yd/158m – could easily claim to be one of the best short holes in the British Isles. You are required to hit a tee shot across wild duneland to an elevated green and, depending on the wind, the club in your hand could range from a nine-iron to a seven-wood. The 7th is a classic par 4 of 374yd/340m, and the new tee back in the dunes gives the tee shot a tunnel-like effect.

So it continues until you leave the coast and head inland from the 11th. Though this stretch of finishing holes is less interesting, it is every bit as challenging, as it is played on a hilly section of the course.

9 Portsalon

Portsalon Golf Club, Fanad, County Donegal
TEL: +353 (0)71 59459 **FAX:** +353 (0)74-59459
LOCATION: *20 miles/32km north of Letterkenny*
COURSE: *18 holes, 5913yd/5376m, par 69, SSS 68*
GREEN FEES: €€€
FACILITIES: *Changing rooms and showers, full catering, bar, practice area, buggy hire, trolley hire*
VISITORS: *Welcome*

Many people believe that the beach that adjoins Portsalon, an inescapable part of the place's magical appeal, is among the very best in the world. The course itself, one of the oldest in the country, also has a good deal going for it. Its greens have recently been remodelled, without altering its essential character, and the links should be even better when some upgrading, designed to make it safer and longer, is completed.

Located on the north-west shore of Lough Swilly and overlooking the magnificent Ballymastocker Bay, Portsalon holds many attractions for the visiting golfer. There are two terrific par 4s on the homeward run: the 13th, known as the Matterhorn, has a view off the tee box that takes in the harbour. An awesome par 4 of 433yd/394m, it is probably the most testing drive in the north-west; if the shot isn't perfectly struck to the left of centre, over the rock that gives the hole its name, then it will find the gully on the right.

The 15th, a par 4 that swings inland, demands a very good drive followed by an approach that must carry a dyke to find the green. While these two holes on the homeward stretch capture the essence of true links golf, the course has been considerably toughened by the transformation of 11 holes by the golf architect Pat Ruddy. The ambience of Portsalon has been retained, however, and the island tee at the 6th hole offers a clear example of the unique character that can be found on this often wind-blown links terrain.

10 Ballyliffin (Old)

Ballyliffin Golf Club, Ballyliffin, Inishowen, County Donegal
TEL: +353 (0)77-76119 **FAX:** +353 (0)77-76672
EMAIL: *ballyliffingolfclub@eircom.ie*
WEBSITE: *www.ballyliffingolfclub.com*
LOCATION: *6 miles/9.5km from Carndonagh, on the R238*
COURSE: *18 holes, 6612yd/6011m, par 71, SSS 72*
GREEN FEES: €€€
FACILITIES: *Changing rooms and showers, full catering, bar, shop, practice area, buggy hire, trolley hire*
VISITORS: *Welcome – booking advisable*

Golf's inventor would surely approve of the fairways that can be found on the Old Course at Ballyliffin, located at Ireland's northernmost tip. It's a links course in the old tradition, with the fairways created by Mother Nature, tumbling first one way and then another, with no chance of getting an unimpeded lie. However, the course oozes character and charm, and anyone who plays here remembers it fondly. Nick Faldo, for one, called it 'the most natural course ever,' and there is a lot of truth in that.

Ballyliffin's Old Course is truly magical, with the rippling fairways – set amidst dunes and with the sea never far away – playing tricks on you at every opportunity.

The holes are tough, yet fair. The 2nd is a par 4, measuring 432yd/393m, that moves uphill to a green surrounded by dunes and gives a very early taste of the fine golf that awaits.

You don't have to wait too long to reach the 5th – called The Tank – which is a fantastic par 3. The green is perched between two sandhills, and only a perfectly struck tee shot will find it some 176yd/160m away.

It once took an hour-and-a-half-long car drive to reach Portrush from Ballyliffin. However, the advent of a new ferry service from Greencastle in County Donegal to Magilligan Point in County Derry has now cut this journey in half.

11 Ballyliffin (Glashedy)

Ballyliffin Golf Club, Ballyliffin, Inishowen, County Donegal
TEL: *+353 (0)77-76119* **FAX:** *+353 (0)77-76672*
EMAIL: *ballyliffingolfclub@eircom.ie*
WEBSITE: *www.ballyliffingolfclub.com*
LOCATION: *6 miles/9.5km from Carndonagh, on the R238*
COURSE: *18 holes, 7135yd/6487m, par 72, SSS 74*
GREEN FEES: *€€€€*
FACILITIES: *Changing rooms and showers, full catering, bar, shop, practice area, buggy hire, trolley hire*
VISITORS: *Welcome – booking advisable*

BALLYLIFFIN GLASHEDY							
HOLE	YD	M	PAR	HOLE	YD	M	PAR
1	426	387	4	10	397	361	4
2	432	393	4	11	419	381	4
3	428	389	4	12	448	408	4
4	479	435	5	13	572	520	5
5	177	161	3	14	183	167	3
6	361	328	4	15	440	400	4
7	183	166	3	16	426	387	4
8	422	384	4	17	549	99	5
9	382	347	4	18	411	374	4
OUT	3290	2990	35	IN	3845	3497	37

7135YD • 6487M • PAR 72

For many years, golf was an alien sport to the people of Ballyliffin, which is situated near Malin Head on the Inishowen Peninsula. It wasn't until after the Second World War that a crude 9-hole course was laid out on poor ground close to the village.

How times have changed. Now Ballyliffin has two prized courses: the Old, so called simply because it was the first, and the Glashedy, named after the Glashedy Rock that sits imposingly out in the Atlantic Ocean, not far from the links.

The Glashedy course only opened for play in August 1995, but already it has taken its rightful place among the great links courses of the world. It was designed by Pat Ruddy, owner and designer of The European Club in County Wicklow, and Tom Craddock, one of Ireland's finest amateur golfers. Between them, they have created a masterpiece; the course enjoys a stunning location and has no obvious weakness.

Unlike the Old Course, with its rippling effect fairways, the Glashedy fairways are flatter and flow along natural valleys through the dunes. The course throws out a challenge from the very first tee shot – a par 4 of 426yd/387m – followed by two even longer par 4s.

This is a technical player's links. You need to know how to play the ball low, into and with the wind, and how to shape shots and to draw and fade. You need to be able to play bump-and-run shots when the occasion requires, and to putt over undulating and tiered greens.

Take one glance at Glashedy Rock from the links on the 4th and it becomes your companion for the rest of the round. The first of the par 3s is the 5th, and it's stunning. The Rock dominates the backdrop to the green, and it is only too easy to lose concentration and discover that your next action is to climb into one of the deep bunkers that practically encircle the green.

The 7th is another super shot hole, where you play from an elevated tee to a green far below with a lake on the right and pot bunkers left. Again, there is no room for error here.

If anything, the second nine is even tougher than the front. There is a wonderful run of holes, from the par 4 12th, a sharp dogleg right and a whopping 448yd/408m. The challenge doesn't abate until it is time to take the ball out of the tin cup on the 18th for a last time and look wistfully back down the fairway, probably wishing you could do it all over again.

Glashedy is one of the world's great links courses – this is the 7th, a par 3 of 183yd/166m played from an elevated tee past an inviting lake on the right.

Roe Park

Radisson Roe Park Hotel and Golf Resort, Limavady, County Derry
TEL: *+44 (0)28-77760105*
FAX: *+44 (0)28-77760105*
EMAIL: *reservation@radisson.nireland.com*
LOCATION: *1 mile/1.6km west of Limavady, off the B192*
COURSE: *18 holes, 6318yd/5744m, par 70, SSS 71*
GREEN FEES: *££*
FACILITIES: *Changing rooms and showers, full catering, bar, pro shop, golf academy, practice area, buggy hire, trolley hire, on-site accommodation*
VISITORS: *Welcome – booking advisable*

Roe Park, an inland course set in a historic riverside estate on the edge of Limavady, has had the benefit of some words of wisdom from one of the USA's leading designers. During the British Seniors' Open, which was held at Royal Portrush in 1996, Ed Seay, design partner to Arnold Palmer, was staying at the five-star hotel and offered valuable help in course presentation.

Overlooking the River Roe and Lough Foyle, the golf course is a very nice parkland layout that takes full advantage of the large number of mature trees on the estate. Among the feature holes is the 6th, a par 3 of 144yd/131m, which rises to an elevated green beside a walled garden.

The 15th is an interesting par 4. Although it measures a mere 272yd/250m, the major deterrent for anyone considering going for the green is that there is a carry of almost 250yd/227m over water. Safety and astute course management normally decree skirting the water to find the fairway with an iron off the tee and then a short iron approach.

As if to emphasize the variety of finishing holes, this short par 4 is followed by a par 5 that offers the prospect of getting something back from the course and, then, two of the toughest holes on the course, a long par 3 17th, often requiring a fairway-wood off the tee, and a long par 4 finishing hole.

13 Castlerock

Castlerock Golf Club, Castlerock, County Derry
TEL: +44 (0)28-70848314
FAX: +44 (0)28-70848215
EMAIL: castlerock18@hotmail.com
LOCATION: 6 miles/9.5km west of Coleraine, off the A2
COURSE: 27 holes, 6687yd/6080m, par 73, SSS 72
GREEN FEES: ££££
FACILITIES: Changing rooms and showers, full catering, bar, pro shop, tuition, practice area, buggy hire, trolley hire
VISITORS: Welcome – essential to book in advance

Castlerock is a gem of a links, sandwiched between the mouth of the Bann and the Derry–Belfast railway line, and in an area on the Derry coastline that is steeped in history. The sand dunes through which part of the course runs were inhabited during the Neolithic and early Bronze Ages, and the links is protected under the Historic Monuments Act of Northern Ireland.

Some famous hands were also involved in the golf course's design. Ben Sayers originally upgraded the course from nine holes to 18 in 1909, and Harry Colt and Eddie Hackett, in the 1930s and 1970s respectively, also contributed their ingenuity. The result is a course, with another nine holes in the dunes, that is considered a classic links and a test for the best – as was discovered in the 2001 Irish PGA Championship staged here and won by Des Smyth.

The course is long, and longer when the wind blows hard, and has an interesting start beside the railway line. Indeed, the 4th hole, a par 3 of 200yd/182m and known as The Leg O' Mutton, is a classic short hole protected on the right by the railway line, a stream on the left and a number of bunkers for good measure.

The 7th, called The Armchair because the plateau green sits into the sandhills, is an extremely demanding par 4, where the number of bunkers is sure to make you think twice about your strategy.

14 Portstewart (Strand Course)

Portstewart Golf Club, Portstewart, County Derry
TEL: +44 (0)28-70832015 **FAX:** +44 (0)28-70834097
EMAIL: bill@portstewartgc.co.uk
WEBSITE: www.portstewartgc.co.uk
LOCATION: 4 miles/6.4km west of Portrush
COURSE: 54 holes (3 courses), Strand: 6817yd/6198m, par 72, SSS 73
GREEN FEES: ££££££+
FACILITIES: Changing rooms and showers, full catering, bar, pro shop, practice area, club hire, buggy hire, trolley hire
VISITORS: Welcome – restrictions at weekends

The first time any golfer stands on the first elevated tee box on the championship course at Portstewart, they can't help but survey the landscape with appreciation. Strangely, the same thing happens again on the second occasion, and on the third, and on the fourth… For each time, the sight of the sea and beach to the right and the fairway far below is always wondrous to behold.

Portstewart's 1st hole has been called 'the best opening hole in the world'. Though it is an intimidating first shot, it is also inviting. Even if you do get away with a good drive, the approach to the green must be shaped over or around a giant dune.

After such a dramatic opening hole, there is a sense that whatever follows must be a let-down. Fortunately, that is not the case; the course winds its way through majestic dunes, and each hole manages to hold your interest and earn your respect.

There is enormous variety in the holes, and the course, the No. 1 of three courses, is always in magnificent condition. This has no doubt helped the club, along with its famous neighbour Royal Portrush, make this region a hotbed for golfing tourists.

Once you have negotiated a route back to the clubhouse, enjoy the atmosphere and look forward to the next time that you will stand on that 1st tee.

Royal Portrush
(Valley Course)

Royal Portrush Golf Club, Dunluce Road, Portrush, County Antrim
TEL: *+44 (0)28-70822311* **FAX.** *+44 (0)28 70823139*
EMAIL: *rpgc@dnet.co.uk*
WEBSITE *www.royalportrushgolfclub.com*
LOCATION: *1 mile/1.6km east of Portrush, on the Bushmills road*
COURSE: *18 holes, 6273yd/5702m, par 70, SSS 71*
GREEN FEES: *£££*
FACILITIES: *Changing rooms and showers, full catering, bar, pro shop, tuition, practice area, buggy hire, trolley hire*
VISITORS: *Welcome – booking advisable*

The second course at Royal Portrush Golf Club, the Valley Course, is more basic than its grand neighbour, the Dunluce course (see pages 156–7). Originally designed to facilitate lady club members, back in 1894, the quality of this course will still come as a surprise to many. Indeed, it is used annually as a qualifying course for the North of Ireland amateur championship. The Valley Course is located in a valley, as its names suggests, between dunes and close to the Atlantic Ocean, and has been created on terrain that is playable virtually all year round.

Though there are surprisingly few bunkers on the course and the greens are small, there are plenty of bushes, the fairways are relatively generous and there are sufficient holes to keep your attention.

Indeed, if this course were not situated in the shadow of the championship course at Dunluce (you can see a number of holes on the adjoining course from the 4th green on the Valley Course), then it would certainly be far better known. This is a course with huge appeal; once you've discovered it, you won't soon forget it.

Set in towering duneland on the Atlantic coast, much of the Valley Course at Royal Portrush is below sea level.

10 *Royal Portrush (Dunluce Course)*

Royal Portrush Golf Club, Dunluce Road, Portrush, County Antrim
TEL: *+44 (0)28-70822311* **FAX:** *+44 (0)28-70823139*
EMAIL: *rpgc@dnet.co.uk*
WEBSITE: *www.royalportrushgolfclub.com*
LOCATION: *1 mile/1.6km east of Portrush, on the Bushmills road*
COURSE: *18 holes, 6782yd/6170m, par 72, SSS 73*
GREEN FEES: *££££££+*
FACILITIES: *Changing rooms and showers, full catering, bar, shop, practice area, buggy hire, trolley hire*
VISITORS: *Welcome – booking essential*

ROYAL PORTRUSH DUNLUCE COURSE

HOLE	YD	M	PAR	HOLE	YD	M	PAR
1	389	354	4	10	480	436	5
2	497	452	5	11	166	151	3
3	159	146	3	12	395	359	4
4	455	414	4	13	371	338	4
5	384	350	4	14	213	194	3
6	193	175	3	15	366	333	4
7	432	393	4	16	432	393	4
8	376	342	4	17	517	470	5
9	476	433	5	18	481	437	5
OUT	3361	3059	36	IN	3421	3111	37

6782YD • 6170M • PAR 72

The lure of the Dunluce course at Royal Portrush is compelling. Situated on the dramatic Giant's Causeway coastline, just a good drive and long-iron away from one of Ireland's most popular seaside resorts, it is the most perfect links terrain that can possibly exist. It is the only Irish course ever to play host to the British Open, won here by Max Faulkner in 1951.

Harry Colt, who designed the course, considered it his masterpiece; nobody could object, for Dunluce is, indeed, a majestic piece of golfing land with few superiors anywhere in the world.

Unfortunately, Royal Portrush has been involved in an ongoing battle with coastal erosion, resulting in huge boulders being placed

down by the cliffs as a protective barrier against the sea. The good news is that the quality and appeal of the links endure.

From the time that you stand on the 1st tee, the sense of duty to perform – not to let yourself down when playing this course – is overwhelming. How could anyone not rise to the challenge?

The 1st is a tough hole, and the course gets harder thereafter. It is an uphill par 4 that brings you up into the dunes. There is out-of-bounds to the right and to the left, bunkers in front of the green and gorse behind it.

Don't be lulled into a false state of security by the relatively gentle 2nd hole. The view from the 3rd is inspiring, with Dunluce Castle and the White Rocks coastline catching your eye. By the time you reach the 5th green, that scenery is almost in play, as the green is perched virtually on the edge of the cliff.

There is no real let-up, even if the holes between the 8th and 13th allow you to draw your breath just a little, and the run for home is relentless once you walk onto the 14th tee box. This is one of the most famous par 3s in the world of golf – perhaps the most famous. It is called Calamity and never has a hole been better named. Though it measures 213yd/194m, length, on this occasion, is not the real issue. The route to the green lies over a chasm, and nothing other than the perfect shot will find the green. Bobby Locke's hollow offers a small bail out on the left, but anything mishit to the right will be next to unplayable and will finish up 50 feet/15m below the green.

The next hole is called Purgatory, maybe because there is some hope left yet. It is a par 4 that sweeps downhill, with dunes on the left. The 16th is the last of the truly great holes – a dogleg right par 4 of 432yd/393m with an out-of-bounds left – that is played to a relatively small green with bushes lying at the back.

From the start, the Dunluce course places a heavy emphasis on accuracy. The 1st is a par 4 of 389yd/354m.

Ballycastle

Ballycastle Golf Club, Ballycastle, County Antrim
TEL: *+44 (0)28-20762536*
FAX: *+44 (0)28-20762536*
LOCATION: *1 mile/1.6km east of Ballycastle, on the coast road*
COURSE: *18 holes, 5946yd/5406m, par 71, SSS 70*
GREEN FEES: *£££*
FACILITIES: *Changing rooms and showers, full catering, bar, pro shop, practice area, trolley hire*
VISITORS: *Welcome – booking advisable*

Ballycastle Golf Club has a place in history as one of the founding members of the Golfing Union of Ireland back in 1891. It also has a beautiful setting, nestling at the foot of Glenshesk with Rathlin Sound lapping up onto the coastline beneath.

The course offers a wild array of choices. There is parkland, links and heathland over cliffs and, on the front nine, six successive par 4s, all played over different types of terrain. The first five parkland holes are bounded by the Margy and Carey rivers. The 2nd is a fearsome hole, measuring just 339yd/309m, but with a drive that needs to be sublimely hit to carry the River Carey. From the 5th hole, there is a fine stretch of links along the coast to the 9th, which rises to an elevated green that has a sheer drop behind it to the shoreline far below.

The 10th is one of those lovely little holes that manages to captivate even the hard-hearted. It only measures 105yd/96m, but it lies across a chasm and has splendid views across the sea to Rathlin Island and its white cliffs. These views stay with you all the way along the high ground to the 17th, which offers panoramic views of Glenshesk and Ballycastle. This hole is a testing par 3 to a well-protected green.

Ballycastle is always in wonderfully good condition, and the 19th hole is undoubtedly one of the friendliest to be found in the whole of Northern Ireland.

REGIONAL DIRECTORY

Where to Stay

Cavan **The Slieve Russell Hotel** (+353 (0)49-9526474) is set in the heart of drumlins countryside and has excellent accommodation and golf.

Sligo **Coopershill House** (+353 (0)71-65108) in Riverstown is a fine example of a Georgian house and offers rooms with four-poster beds. **Yeats Country Hotel** (+353 (0)71-77211) is across the road from the County Sligo golf links and has its own modern leisure complex. **The Tower Hotel** (+353 (0)71-44000) in Sligo Town is a good base for exploring the courses on Sligo's coastline.

Fermanagh **Arch Tullyhona Farm Guesthouse** (+44 (0)28-6634 8452) in Florencecourt is an award-winning Grade A guest-house close to the Marble Arch caves. **The Killyhevlin Hotel** (+44 (0)28-6632 3481) is situated on the shores of Lough Erne, close to the historic town of Enniskillen.

Donegal **The Great Northern Hotel** (+353 (0) 72-41204) in Bundoran is located in the middle of its own cliff-top championship course. **Jackson's Hotel** (+353 (0)74-31021) in Ballybofey is a modern hotel set on the banks of the River Finn. **Kee's Hotel** (+353 (0)74-31018) is situated in the village of Stranorlar. It has two excellent restaurants and you can choose between fine French cuisine or the best of Ulster food! **Rosapenna Hotel** (+353 (0)74-55301) in Downings is situated beside the two championship courses and also offers a series of golf schools throughout the year. **The Inishowen Gateway Hotel** (+353 (0)77-61144) in Buncrana is a very fine base from which to explore the northernmost courses in Ireland. Away from the hotel scene, **Donegal Thatched Cottages** (+353 (0)71-77197) at Cruit Island, Kincasslagh, offers thatched roofs, roaring turf fires and the unique course at Cruit Island for your golfing needs.

Derry **Beech Hill Country House Hotel** (+44 (0)28-7134 9279) is set in 32 acres of tranquil woodlands. **Everglades Hotel** (+44 (0)28-7134 6722) on the outskirts of Derry City is situated on the banks of the River Foyle; courses in the vicinity are City of Derry, Roe Park, North-West and Castlerock. **Radisson Roe Park** (+44 (0)28-7772 2212) in Limavady is a luxury development with its own championship course.

Antrim **Magherabuoy House Hotel** (+44 (0)28-7082 3507) in Portrush overlooks the splendour of the Causeway Coast. **Marine Hotel** (+44 (0)28-2076 2222) in Ballycastle is located on the seafront.

Where to Eat

Cavan **The Mac Nean Bistro** (+353 (0)72-53022) in Blacklion is an award-winning family restaurant and a memorable dining experience.

Sligo **Cromlech Lodge** (+353 (0)71-65155) is set in a quiet hill overlooking Lough Arrow where Moira, the Irish Chef of the Year in 2000, will prepare a gastronomic delight for you.

Donegal **Rathmullan House** (+353 (0)74-58188) in Rathmullan, renowned for its good food, is set on the shores of Lough Swilly amid an award-winning garden; reservations advised. **St John's Country House and Restaurant** (+353 (0)77-60289 in Fahan, on the Inishowen peninsula, is an 18th-century house that uses the freshest Donegal produce – mountain lamb, fresh fish, home-cooked bread – and has a cosy bar with a turf fire. **St Ernan's House Hotel** (+353 (0)73-21065) in Donegal offers the finest tradition of Irish country home cooking.

Derry **Browns Bar and Bistro** (+44 (0)28-7134 5180) in Bonds Hill is a modern European-style bar and brasserie serving food in an atmosphere that is 'fun 'n' funky'. **Brown Trout Inn** (+44 (0)28-7086 8209) in Aghadowey, near Coleraine, overlooks the most magnificent oak tree; the upstairs restaurant is non-smoking – but there is more casual dining downstairs.

Antrim **Bushmills Inn Restaurant** (+44 (0)28-2073 2339) in Bushmills has turf fires, oil lamps and stripped pine in the public rooms, and an award-winning restaurant with intimate snugs. Make sure you try a glass of 25-year-old Bushmills malt whiskey from the hotel's private cask.

What to Do

Cavan Some of the best coarse-fishing waters can be found in the lakelands of **County Cavan**. **Killykeen Forest Park**, set around the lake and islands of Lough Oughter, has a different outdoor offering, with marked trails flanked by tall Norwegian spruce, ash, birch, oak, beech, sycamore and alder, as well as sites of great historical interest, including an Iron Age ringfort. You can take a two-hour boat trip on the **Ballyconnell–Ballinamore Canal**, which connects the River Shannon with Lough Erne.

Fermanagh **Belleek** is famous for its pottery and china and there is a visitors' centre in the factory where you can see the potters at work. There are guided tours of the **Marble Arch caves** on the Marlbank scenic loop, about 12 miles/19km from Enniskillen. **Devenish Island** on Lough Erne is famous for its 12th-century round tower and ruined Augustinian abbey. You need to take a short ferry ride to access the island.

Sligo The favourite sons of County Sligo are, unquestionably, poet W. B. Yeats and the painter Jack Yeats. **The Municipal Art Gallery** and **Yeats Memorial Museum** in Sligo Town house some of Jack's drawings and paintings and a

Carrick-a-Rede rope bridge spans a chasm 80 feet/24m above the sea across to a small island.

collection of Yeats family memorabilia. Yeats is buried in **Drumcliffe Church** and there is a visitor centre there to extol the virtues of the poet. For the more energetic, a walk – or should that be a climb? – up Knocknarea, otherwise known as **Queen Méabh's Grave**, can be attempted. The mount is 1,078 feet/329m high and has a cairn on its peak made up of 40,000 tons of rock placed here by Neolithic farmers. Legend has it that the warrior chief Méabh is buried here. More ancient monuments are to be found 3 miles/4.8km away

at the **Carrowmore Megalithic Cemetery**, one of the largest of its kind in western Europe.

Donegal A slight detour on the way into Donegal Town will bring you to **Lough Derg**. Here you will find St Patrick's Purgatory. Ireland's patron saint apparently spent 40 days praying and fasting on the island in the lake, and thousands of visitors come here each summer to continue the tradition of self-sacrifice and penance. Elsewhere in County Donegal, the welcome is far more jovial. Nowhere is this more so than in the village of **Kincasslagh**, home to the singer Daniel O'Donnell, who has been known to host tea parties. The singer Enya hails from the village of **Crolly**, where traditional music sessions are regularly held in the family pub. The **Donegal County Museum** is in Letterkenny. You may also wish to visit the **Glenveagh National Park** and **Glenveagh Castle**.

Derry To learn the story of the historic city of Derry, visit the museum in **O'Doherty's Tower**. **St Columb's Cathedral** was built in 1633 and stained glass depicts heroic scenes from the great siege of 1688–9. **The Earhart Centre and Wildlife Sanctuary** at Ballyarnet is a cottage exhibition on Amelia Earhart, the first woman to fly the Atlantic solo, and who landed in the field here in 1932.

Antrim Further along the coast, past the resort of Portrush, is the town of Bushmills. Here, the **Bushmills Distillery**, the world's oldest licensed distillery, offers guided tours. Though it was first officially used as a distillery in 1608, 13th-century records tell of soldiers being fortified with *uisce beatha*, the Irish for 'water of life'. It is possible to have what locals here call a 'wee snifter' in the 1608 Bar before moving a little further east along the coast to one of the most famous and distinctive landmarks in Ireland, the **Giant's Causeway**. The rope bridge at **Carrick-a-Rede** is not for the faint-hearted, swaying some 80 feet/24m above the sea, but a crossing will bring you to the salmon fishery on the small island.

Tourist Information Centres
Sligo Tourist Information Centre, Aras Reddan, Temple Street, Sligo Town (+353 (0)71-61201)
Donegal Tourist Information Centre, The Quay, Donegal Town (+353 (0)73-21148)
Fermanagh Information Centre, Wellington Road, Enniskillen (+44 (0)28-6632 3110)
Derry Information Centre, 44 Foyle Street, Derry City (+44 (0)28-7126 7284)
Giant's Causeway Centre, 44 Causeway Road, Bushmills (+44 (0)28-2073 1855)
Ballycastle Centre, Sheskburn House, 7 Mary Street, Ballycastle (+44 (0)28-2076 2024)

Chapter 8

Belfast & the Mournes

Belfast City, for all its troubles, is the most charming of cities. You can walk around Donegall Square, which is the city's hub, and be close to everything – shops, theatres and restaurants. Moreover, Belfast is only 100 miles/160km north of Dublin, just a two-hour drive away. Add to all this excellent inland courses, both on the outskirts of the city limits and a short drive away in north Down, and the attraction for visiting golfers is great.

Belfast is by far the biggest city in Northern Ireland; more than a third of the population of Northern Ireland lives here. In appearance at least, Belfast bears a strong resemblance to the industrial city of Glasgow, with which it shares so much of its culture.

Left: Belfast City Hall is built in Classical Renaissance style. Above: Early settlements at the Ulster History Park near Gortin Glen Forest Park in County Tyrone.

Much of the inner city is characterized by elegant Victorian buildings, far removed from the town's origins as a cluster of forts that were built in ancient times to guard a ford across the River Farset. The river now runs underground, beneath the High Street. The Farset and Lagan rivers form a valley that marks a geographical boundary between the basalt plateau of Antrim and the slate hills of Down.

The Crown Liquor Saloon – across from the Europa Hotel – acts as a magnet for visitors. It is located on the Golden Mile, so called because it boasts some of the best pubs and restaurants that you will find in any Irish city. As a rule, though, the cheaper restaurants can be found towards the city end, with some more expensive ones clustered around the BBC building in Bedford Street.

There are 11 parkland courses in the Belfast area, and many have been in existence since the early days of golf in this country. The two best courses lie near each other and just off the southern part of the M1; Malone and Belvoir (pronounced Beaver) Park are two of the finest inland courses in the country, the latter a design of the famed Harry Colt.

In either place, you can imagine yourself to be in a lush country estate, many miles from the hustle and bustle of a major city. Still, the city is present in some ways; every so often you catch a glimpse of the Harland and Wolff shipyard, one of Belfast's famous landmarks. The ill-fated *Titanic* was built there, and the city still maintains a strong shipbuilding tradition.

There are also some magnificent golf courses outside the city and along the north Down coast. You will find the Royal Belfast course in a tranquil setting

The Palm House at the Botanic Gardens in Belfast dates from 1839 and is well worth a visit.

overlooking Belfast Lough, and the area around Bangor has a share of golf courses that is disproportionate to its small size. This region is very popular with Belfast natives, who regularly make the short journey for a round of golf.

Unlike Dublin, Belfast doesn't have any links courses. Arguably the best course in the world is situated about an hour's drive from the city, however, down along the coast and skirting the Mournes. Royal County Down, set at the foot of the mountains made famous by the songwriter Percy French, is a course thrown down by nature and one that has captivated and enchanted members and visitors ever since.

County Down has more golf courses than any other county in Northern Ireland, each one more beautiful and challenging than the next. Even the area around the Mournes features a wide range of courses, from Clandeboye's 36 holes in

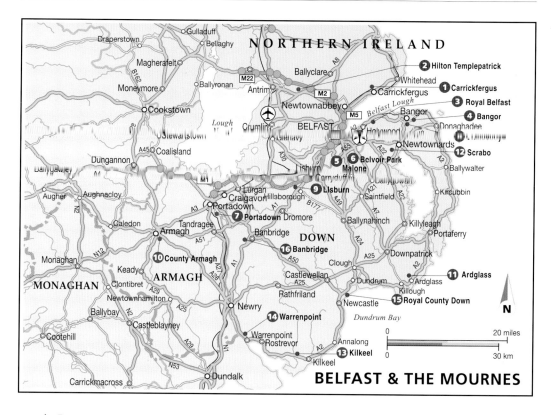

BELFAST & THE MOURNES

north Down to nine-hole courses such as Helen's Bay. Newcastle is the main attraction for golfers, however, and this has benefited many other courses in the vicinity. Kilkeel, for instance, which has perhaps been overlooked in the past, shared the qualifying stages for the British Amateur championship when it was held at Royal County Down, and word of its charms and challenge has since spread.

This area also has a strong association with St Patrick, Ireland's patron saint. When St Patrick was shipped to Ireland from Wales as a slave in AD432, the intention was to sail up the coast to County Antrim. His boat was driven through Strangford Lough, however, where he landed. Downpatrick's 12th-century Down Cathedral, which rises above the Quoile river, has St Patrick's grave in its grounds, and is a monument to the saint's great impact on Ireland.

Open-air cafés and bars testify to Belfast's newly discovered cosmopolitan tastes.

1 Carrickfergus

Carrickfergus Golf Club, Carrickfergus, County Antrim
TEL: *+44 (0)28-9336 3712*
FAX:: *+44 (0)28-9336 3023*
EMAIL: *carrickfergusgc@talk21.com*
LOCATION: *9 miles/14.5km north of Belfast, off the A2 on the outskirts of Carrickfergus*
COURSE: *18 holes, 6344yd/5768m, par 68, SSS 68*
GREEN FEES: *££*
FACILITIES: *Changing rooms and showers, full catering, bar, pro shop, practice area, trolley hire*
VISITORS: *Welcome – except Saturdays; booking is advised*

Carrickfergus Golf Club, set in the heart of this north Antrim town, is a green oasis. A relatively flat parkland course with plenty of mature trees, it is located in a well-developed area just off the North Road.

The course itself has matured nicely and offers a good test for players, especially on approach play into the greens. It is tight, so it pays to be accurate off the tees. At the very first tee box, you are introduced to a natural feature called The Dam, which is an old quarry filled with rocks and water. The opening drive on this 418-yd/380-m hole must clear the dam and then find a fairway that isn't entirely generous. The 6th hole, a par 4 of 426yd/388m, also brings the quarry into play, and you are required to play an approach to a green in a valley.

Former European Tour player David Jones has redesigned the greens on many of the back nine holes, adding undulations on the putting surfaces and building mounds around them. The 14th is a 200-yd/182-m par 3 with a shot to just such an undulating green, but it is the 16th – a classic short par 4 of only 340yd/310m – that will probably stay in the memory. It demands a precise approach shot over water to a green that slopes severely.

The course at Carrickfergus is extremely well maintained and is well worth a stop-off if you are in the region.

2 Hilton Templepatrick

Hilton Templepatrick Hotel and Golf Resort, Castle Upton Estate, Templepatrick, County Antrim
TEL: *+44 (0)28-9443 5510*
FAX: *+44 (0)28-9443 5510*
LOCATION: *Just off Junction 5, on the M2 motorway between Belfast and Antrim town*
COURSE: *18 holes, 7342yd/6675m, par 71, SSS 72*
GREEN FEES: *££££*
FACILITIES: *Changing rooms and showers, full catering, bar, pro shop, practice area, club hire, buggy hire, trolley hire, golf academy, on-site accommodation*
VISITORS: *Welcome – booking advisable*

Over a thousand years ago, so legend tells us, St Patrick blessed a well on what later became the Castle Upton Estate, located just off the M2 motorway, five minutes from Belfast International Airport and 20 minutes from Belfast City. This well, it is alleged, has never since run dry.

Somewhat appropriately, given the reliance that modern golf courses' place on proper irrigation, that blessed well is now sited on Hilton Templepatrick, a championship golf course that has been developed on the old estate. Designed by David Jones, a former European tour player, it measures 7342yd/6675m off the back stakes and has five sets of tees in operation, which make the course playable for all levels. A golfing academy, used by the Golfing Union of Ireland, is also located here.

The front nine is the more open part of the course, but the 3rd hole, a par 5 of 564yd/513m, does have the added difficulty of Neill's burn – a ditch – running along the left-hand side.

The holes on the homeward journey enjoy some spectacular settings; the 11th, in particular, is a par 3 with a line of poplar trees on the left and the river to the right. The 18th is a 444-yd/404-m hole that offers scope for those brave enough to carry bunkers and water. It has an alternative safe route to make the hole less treacherous but longer.

Royal Belfast

Royal Belfast Golf Club, Holywood, County Down
TEL: +44 (0)28-9042 8165 FAX: +44 (0)28-9042 1404 EMAIL: royalbelfastgc@btclick.com
LOCATION: 2 miles/3.2km east of Holywood, off the A2
COURSE: 18 holes, 6936yd/6300m, par 70, SSS 71
GREEN FEES: ££££
FACILITIES: Changing rooms and showers, full catering, bar, pro shop, practice area, club hire, buggy hire, trolley hire
VISITORS: Welcome – booking essential

As you would expect from the oldest established club in Ireland, Royal Belfast is an exclusive place, and anyone wishing to play here should definitely book in advance. Royal Belfast is well worth the forward planning, though, for it is an excellently maintained course.

Royal Belfast was designed by the illustrious Harry Colt. Built on Craigavad House and its demesne, on the shores of Belfast Lough, the course gently slopes down towards the water's edge and is a place of genuine beauty. Colt has made the most of the location: mature trees are complemented by the strategic placement of bunkers (there were once 365, one for every day of the year, but that number has been reduced considerably) and the greens have always been very tricky. The 9th and 10th holes down by the Lough are considered the feature holes, but this course is a tough par of 70 and extreme precision is required to avoid the well-positioned sand traps.

Bangor

Bangor Golf Club, Bangor, County Down
TEL: +44 (0)28-9127 0922
FAX: +44 (0)28-9145 3394
EMAIL: secretary@bangorgolfclub.co.uk
LOCATION: 1 mile/1.6km from the centre of Bangor, on the Donaghadee road
COURSE: 18 holes, 6410yd/5820m, par 71, SSS 71
GREEN FEES: £££
FACILITIES: Changing rooms and showers, full catering, bar, shop, practice area, buggy hire, trolley hire
VISITORS: Welcome – restrictions on Tuesdays and Saturdays; booking advised

Bangor golf course can hold its head high as, over the years, it has nurtured Ryder Cup players Norman Drew and David Feherty, as well as British amateur champion Garth McGimpsey.

A tree-lined inland course, with views over Ballyholme Bay, Bangor has undergone a series of improvements in fairway drainage and in the treatment of greens. Although not a physically demanding course, it has a number of testing holes. The 5th is a long par 4 of 473yd/430m that demands length and accuracy. On the homeward run, the best and toughest hole is probably the 15th, a par 4 of 415yd/377m, which requires accuracy both off the drive and on the approach to the green.

A course with many mature trees, Royal Belfast's parkland slopes gently down to Belfast Lough.

Malone

Malone Golf Club, Upper Malone Road, Dunmurry, Belfast BT17
TEL: *+44 (0)28-9061 2758* **FAX:** *+44 (0)28-9043 1394*
EMAIL: *manager@malonegolfclub.co.uk*
WEBSITE: *www.malone.guiclubs.com*
LOCATION: *2 miles/3.2km south-east of Junction 2, on the M1 motorway to Belfast*
COURSE: *27 holes, 6599yd/5999m, par 71, SSS 72*
GREEN FEES: *££££*
FACILITIES: *Changing rooms and showers, full catering, bar, pro shop, practice area, club hire, buggy hire, trolley hire*
VISITORS: *Welcome – Monday to Thursday; restrictions Fridays and weekends; booking essential*

Set in an old estate, its age reflected by the mature trees that play such a large part in the course's layout, Malone Golf Club should be included on any golfer's itinerary.

Despite its lack of length when compared to some of the newer parkland courses, it has enormous appeal, and there is a huge emphasis on course management throughout.

An indication of the high regard in which Malone is held by the decision-makers in Irish golf is its role as host to numerous professional tournaments and amateur championships through the years. Three years before he went on to win the British Open, Tony Jacklin won his first professional title here in 1966 when the course staged the Blaxnit Tournament.

The trees, along with over 40 strategically placed bunkers and water hazards, make this a course that demands your utmost attention. The huge 25-acre lake, which serves as a trout fishery for members of the local angling club, comes into play on the 15th, 16th and 18th holes.

The short 15th, a mere 132yd/120m, has been the ruin of many a potentially good card, as the green protrudes out into the lake and it takes an extremely precise shot to find the putting surface. The finishing hole requires a brave drive off the tee over water.

A 25-acre trout-filled lake forms the centrepiece to the beautiful Malone course.

Belvoir Park

Belvoir Park Golf Club, Newtownbreda, Belfast
BT8 7AN
TEL: +44 (0)28-9049 1693 **FAX:** +44 (0)28-9064 6113
LOCATION: 4 miles/6.5km south of Belfast City
Centre, off the Ormeau Road
COURSE: 18 holes, 6516yd/5921m, par 71, SSS 71
GREEN FEES: ££££
FACILITIES: Changing rooms and showers, full catering,
bar, pro shop, tuition, practice area, buggy hire, trolley hire
VISITORS: Welcome – booking essential

There are few better parkland courses within such easy striking distance of a major city. Belvoir Park is probably the premier course in the Belfast area. Although ongoing work has taken place to ensure it keeps its place amongst Irish golf's hierarchy, it still retains the charms of Harry Colt's original design from the 1920s.

Set in rolling parkland with thousands of mature trees to block out the city's traffic, Belvoir Park requires unfailing accuracy off the tee, for trees come into play time and time again. Still, the fairways are sufficiently wide to reward accurate driving, and it is not the end of the world to find yourself in one of the fairway bunkers.

Unlike many modern inland courses, which place a heavy emphasis on water hazards, there are no lakes, and only two ditches that may potentially cause duress.

Apart from the 3rd and 17th holes, Belvoir Park is not too hilly. The 16th is a formidable short hole of 204yd/185m; the 17th is a rather special par 4, measuring 449yd/408m, and located on undulating terrain. The last hole is a dogleg to the right, with the demands on an accurate tee shot if you are not to be blocked out by trees on the approach to the green.

The course is always in good condition, and when the Irish PGA was played here in 1995, the greens were found to be among the fastest in the country.

Portadown

Portadown Golf Club, Portadown, County Armagh
TEL: +44 (0)28-3835 5356
FAX: +44 (0)28-3839 1394
LOCATION: 2 miles/3.2km south-east of Portadown
COURSE: 18 holes, 6132yd/5575m, par 70, SSS 69
GREEN FEES: ££
FACILITIES: Changing rooms and showers, full catering,
bar, shop, practice area, trolley hire
VISITORS: Welcome – except Tuesdays or Saturdays;
booking advisable

There was a touch of destiny in Portadown Golf Club finally settling for good on its current location at Carrickblacker, on the outskirts of the town, in 1934. The club's home at its four previous sites – in Lisniskey, Drumcree, Seagoe and the Mahon – all had a familiar theme in that the River Bann came into play on each course. It is no surprise, then, to discover that the Bann is an integral part of the 18-hole stretch at Carrickblacker.

The 9th hole, measuring all of 497yd/451m, is actually played over the river, while both the 14th and 17th holes have the waterway as company all the way up the right-hand side.

The course itself is not long, but that doesn't lessen the stringent demands placed on the player. Although it starts off with two short par 4s, there are times when length is required to match the necessity for accuracy. Nowhere is this more true than on the 17th, a par 5 of 534yd/486m, which sets you up nicely for the finishing hole, a par 4 that is the longest on the course.

Anyone who plays to their handicap at Portadown can feel justly proud. The members of this welcoming club should feel proud, too. After many years spent jumping back and forth across the River Bann, they have finally found their spiritual home, and they now have a magnificent clubhouse in which to fête their visitors.

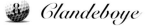 *Clandeboye*

Clandeboye Golf Club, near Conlig Village,
Newtownards, County Down
TEL: *+44 (0)28-9127 1767* **FAX:** *+44 (0)28-9147*
3711 **EMAIL:** *clandeboyegolf@dnet.co.uk*
LOCATION: *In the village of Conlig, off the Belfast–*
Bangor road at Newtownards
COURSE: *36 holes (2 courses), Dufferin Course:*
6559yd/5963m, par 71, SSS 71
GREEN FEES: *£££*
FACILITIES: *Changing rooms and showers, full catering,*
bar, pro shop, practice area, buggy hire, trolley hire
VISITORS: *Welcome – restrictions at weekends;*
booking essential

The narrow and steep incline that brings you up towards Clandeboye doesn't sufficiently hint at the delights to come once your journey has been completed.

There are two courses here – Dufferin, the longer championship course, and Ava, a lovely, tight, tree-lined course that hardly requires a driver. The vista from the top of the hill takes in Belfast Lough on one side and Strangford Lough on the other. A mixture of parkland and heathland, Dufferin states its

intent straight away with a tough par 4 – one of a series that is on the course – where you are required to drive over gorse to a fairway that sweeps away to the left.

With numerous streams and ditches winding their way through this layout, there is a great onus on accuracy. Still, anyone who enjoys length and precision off the tee will find some generous landing areas.

The 4th hole, however, is sure to intimidate any golfer. It requires a drive to a narrow-necked fairway with gorse, heather and trees on either side. If that initial task is successfully accomplished, there is then an approach to a small, raised green that requires considerable finesse.

There are many other demanding holes: the 8th needs a player's full attention, and the inward run has many strategically placed bunkers to add to the challenge.

Perched on a hillside overlooking Bangor, Dufferin has a
great deal of gorse, so you'll pay a high price if you
miss the fairway.

9 Lisburn

Lisburn Golf Club, Eglantine Road, Lisburn, County Antrim
TEL: +44 (0)28-9267 7216
FAX: +44 (0)28-9260 3608
EMAIL, lisburngolfclub@aol.com
LOCATION: 2 miles/3.2km south of Lisburn, off the A1 to Hillsborough
COURSE. 18 holes, 6685yd/6078m, par 70, SSS 72
GREEN FEES: ££££
FACILITIES: Changing rooms and showers, full catering, bar, shop, practice area, club hire, buggy hire, trolley hire
VISITORS: Welcome

The avenue up to Lisburn Golf Club is lined with trees, setting the tone for what lies ahead. This is a lovely parkland course, designed by Fred Hawtree. Admittedly, Hawtree had much to work with, including mature trees, water courses and rolling terrain, but he made the most of it, adding some strategic bunkering of his own for good measure.

However, this lovely course, which gets better with each passing year, has a little sting in the tail. The 17th is an extremely tricky par 4 of 449yd/408m – the tee shot is almost blind – and it demands both length and accuracy. Then, the 18th, a par 3 of 217yd/197m, is a spectacular downhill finish.

Comprising two loops of nine holes, with the finishing hole on each loop bringing the player back to the clubhouse, Lisburn is a well thought-out course with a degree of difficulty. However, when David Feherty, now a noted golf television commentator in the United States, won the Ulster Professional championship here in 1989, he did so with rounds of 65-64-68-65 to win by 18 shots.

10 County Armagh

County Armagh Golf Club, Newry Road, Armagh BT60 1EN
TEL: +44 (0)28-3752 5861 **FAX:** +44 (0)28-3752 5861 **EMAIL:** info@golfarmagh.co.uk
WEBSITE: www.golfarmagh.co.uk
LOCATION. Located close to Armagh city centre, off the Newry Road; the course is signposted
COURSE: 18 holes, 6212yd/5646m, par 70, SSS 69
GREEN FEES: ££££
FACILITIES: Changing rooms and showers, full catering, bar, shop, practice area, buggy hire, trolley hire
VISITORS: Welcome – Mondays, Tuesdays and Fridays; restrictions at weekends and booking advisable

As you drive into the ancient Cathedral City of Armagh with its towering church spires, a little sign on the left points to a golf club that is situated almost in the centre of the cityscape. The course enjoys a perfect location – it is laid out within the walled demesne of the former palace of the archbishop of Armagh – and the thousands of mature trees on the rolling terrain give it a country feel. A massive limestone obelisk that stands on the highest part of the course is a dominant feature.

The Obelisk, erected in 1783, forms part of the County Armagh club emblem.

Trees are the main hazard at County Armagh golf course. There are very few bunkers on the outward run, and none at all on the way home. However, over the years the course has undergone continuous improvements, and it now has sufficient challenging holes to sustain a player's interest. The 1st is a tough par 4, but it is the par 3s, especially the downhill 11th, which provide the highlights. There are three tight finishing holes, starting with the 446-yd/406-m 16th, which have the ability to ruin a card.

11 Ardglass

Ardglass Golf Club, Castle Place, Ardglass, County Down
TEL: *+44 (0)28-4484 1219* **FAX:** *+44 (0)28-4484 1841*
EMAIL: *golfclub@ardglass.force9.co.uk*
WEBSITE: *www.ardglass.force9.co.uk*
LOCATION: *7 miles/11km south-east of Downpatrick*
COURSE: *18 holes, 6671yd/6065m, par 70, SSS 69*
GREEN FEES: *£££*
FACILITIES: *Changing rooms and showers, full catering, bar, practice area, buggy hire, trolley hire*
VISITORS: *Welcome – except Wednesdays and Saturdays; restrictions on Sundays; booking essential*

Ardglass, this most picturesque of places with its jagged coastline, is steeped in history. It was once occupied by the Vikings, and the vestiges of a Norman castle can be found alongside the clubhouse.

The course runs impressively along coastal cliffs for much of the outward journey, and it doesn't take long to get to the club's feature hole. The 2nd, measuring 160yd/147m, is a par 3 with a rocky inlet between the tee box and the green.

Elsewhere, Ardglass offers a number of blind tee shots, while the greens are relatively small. The course is a very good test, with another par 3 on the homeward run – the 11th, which invariably plays into the wind coming off the Irish Sea.

The outward run at Ardglass has some spectacular holes right next to the Irish Sea.

12 Scrabo

Scrabo Golf Club, Newtownards, County Down
TEL: *+44 (0)28-9181 2355*
FAX: *+44 (0)28-9182 2919*
EMAIL: *scrabogc@compuserve.com*
WEBSITE: *www.scrabo-golf-club.com*
LOCATION: *1 mile/1.6km south of Newtownards, off the A21; the course is signposted*
COURSE: *18 holes, 6294yd/5722m, par 71, SSS 71*
GREEN FEES: *£££*
FACILITIES: *Changing rooms and showers, full catering, bar, pro shop, practice area, club hire, trolley hire*
VISITORS: *Welcome – except Wednesdays and Saturdays; booking advisable*

It is no wonder that the local golfers kept Scrabo a secret for so long. This is a unique and rather special place, dominated by Scrabo Tower, which was built as a memorial to the third Marquis of Londonderry in 1857.

It seems strange that a man-made object should have such a dominant presence in a landscape that is so natural. Gorse bushes are plentiful, and they provide the main hazard for the golfer, rendering bunkers unnecessary.

Scrabo doesn't waste any time letting the toughest hole of all rough you up a bit. The 1st was once described by Christy O'Connor Snr as among the best opening holes in the country. It is a par 4 of 466yd/424m, and it rises uphill to a green that is surrounded by gorse bushes. Scrabo is not a place to be wild off the tee, but it is a place that you must definitely visit.

13 Kilkeel

Kilkeel Golf Club, Mourne Park, Ballyardle, Kilkeel, County Down
TEL: *+44 (0)28-4177 65095* **FAX:** *+44 (0)28-4176 5579*
EMAIL: *kilkeelgolfclub@tinyonline.co.uk*
LOCATION: *3 miles/4.8km west of Kilkeel, just off the Newry road*
COURSE: *18 holes, 6615yd/6014m, par 72, SSS 72*
GREEN FEES: *££*
FACILITIES: *Changing rooms and showers, full catering, bar, practice area, buggy hire, trolley hire*
VISITORS: *Welcome*

Royal County Down is not the only course that can lay claim to a backdrop of the Mournes. So, too, can Kilkeel, even if its view of the mountain range is not as spectacular. Kilkeel, an attractive parkland course located within the walls of the Kilmore Estate at the foot of the mountains – has gradually established a reputation as an ideal golfing stop-off on the way to Royal County Down.

In 1993, Kilkeel was extended to 18 holes, making the course even more attractive. With its mature trees and masses of rhododendron bushes, it really is a very pretty place in which to play golf. It is also a good challenge, as evidenced by the decision to use it as a strokeplay qualifying course when the British Amateur championship was played at Royal County Down in 1999.

Kilkeel has some extremely good holes that require plenty of attention. After a gentle start, the pressure is on straight away, with the 2nd hole, a par 4 of 450yd/409m, setting the trend for a good mix to come.

Tree-lined Kilkeel has acted as a qualifying course for the British Amateur championship.

14 Warrenpoint

Warrenpoint Golf Club, Lower Dromore Road, Warrenpoint, County Down
TEL: *+44 (0)28-4175 3695*
FAX: *+44 (0)28-4175 2918*
EMAIL: *warrenpointgolfclub@talk21.com*
LOCATION: *1 mile/1.6km west of Warrenpoint, on the A2 Newry road*
COURSE: *18 holes, 6161yd/5601m, par 71, SSS 70*
GREEN FEES: *£££*
FACILITIES: *Changing rooms and showers, full catering, bar, shop, practice area, buggy hire, trolley hire*
VISITORS: *Welcome – booking essential*

Warrenpoint doesn't have much room to breath, squeezed as it is into land that is surrounded by busy roadways. Yet, with the view from the north shore of Carlingford Lough and the beautifully manicured condition of the course, members should still be thankful for what they have.

This course, which was the nurturing ground for Europe's number one golfer of 1989, Ronan Rafferty, is an example of how much can be compressed into a small space. Warrenpoint has even managed to squeeze in three par 5s on the front nine!

There is a remarkable variety on this course, though it only just about breaks the 6000-yardage barometer. The par 4 7th hole is a little quirky, with trees in unusual positions, and accuracy off the tee is absolutely crucial if a shot to a well-protected green is to be achieved; while the 12th and the 13th (which has out-of-bounds on the right) are two fine par 4s. Everywhere on this course the real emphasis is on short game skills, but there is certainly no harm in that.

Royal County Down

Royal County Down Golf Club, Newcastle,
County Down
TEL: *+44 (0)28-4372 3314* **FAX:** *+44 (0)28-4372 6281*
EMAIL: *golf@royalcountydown.org*
WEBSITE: *www.royalcountydown.org*
LOCATION: *30 miles/48km south of Belfast, off the*
A2 approximately 2/3 mile/1km north of Newcastle; the
course is signposted
COURSE: *36 holes (2 courses), Championship course:*
7037yd/6397m, par 71, SSS 74
GREEN FEES: *££££££+*
FACILITIES: *Changing rooms and showers, full catering,*
bar, pro shop, practice area, club hire, trolley hire; the
terrain of the course makes it unsuitable for buggies
VISITORS: *Welcome – except Wednesdays and*
Saturdays; booking essential; visitors may be admitted to
the Members' Bar and Dining Room when introduced by
a member; jackets and ties must be worn, but casual dress
is permitted in the Centenary Room

ROYAL COUNTY DOWN

HOLE	YD	M	PAR	HOLE	YD	M	PAR
1	506	460	5	10	197	179	3
2	421	383	4	11	438	399	4
3	474	431	4	12	525	477	5
4	212	192	3	13	443	402	4
5	438	398	4	14	213	194	3
6	396	360	4	15	464	422	4
7	145	132	3	16	276	251	4
8	429	390	4	17	427	388	4
9	486	442	4	18	547	497	5
OUT	3507	3188	35	IN	3530	3209	36

7037YD • 6397M • PAR 71

Anyone visiting Royal County Down for the first time does so with a great sense of expectation for, quite rightly, this course is rated as one of the best in the world. Anyone making a return visit does so with an even greater sense of anticipation, for once you have played here, the links has a spellbinding effect that draws you back time after time.

There are few, if any, better locations in golf. The Old Head of Kinsale may be more dramatic, and Pebble Beach may have its fans, but the unique appeal of Newcastle – with the Mountains of Mourne sweeping down to the sea – is that this links, which Old Tom Morris laid out in 1889, has been effectively created by Mother Nature. It is the most genuine and natural test of golf, as well as one of the toughest, to be found anywhere on earth.

It doesn't matter what type of weather unfolds, good or bad; not even low clouds and driving rain can diminish the appeal of playing here. The course has its eccentricities, with wild grass surrounding the fringes of the bunkers – almost giving the sand traps an unkempt appearance – and, of course, there are the blind tee shots. There are five of these in all, at the 2nd, 5th, 6th, 9th and 15th holes. While it may be worthwhile investing in a caddie for your first time here, these blind shots are played to quite generous landing areas, and in no way do they blight this fantastic links.

Donald Steel has skilfully reshaped the 18th, a hole traditionalists perceived to be the one weakness in the course. By doing so, he has managed to recreate the character that Old Tom achieved on the other 17 holes.

The drive off the 5th hole at Royal County Down is one of five blind tee shots on the championship course.

The first three holes work their way up along high dunes and the fourth, a par 3 of 212yd/192m, is played back towards the direction of the clubhouse and offers a stunning vista of the Mournes. The 5th is one of the toughest holes to be found on any course. The drive over a marker stone must also carry a huge amount of rough – go too far left, and the ball will find a fairway bunker; go too far right, and it will be almost unplayable. Assuming you're safe off the tee, the approach is to a small green, with yet more trouble awaiting any loose shot.

Then there is the 9th, one of the greatest holes in golf. It is a monster, a par 4 measuring 486yd/442m from the championship tees with dunes on either side and a large carry over a valley to find the fairway. The approach, if you're lucky, is to a raised green.

The back nine starts with a demure-looking short hole that is actually nothing of the kind. It then continues in a similar vein to the front nine, with a sequence of holes, one after the other, that test every golfing skill. Of these, the 13th, played down a corridor of dunes and gorse, encapsulates the special affinity that a golfer must have with a course. It's the same all the way back to the clubhouse – one magical moment after another.

16 *Banbridge*

Banbridge Golf Club, Banbridge, County Down
TEL: *+44 (0)28-4066 2211* **FAX:** *+44 (0)28-4066 2342*
EMAIL: *info@banbridge-golf.freeserve.co.uk*
WEBSITE: *www.banbridge-golf.freeserve.co.uk*
LOCATION: *1 mile/1.6km north of Banbridge, just off the A50; from Dublin, take the third Banbridge Junction on the A1 Belfast Road; from Belfast, take the first Banbridge Junction on the Dublin Road; then proceed through two sets of traffic lights, turn right at the third set, and the golf club is approximately 1 mile/1.6km on the left*
COURSE: *18 holes, 5590yd/5082m, par 69, SSS 67*
GREEN FEES: *££*
FACILITIES: *Changing rooms and showers, full catering, bar, shop, practice area, trolley hire*
VISITORS: *Welcome – booking advisable*

Located just off the main Belfast to Dublin road, on the outskirts of Banbridge, this parkland course has been upgraded by Frank Ainsworth to 18 holes, and the benefits are clear.

An obvious example of the course's modernization is the dogleg 6th hole, known as The Pond, which measures only 346yd/315m. This is a classic little hole that puts a heavy emphasis on accuracy, both off the tee and on the approach shot to the green.

The designer has made clever use of the land at Banbridge, and there are a number of classic short par 4s. There are just two par 5s, and the longest, the 14th, has been redesigned and needs a good drive over an intimidating ravine.

The earlier 10th, a par 3 of 221yd/201m is the course's signature hole. It shares the name of The Dell with another more famous short hole on the old course at Lahinch, but a measure of this northern hole's difficulty is that it is stroke index 2 on the card, which tells its own story.

All in all, Banbridge is an extremely pleasant course that caters well for handicappers of all levels. It may not be the toughest course around, but it has a welcome that is second to none.

REGIONAL DIRECTORY

Where to Stay
Belfast **Benedicts Hotel** (+44 (0)28-9059 1999) has a great location close to the city centre. **Madisons Hotel** (+44 (0)28-9050 9800) on Botanic Avenue is situated near many lively bars and restaurants. **McCausland Hotel** (+44 (0)28-9022 0200) on Victoria Street is an oasis of quiet elegance in the heart of Belfast. **Malone Lodge Hotel** (+44 (0)28–9038 8000) on Eglantine Avenue is near the University. **Hilton Hotel** (+44 (0)28-9027 7000) in Canyon Place is in the heart of the city centre, beside the Waterfront Hall. **The Europa Hotel** (+44 (0)28-9032 7000) is within walking distance of some of the city's best restaurants and historic landmarks. **The Stormont Hotel** (+44 (0)28-9065 8621) on the Newtownards Road is on the outskirts of the city, but is well placed for exploring the region's courses. *Down* **The Royal Hotel** (+44 (0)28–9127 1866) in Bangor overlooks the Marina. **The Marine Court Hotel** (+44 (0)28-9145 1100) in Bangor is well aware of the needs of visiting golfers. **The Old Inn** (+44 (0)28-9185 3255) in Crawfordsburn is one of Ireland's oldest hostelries, dating back to 1614. **The Clandeboye Lodge** (+44 (0)28-9185 2500) is set between the countryside and the coast and boasts the award-winning Lodge Restaurant. **The Burrendale Hotel and Country Club** (+44 (0)28-4372 2599) in Newcastle is only a five-minute drive from the Royal County Down links courses and has a health and beauty clinic. **The Slieve Donard Hotel** (+44 (0)28-4372 3681) rises majestically above the sand dunes that have made Royal County Down the world's best golf course.

Where to Eat
Belfast **Harlequin Restaurant** (+44 (0)28-9066 9191) specializes in modern Irish dishes. **McHugh's Restaurant** (+44 (0)28-9050 9999) on Queen's Square is a bar-cum-eatery that offers good food at pleasing prices. **Olio Restaurant** (+44 (0)28-9024 0239) on Brunswick Street has an excellent wine list. Enjoy TV chefs' Paul and Jeanne Rankin's gastronomic global delights at **Cayenne** (+44 (0)28-9033 1532) on Shaftesbury Square. **Tedford's Restaurant** (+44 (0)28–9043 4000) on Donegal Quay, located in a former ships' chandler's, specializes in seafood. *Down* **Glassdrumman Lodge Restaurant** (+44 (0)28-4376 8451) in Annalong has earned a widespread reputation for its food. **The Buck's Head** (+44 (0)28-4375 1868) in Dundrum is a country pub dating back to the 18th century. **The Cuan** (+44 (0)28-4488 1222) is a family-run business in the picturesque village of Strangford.

The Lobster Pot (+44 (0)28-4488 1288) in Strangford uses only the freshest local produce in its dishes. **The Slieve Croob Inn** (+44 (0)28-4377 1412) in Castlewellan includes such specialities as Dundrum oysters and Rockerfeller and fresh darne of local salmon on its menu.

What to Do
Belfast Situated in the heart of West Belfast, **Colin Glen Forest Park** is a beautiful wooded river glen consisting of 200 acres of woodland, grassland, waterfalls and ponds. **The Giant's Ring** is a prehistoric enclosure, and is 1 mile/1.6km south of Shaw's Bridge. **The Botanic Gardens** has some excellent examples of Victorian horticulture, while **Malone House** in Barnett demesne, Upper Malone Road, is a 19th-century house in beautiful parkland with a restaurant and an art gallery. **Belfast Zoo** has 160 species of rare and endangered animals, while the **Odyssey** includes a 10,000-seater indoor arena.
Down **The Ulster Folk and Transport Museum** at Cultra illustrates the traditions of the people of the North of Ireland. **The Brontë Homeland Interpretative Centre** near Rathfriland is where Patrick Brontë, father of the novelist sisters, taught and preached. **The St Patrick Centre** in Downpatrick explores the legacy of Ireland's national saint. **Murlough National Nature Reserve** is a sand-dune system near Dundrum with a nature trail. **Tollymore Forest Park** near Newcastle has numerous stone follies and bridges and a magnificent Cork Oak in the arboretum. **Strangford Lough Wildlife Centre** has guided tours and boat trips. **Hillsborough Castle and Gardens** is an 18th-century mansion, formerly the home of the Governor of Northern Ireland and now the official residence of the Secretary of State.
Armagh **Oxford Island/Lough Neagh Discovery Centre** near Craigavon has woodlands and bird-watching hides, as well as picnic and play areas. **Mullaghbawn Folk Museum** is a thatched roadside museum. **St Patrick's Visitor Complex** features the Armagh Story and the Land of Lilliput (an adaptation of *Gulliver's Travels*).

Tourist Information Centres
Belfast Welcome Centre, 35 Donegall Place, Belfast (+44 (0)28-9024 6609)
Gateway Tourist Information, Newry Road, Banbridge (+44 (0)28-4062 3322)
Tourist Information Centre, Tower House, 34 Quay Street, Bangor (+44 (0)28-9127 0069)
The St Patrick Centre, Market St, Downpatrick (+44 (0)28-4461 2233)
Newcastle Centre, 10-14 Central Promenade, Newcastle (+44 (0)28-4372 2222)

Index

Acknowledgements

Author's Acknowledgements
The author would like to acknowledge the assistance of the many Irish club secretary-managers,
Irish PGA professionals and club members and officials who helped with the research for this book,
and to friends who sampled some of the courses in the line of duty. Thanks also to Damian Ryan, the Director of Golf
with Bord Failte, who does a splendid job in letting the world know that the grass really is greener in Ireland.
And special thanks to my two young caddies, Conor and Evan, and wife Barbara for their support.